Ethnicity, Race, and Nationality in Education

A Global Perspective

THE RUTGERS INVITATIONAL SYMPOSIUM ON EDUCATION SERIES

O'Donnell/King, Eds.
Cognitive Perspectives on Peer Learning

Vitello/Mithaug, Eds.
Inclusive Schooling: National and International Perspectives

Golbeck, Ed.
Psychological Perspectives on Early Childhood Education: Reframing Dilemmas in Research and Practice

Shimahara/Holowinsky/Tomlinson-Clarke, Eds.
Ethnicity, Race, and Nationality in Education: A Global Perspective

Ethnicity, Race, and Nationality in Education

A Global Perspective

Edited by

N. Ken Shimahara
Ivan Z. Holowinsky
Saundra Tomlinson-Clarke
Rutgers, The State University of New Jersey

LEA LAWRENCE ERLBAUM ASSOCIATES, PUBLISHERS
2001 Mahwah, New Jersey   London

Lawrence Erlbaum Associates, Inc., Publishers
10 Industrial Avenue
Mahwah, New Jersey 07430

Cover design by Kathryn Houghtaling Lacey

Library of Congress Cataloging-in-Publication Data

Ethnicity, race, and nationality in education : a global perspective / edited by N. Ken
Shimahara, Ivan Z. Holowinsky, Saundra Tomlinson-Clarke.
    p. cm. – (The Rutgers invitational symposium on education series)
    "This volume is based on original papers presented by the authors at the symposium on
Diversity in the New Millennium: an International Perspective, held on October 26,
1999, in New Brunswick, New Jersey, at the Rutgers Graduate school of
Education"—Series foreword.
    Includes bibliographical references and index.
    ISBN 0-8058-3837-6 (cloth : alk. paper)
    1.   Educational anthropology—Cross-cultural studies—Congresses. 2.
Ethnicity—Cross-cultural studies—Congresses. I. Shimahara, Nobuo. II. Holowinsky,
Ivan Z. III. Tomlinson-Clarke, Saundra. IV. Series.

LB45 .E835 2001
306.43—dc21

                                                                                    2001023920

Printed in the United States of America
10   9   8   7   6   5   4   3   2   1

TABLE OF CONTENTS

PART III: CHANGING ETHNIC AND RACIAL MAPS AND EDUCATION

PART IV: LANGUAGE AND NATIONAL IDENTITY

SERIES FOREWORD

RUTGERS INVITATIONAL SYMPOSIA ON EDUCATION
RUTGERS GRADUATE SCHOOL OF EDUCATION

The profession of education was shaken to its roots nearly two decades ago, when national attention focused critically on education and on educators. Beginning with the highly publicized *A Nation at Risk* (1983), often contradictory criticisms, analyses, and recommendations on American education appeared from virtually every segment of contemporary U.S. society. Critics and friends have raised basic questions about our profession, including whether educators have met the challenges successfully that the students and the schools present, and, even more fundamentally, if we are able to meet those challenges.

In this explosion of concern and ideas for educational reform, there has been a need for a national forum in which the problems of education can be examined in light of research from a range of relevant disciplines. Too often, analyses of complex issues and problems occur within a single discipline. Aspects of a problem that unfamiliar to members of the discipline are ignored, and the resulting analysis is limited in scope and thus unsatisfactory. Furthermore, when educational issues are investigated by members of only a single discipline, there is seldom an attempt to examine related issues from other fields or to apply methods developed in other fields. Such applications may prove to be illuminating.

The national debate on educational reform often has suffered from a myopia, as problems and issues are identified and analyses and solution soften proposed within the limited confines of a single disciplinary boundary. In the past, national discussions have been ill informed or uninformed by current research, partly because there are far too few mechanisms for interdisciplinary analyses of significant issues.

In response to the call for educational reform in our country, the faculty of the Rutgers Graduate School of Education developed the *Rutgers Invitational Symposia on Education* (RISE), which is both a live forum at rutgers and a published scholarly series. Taking a multidisciplinary and interdisciplinary perspective, the *Symposia* focus on timely issues and problems in education. Because there is an accumulating corpus of high-quality educational research on topics of interest to practitioners and policymakers, each symposium focuses on a particular issue, such as potential teacher shortage, how to assess literacy skills, the optimal structure of schools, or the effects of cognitive psychology on teaching mathematics. Each volume in the *Symposia* series provides an interdisciplinary forum through which scholars interpret and disseminate their original research and extend their work to potential applications for practice, including guides for teaching, learning, assessment, intervention, and policy formulation. These contributions increase the potential for significant analysis and positive impact on the problems of educational improvement for American children.

The present volume, the 14th symposium, concerns cultural, ethnic, and national diversity in education. With the arrival of the 21st century, it is clear that as educators we will have to deal increasingly with issues related to diversity. No longer do we work in homogeneous neighborhood schools. No longer are students and colleagues defined in terms of simple traditional categories. Increasingly, individuals are identified and identify themselves by reference to particular cultural or ethnic groups or, on the international level, by reference to nationality. This has fundamental implications for educational practice and policy that are just beginning to be explored. This volume is based on original papers presented by the authors at the symposium on *Diversity in the New Millennium: An International Perspective*, held on October 26, 1999, in New Brunswick, New Jersey, at the Rutgers Graduate School of Education. In this context, the 14th RISE is an important contribution to our understanding and improvement of how students learn and should be taught all over the world.

It is with great pleasure that we contribute this volume to the series, *The Rutgers Invitational Symposia on Education.*

Louise C. Wilkinson
Dean and Professor of
Educational Psychology
Rutgers Graduate School of
Education

PREFACE

This volume, *Ethnicity, Race, and Nationality in Education: A Global Perspective*, comprises 12 papers originally presented at the 14th Rutgers Invitational Symposium on Education in October 1999. The symposium explored contemporary issues of ethnic, cultural, and national identities and their influence on the social construction of identity. These issues were analyzed from the perspectives of seven nations: China, Israel, Japan, South Africa, Ukraine, Wales, and the United States. Although different, these perspectives are not mutually exclusive lenses through which to review the discourse between ethnic and educational dynamics. This volume illustrates how these seven perspectives differ as well as overlap.

The book is thematically organized and divided into four parts. Part I explores ethnicity and race as important variables in explaining minority students' academic performance and schooling in the United States and China. Past and emerging paradigms of explanation are offered. Part II focuses on ethnic and racial identity issues in Israel, Japan, and South Africa. The construction of cultural identity in school settings is not a uniform mechanism of social reproduction, but a quite complex process, involving interactive and situational as well as contentious discourse. This process empowers students to cope with interethnic and racial problems that they encounter. Part III addresses ethnic and racial identity as it affects racial integration at different levels of education in post-apartheid South Africa, and the effects on schooling of a rapidly changing ethnic map in the United States. And finally, in Part IV attention is given to issues of language and national identity. A national language is central to nation building in Ukraine and Wales, whereas promotion of bilingual education is essential in enhancing national literacy and communication among ethnic groups in China, where 61 languages are in use. The detailed chapter synopses in the Introduction guide the reader in selecting chapters of interest.

ACKNOWLEDGMENTS

We began planning the 14th Rutgers Invitational Symposium on Education in the winter of 1998. We invited scholars from seven countries, including the United States, to present papers at the symposium. This volume is based on the papers presented at the symposium held at Rutgers University in October 1999. Prior to the conference, we held a work session to review the participants' draft papers. We are grateful to our colleagues who generously devoted their time to review and critique them. We wish to acknowledge the following colleagues who contributed to the work session: James Bliss, Sarane Boocock, Ken Carlson, William Firestone, John Fizer, David Muschinske, Adam Scrupski, Dorothy Strickland, and Ching-I Tu. Their reviews helped us consider the suggestions to the authors to revise their papers.

We are especially indebted to David Muschinske, Executive Director of Continuing Education at the Graduate School of Education, Rutgers University, for the unwavering support and advice, both intellectual and financial, that he offered us from the outset of the planning process to the final stage of editing the manuscript. His interest in the symposium immensely contributed to its success and the publication of this volume. We would also like to express our appreciation to Dean Louise C. Wilkinson for her support in making the symposium and the publication of its volume possible.

Editors

INTRODUCTION

N. Ken Shimahara
Rutgers, The State University of New Jersey

CONTEMPORARY CONSTRUCTIONS OF ETHNICITY AND RACE

Past geography of ethnicity and race is becoming complex and globalized, as the movement of capital and labor has internationalized all regions, transcending national boundaries (Omi & Winant, 1994). Lazarus (1999), for example, maintained: "The singularity of capitalism as an historical formation consists precisely in this relentless and almost irresistible tendency toward universalization" (p. 16). Yet ethnicity provides a powerful cultural basis for group solidarity and national identity, both of which people struggle to preserve across the globe. As the 20th century comes to a close, ethnic civil and national liberation wars have intensified worldwide, most recently in Kosovo, Bosnia, Croatia, Rwanda, Burundi, Indonesia, Sudan, Kurdistan, Azerbaijan, Georgia, Chechnya, Tajikistan, Kashmir, Myanmar, and Sri Lanka. It is no wonder that policy makers and journalists often ascribe the driving forces behind these wars to deep-seated ethnic conflicts, although more complex accounts of such conflicts must take into account the structural, political, and economic factors that intersect with intense ethnic conflicts (Brown, 1997).

Ethnicity is often interpreted from two related but analytically different perspectives: the primordial and the instrumental views. In anthropology, these two views provided frameworks by which ethnicity and ethnic conflicts have been studied and brought into academic and social discourse (Jenkins, 1999). Geertz (1973) represented the primordial view of ethnicity, which emphasizes "primordial attachments" embedded in kinship, locality, and culture as the basis for ethnic cohesiveness. Although these attachments form a cohesive force for each ethnic group, they can more often than not become obstacles to the development of civic political sentiments. The instrumental view, which derives from Barth's (1969) *Ethnic Groups and Boundaries*, emphasizes situational

1

factors, such as economic and political interests, and plasticity as important characteristics of ethnicity. Although ethnicity is nested in primordial sentiments, people are not necessarily bound by cultural promordiality in their pursuit of political and economic interests. Thus, understanding of ethnic dynamics does require consideration of both the changing and contingent variables of interpersonal interaction embedded in social situations and also deeply held ethnic loyalty and sentiments.

From an anthropological perspective (Jenkins, 1999), therefore, ethnicity is about cultural differentiation "externalized in social interaction and internalized in personal self-awareness" (p. 88). Ethnicity and race are not just natural categories; instead they are socially constructed and their boundaries and membership are negotiated (Bulmer & Solomos, 1999).

These views were reflected in heated debates on ethnicity in the United States during the 1970s, when cultural and structural approaches were contrasted. The cultural approach emphasized the value orientation, religious beliefs, linguistic differences, and other customs of ethnic groups as most crucial to understanding ethnic phenomena, such as interethnic inequality and conflict, discrimination, and prejudice. On the other hand, the structural approach gained attention from social scientists, and was the central thrust of *Ethnicity: Theory and Experience*, compiled by Glazer and Moynihan (1975). The thesis of this book was that the structural conditions of national society viewed, in terms of institutional arrangements, constitute one of the most important conditions influencing the formation, development, decline, and assimilation of ethnic groups and communities. Therefore, these groups' social success or failure is not entirely determined by their cultural orientations. To understand their social position requires an illumination of their positions in the structural conditions of society at the local and national levels. Sensitivity to cultural orientations is undoubtedly important, but not always primary. It is the economic and political conditions of society to which attention must be given if one is to gain insight into the dynamics of ethnicity.

As mentioned earlier, the concept of race is a social category. The meaning of race changes as a function of social, political, and economic circumstances. As Omi and Winant (1994) asserted, "The main task facing racial theory today . . . is no longer to problematize a seemingly 'natural' or 'common sense' concept of race. . . . Rather our central work is to focus attention on the *continuing significance and changing meaning of race*" (p. 3). Bulmer and Solomos (1999) contended that "racial and ethnic groups, like nations, are imagined communities" (p. 5) and ideological entities.

In the United States, in the first half of the 20th century, for example, ethnicity was a major ideological concern in immigration and assimilation, and the social patterns resulting from them, whereas race was measurably disregarded. Put differently, the ethnicities of European immigrants were a preoccupation of American society; racial makeup was not considered in the prevailing ethnic frame of reference (Omi & Winant, 1994). In the 1950s and 1960s, however, integration and assimilation of Blacks became a focal political issue and was, initially, guided by the existing paradigm of ethnic assimilation. Given the entrenched structural barriers for the integration of Blacks, however, the model of ethnic assimilation did not offer an account of Black social life, as it did for European immigrants. Hence Blacks and other racial minorities resorted to their racial identities to demand group rights and recognition, which represented a more radical approach than seeking ethnic assimilation. In this context, race gained a new social and political meaning. The growth of a substantial Black middle class, however, later resulted in some attempts to reexamine the preeminence of race as a determinant of social placement. Suffice it to recall Wilson's (1978) *The Declining Significance of Race*, which exemplifies these attempts. As Bulmer and Solomos (1999) suggested, racial and ethnic groups are discursive formations in which the social significance of differences is accorded and explained.

Nationality is a broader social category than ethnicity. But, like ethnicity, it is a mobile category, as illustrated, for example, by the independence movements by Wales and Scotland in the United Kingdom. Wales has moved toward greater autonomy via the creation of local institutions, including an elected National Assembly that recognizes Wales' distinctiveness and manages its affairs. In this sense there is now a stronger recognition of "a nation within a nation." In this context, nationality is a negotiated identity. Likewise, national identity has been a paramount issue in Ukraine since the 18th century, as is discussed in this volume. Because Ukraine was extensively *Russified* prior to its independence in 1991, de-Russification has been slow, as seen by Ukraine's difficulty in replacing the Russian language with Ukrainian in schools.

The contributors to this volume consider ethnicity and race as key concepts in individual and collective identity. Identity is multifaceted. Sociologically, it is viewed as the connectedness between self and society, the symbolic structuring of social relations in which subjectivity is deployed. In other words, an important identity question is how one is represented in a social, educational, and political context. Psychologically, identity refers to self-concept constructed in a complex sociocultural milieu. Ethnicity is a collective identity and influences the construction of self-concept. Furthermore, as Rodriguez and Trueba (1998) observed, "the formation of ethnic identity is an ongoing process" that reflects individual and collective adaptation to social, political, economic, and educational change. They cited for example, Chicanos in northern California who have developed a sense of self-esteem and a new ethnic identity as a result of their active participation in successful political action developed under the leadership of middle-class Chicanos. Their emerging identity signals a departure from Chicanos' traditional racial, ethnic, and class roles in U.S. society and represents a redefinition of their collective identity. They have constructed "situated selves," a new self-concept, through political action (1998, p. 46). The emergence of well-educated Chicano leaders, Rodriguez and Trueba asserted, is a critical factor in transforming Chicanos' social identity and mainstreaming rank-and-file Chicanos.

I have discussed how race and ethnicity are shifting, mobile social categories whose meanings are context dependent. The contributors to this volume focus on formal education in particular as a site where students engage in constructing their ethnic and racial identities. For example, Soudien (chap. 5) illustrates how Black and "colored" adolescents in post-apartheid South Africa negotiate their racial identities in schools. Likewise, Ikeda (chap. 4) provides ethnographic data showing that Japanese minority students "reinvent" their cultural identities through social discourse in everyday life. Foley (chap. 1) points out that valorizing Mexican-American students' new ethnic identity is key to their academic success. As a final example, Horenczyk and Ben-Shalom's (chap. 3) study of Russian immigrant adolescents in Israel focuses on how their multiple ethnic identities are molded in their adaptation to a new country.

Part I

Foley, in chapter 1, focuses on minority school achievement, a major educational as well as social issue since the 1960s. Foley critiques the past accounts of minority school performance and, in turn, presents native ethnographers' perspectives and research on this subject, which, in his view, constitute a promising epistemological alternative to past explanations. He maintains that the new epistemological paradigm calls for reconceptualization of ethnicity. Early paradigms were dominated by "deficit discourse" and/or the concept of genetic deficiency postulated by Jensen (1969) and recently revived by Herrnstein and Murray (1994) in *The Bell Curve*. These paradigms were replaced by social-structural, cultural, and sociolinguistic explanations of school performance in the 1970s. Marxists, such as Bowles and Gintis (1976), offered a theory of social reproduction to interpret functions of schooling, whereas Bourdieu and Passeron (1977) formulated a theory of cultural reproduction. They shifted the blame for minorities' low school achievement from individuals dominant in deficit discourse to institutions and social structure. Furthermore, sociolinguists viewed the school failure of minority youth as caused by everyday miscommunications and cultural misunderstandings. Anthropologist Ogbu (1991), on the other hand, sought to offer a complex, universalistic explanation of minority school failure with "cultural ecological theory."

Foley turns to native ethnographers and scholars, who offer an epistemological grounding of schooling from native cultural perspectives and accounts of cultural production, instead of cultural reproduction. They deconstruct the foundations of the deficit model and search for alternative models to narrow the achievement gap. Native ethnographers are accumulating data to show how minority youth, such as Mexican Americans and African Americans, engage in cultural production in the form of academic success in school with resilience and communicative skills and through participation in political movements and ethnic identity struggles. Native scholars, Foley admits, have not yet developed a coherent paradigm to explain how and why minority students succeed in schooling.

Ota Wang (chap. 2) explores the influence of Confucianism on the Chinese and on the development of Chinese-American students' cultural identities and academic achievement. The moral principles of conduct set out in Confucianism have provided the Chinese with essential aspects of identity formation and development from the fifth century B.C. to present day. The pillar of these principles is filial piety, which underscores Chinese socialization and social relations in general. This moral principle is extended beyond the family to the entire societal sphere, including educational, political, and other social institutions. Ideal social relations are hierarchically structured and social order is maintained through individuals' adherence to specific responsibilities, expectations, and codes of conduct as defined by Confucian teachings.

Recent Chinese school reforms, especially in the 1980s and 1990s, however, have emphasized students' independent initiatives, individual achievement, and competition. Yet the research cited by Ota Wang suggests that students' motivation to do well in school is likely to be based on parental expectations and culturally shared values, which still reflect Confucian norms, rather than self-advancement. But, in concert with the reform initiatives, efforts are now made in Chinese schools to enhance independence and achievement motivation in students, counter to Confucian teachings. Hence, there is discontinuity between formal socialization in school and societal expectations and values that stress noncompetitive and collective orientations.

In contrast, research indicates that Chinese-American families encourage children's independence and individualistic achievement outside the family while encouraging interdependence within the family. This shows a tendency for Chinese-Americans to accommodate American societal values to be successful in society while still stressing traditional interdependence in primary groups. Ota Wang's analysis shows that while individual cultural identity formation is strongly influenced by cultural tradition, it is also context dependent.

Part II

In chapter 3, Horenczyk and Ben-Shalom look at issues of multicultural education and national policy in Israel. Israel is a highly diverse, multicultural society. But Jewish, Arab, and Christian students do not have common experiences in education because they attend separate schools. Since 1989, Israel has swelled with nearly 1 million immigrants, of whom 900,000 are from the former Soviet Union. Horenczyk and Ben-Shalom contend that despite this fact, there is no viable multicultural education in Israel because it does not have coherent policy on this important multicultural issue. Hence, discourse on multicultural education is limited to the education of immigrant students, a discussion that in turn is focused on the assimilation of these students into Israeli society.

The authors' empirical study of Russian immigrant students shows that their multicultural identities and "identity accumulation" have positive effects on their adaptation to Israel. They point out that immigrants' positive cultural identities are a crucial factor in successful adjustment in a new country. Yet, in the absence of a comprehensive national policy of immigrant integration there is a continued emphasis placed on the traditional ideology of assimilation as a policy framework to integrate immigrant students. This represents a major source of adaptation problems for immigrant youth because their cultural identities are disregarded when the one-way process of assimilation is promoted.

In chapter 4, focusing on Burakumin, the largest Japanese minority group in Japan, Ikeda explores the development of minority students' cultural identities based on the ethnographic data he collected over an extended period of time. This minority group came into existence several centuries ago as a result of the rigidly ascribed status system of the Japanese feudal period. Although Burakumin are not distinguishable from majority Japanese by their physical and primary cultural attributes, they still suffer from social disabilities, including prejudice and discrimination. Ikeda's research indicates that Burakumin students construct their identities through interactive and situational discourse in everyday life in school, the youth center, and the community. He argues that their identity formation is significantly influenced by "contingent" forces in these environments. Put differently, minority students' identity development is not uniformly determined by the oppositional culture of the Burakumin community, and their subjectivity plays an important role in shaping their identity.

His findings challenge the theory of cultural reproduction and Ogbu's (1991) ecological theory that children of an involuntary minority develop an oppositional culture embedded in the oppositional community culture of the minority. Ikeda's analysis of identity construction focuses on students' self-concepts, the relationship between their self-esteem and school achievement, and the strategies that they forge to cope with the sense of vulnerability that stems from both their minority status and low school achievement. The author looks at how Burakumin students use multiple strategies to seek a "security basis" to harbor and promote their self-esteem. His findings show that these strategies very among students depending on how they use available resources in the school and community cultures.

Turning to chapter 5, Soudien explores how students' racial and ethnic identities are negotiated within South African apartheid schools through official (formal) and informal discourses. He contends that these negotiations are characterized by "a taught dialectic of choice and compulsion." His thesis is that culture, race, and ethnicity are constructed in particular historical and social contexts and that the construction of individual ethnic or racial identities cannot be totally dictated by the reproductive power of the apartheid structure. To support his thesis, he draws on Sharp (1988), who maintains that race and ethnicity are "mobilizable" concepts, and on critical theory, which emphasizes the role of agency in the social construction of individual or group identity. To illuminate his thesis, Soudien presents data from two secondary schools attended by African and "colored" students. His research participants were engaged in a discursive interplay between official discourses on their ethnic and racial identities and the informal discourses that resist the reproductive structure of the school. Thus, the school becomes a site for symbolic work and a contested terrain. His study shows that the apartheid school offers a process through which young people are actively involved in complex contestation, agreement, and dissonance regarding their identities.

Part III

In chapter 6, Wedekind reflects on the process of desegregation in secondary schools in post-apartheid South Africa, based on his study of school desegregation in Natal. When the legal structure of the apartheid system was repealed in the early 1990s, debates on the future of a new South Africa gained momentum. The government inaugurated after the historic elections in 1994 created a constitutional framework of education to promote school desegregation. This legal infrastructure and the national policy of school desegregation, however, were not sufficient to implement the desegregation process, as was often the case in the United States during the late 1960s and early 1970s. The desegregation process followed different courses depending on local departments of education, and Wedekind's case study shows that the national Department of Education was not proactive in promoting racial integration in Natal. Integration was impeded by a number of structural barriers, including insistence on academic standards, admissions through tests, and ability grouping. These structural barriers have contributed to resegregating students and a new pattern of de facto segregation.

Furthermore, teachers were ill prepared to achieve integration in schooling. As the author states, "None of the schools in the study operated with any policy on the promotion of interethnic, cultural, or racial relationships." They were simply unaware of any policy regarding desegregation. They failed to view the goals of integration in the broader South African society as central to schooling and the curriculum. Consequently, the state's role in moving beyond the identities of the apartheid past is quite limited. As the author argues, the state has a new vision and identity based on striving for a democratic country, but its new identity is impeded by the lack of links between national goals and schooling.

Chapter 7 focuses on crucial problems of race and ethnicity at the level of higher education in South Africa. Stewart and Abrahams discuss the roles of institutions of higher education in transforming a post-apartheid South Africa. The major challenge facing higher education is to provide equitable access to its institutions for members of all groups and to integrate diverse ethnic and racial groups into historically segregated, monocultural institutions. The authors suggest that transforming higher education in South Africa is a monumental task. They address problems that constrain the transformation and reform initiatives based on reform reports, including the *Education White Paper* issued in 1997 by the Department of Education, which presents a national framework for transforming higher education, and the overhaul proposals offered by Christiansen and Slammert (1999). The authors observe that there are parallels between the current demands in South Africa for integration of higher education and those in the United States during the civil rights movement and subsequent two decades.

Integrating historically White universities and Black universities requires not only the bold policy initiatives proposed by the *Education White Paper* and other overhaul proposals, but also public funding. According to the authors, funding is a critical issue in South Africa because it is severely limited. They report that some Black universities have been closed by the elimination of public funding. Other problems that constrain the policy initiatives include linguistic diversity, which constitutes a major challenge; campus unrest caused by charges of racism and discontent with the slow pace of transformation; conflicts over demands to create a multicultural institutional culture; disagreement over conceptions of multicultural education and strategies to diversify the demographic and ethnic composition of students; and affirmative action. The *Education White Paper* emphasizes institutional initiatives at the local level to address these problems and integrate students of diverse racial and ethnic groups at all types of institutions, including historically White, Black, and Africaans-speaking White institutions. South Africa's higher education is a site for contention, negotiation, and coordination in institutional efforts to achieve racial and ethnic integration as well as local and regional development.

In chapter 8, Tomlinson-Clarke discuses the impact of changing racial and ethnic demographics on national and ethnic identity and education in the United States. The United States is witnessing a phenomenal expansion of cultural diversity in the economic, educational, and social spheres, leading to a projected fundamental shift in ethnic and racial patterns by 2050, when the current White majority will constitute less than 50% of the national population. Models of adaptation to American society changed from assimilation in the first half of the 20th century to pluralism in the 1950s and 1960s and to multiculturalism in the 1980s and 1990s. This means that Americans of different ethnic and racial backgrounds must learn to accept, respect, and appreciate cultural differences to nurture national unity in diversity.

In this chapter, the author examines how increased ethnic and cultural diversity has wrought social and cultural changes in American life that have had a major impact on society and schooling. Focusing on issues of access to education and social resources in a multiethnic society, she examines schooling within a transforming sociocultural context. She argues that the current conceptualizations of multicultural education are ineffective in addressing structural issues of social and educational inequality.

Part IV

Chapter 9 concentrates on complex problems in the sociopolitical and historical context of Ukraine. Kononenko and Holowinsky explore the sociopolitical history and contemporary status of these problems. Ukraine's current sociopolitical reality has its roots in its geopolitical past as a buffer between Europe and Asia. "Russification" of Ukrainian culture began as early as 1700 under the Tsars and continued until Ukraine's independence in 1991 from the former Soviet Union. Because national language is central to nation building, the Soviet Union had insisted on Russian as the official language of its republics. The legacy of Russification in Ukraine remains strong even after its independence. Regarding Ukrainian as the national language is a continued struggle. At the level of higher education, for example, Russian continues to be the dominant language used in instruction, academic discourse, and publication. Ukrainian reformers are launching a campaign to restructure the school system, based on the European model, and also to update teacher education. But a national language remains a heated political issue, particularly because the many resident ethnic Russians insist on the use of Russian in Ukraine.

Chapter 10 turns to Wales. Promoting ethnic identity is an intense political issue in the United Kingdom, where England, Wales, and Scotland have a high degree of autonomy as separate political structures. Wales now has the national assembly, an elective legislative body on which power has been devolved from Westminster, and a political party representing the Welsh national interest in the British National Assembly. Wales' institutional system governs its political, economic, and cultural relations as well as its language, Welsh, which is used as the medium of instruction in about 30% of its schools. Fitz examines tensions between Wales' historically rooted commitment to promoting cultural distinctiveness and central control exerted from England. Despite Wales' autonomous status, however, there is little difference between schooling in Wales and England because of constitutional arrangements through which England influences Wales. Such an institutional system constrains the development of distinctive schooling in Wales. Although Wales has progressively gained the opportunity to advance its national identity through the *curriculum cymraeg*, the curricular programs that expose students to Welsh culture, including the Welsh language, history, geography, literature, and music, England's educational policy generally takes precedence over Wales' educational agendas. The emphasis on national curricular standards and accountability, for example, creates pressures on Welsh schools to conform, which causes tensions between Wales and England.

Finally in chapter 11, Xing and Yanheng discuss the development of bilingualism and problems in bilingual policy in People's Republic of China, which consists of 56 ethnic groups or "nationalities." These ethnic groups constitute about 8% of the entire population. China's standard language is Mandarin or the Han language, and there are 61 minority languages. Hence, the Chinese bilingual policy, which is intended to promote literacy in both Mandarin and a local language, is imperative for effective communication among different ethnic groups throughout the country, the development of functional literacy, and the enhancement of national identity. Teng and Weng examine the evolution of national policy on bilingualism over the past two decades and pedagogical strategies to promote it. Given the vast size of the country and its enormous linguistic and ethnic diversity, China's policy to advance bilingualism is highly challenging and calls for a major national commitment.

REFLECTIVE REMARKS

Geography of race and ethnicity will challenge immensely in the first several decades of the 21st century, altering the landscape of schooling throughout the globe. Such a dramatic change will be illustrated by the United States. The current U.S. population is estimated a little more than 270 million, of which Whites, Blacks, Asians/Pacific Islanders, and Amerindians comprise 83.4%, 12.4%, 3.3%, and 0.8%, respectively. Of the U.S. population, 11.2% is of Hispanic origin. By the year 2015, Hispanics will be the largest ethnic group, comprising 15.1%; by 2020, what are currently considered the minority groups (.e., non-whites) will constitute 40% of the U.S. population. They will comprise more than 50% of the population by 2050. As these changes occur, ethnicity and race will be reconceptualized and exert significant impact on education in the United States. Ethnicity, race, and nationality are mobile and shifting social categories whose meanings are dependent on changing sociopolitical contexts. As Foley (chap. 1, this volume) illustrates, ethnic researchers in the United States are reconceptualizing ethnicity to enhance schooling for minority students as a project of cultural "production" (Levinson, Foley, & Holland, 1996), rediscovering resources within ethnic cultures and valorizing ethnic and racial identities. One can no longer explain the changes anticipated in the coming few decades with cultural reproduction theory.

As pointed out at the beginning of this chapter, ethnicity and race are globalized as labor and capital move across the national boundaries in the Euro-American and Asian regions. Collective and individual cultural identities are crucial as a personal and social anchorage in adapting to new environments. The traditional paradigm of integrating immigrants into society through assimilation is ineffective, as Horenczyk and Ben-Shalom (chap. 3, this volume) argue. As Burakumin, a Japanese minority, have gained substantial social and economic liberation, they are now compelled to invent a new identity. Likewise, Burakumin minority adolescents reinvent their cultural identities through discursive discourse in everyday life to find what Ikeda (chap. 4, this volume) calls "a security basis" in school and society. In post-apartheid South Africa, Black and "colored" adolescents negotiate their identities through symbolic discourse by resisting the official ethnic and racial categorizations imposed on them. They are engaged in constructing new identities, reflecting social and political change in South Africa, but as Wedekind (chap. 6, this volume) documents well, change in the highly entrenched structure of a racially segregated society is very slow, often resulting in resegregation and reproduction of previously held individual and collective identities in schools.

National language and national identity are two sides of a coin--closely related political issues. This is illustrated well in newly independent countries, like Ukraine, as well as established countries, such as the United Kingdom and China. In the United States national language and cultural literacy also have been extensively debated controversies. The recent movement to make English the official language, for example, began in 1983 with the establishment of the organization U.S. English. Against the background of the bilingual crusade in the 1970s, 14 states declared English the official state language between 1984 and 1988, in addition to several other states that had earlier established English as the official language. We are also familiar with a prolonged civic controversy on cultural literacy and what is called the "canon debate." Cultural conservatives, such as Hirsch (1987), insist on transmitting Western-centric knowledge to the students. Multiculturalists are opposed to the traditional definition of the canon of culture and knowledge to be taught and make challenges on epistemological grounds (Apple, 1996; Banks, 1994). Multiculturalists insist that Western-centric knowledge represents only the dominant economic and political structure of society and marginalizes the experiences of minorities, including women (Banks, 1994). They demand that the facts, concepts, and explanations of reality that challenge mainstream knowledge be taught for minority students to function effectively in a pluralistic society. They call for civic action, essential in a democratic society, and cultural citizenship (Martin & Noddings, 1997).

This volume illustrates the embeddedness of the contemporary issues of ethnic, racial, and national identities in education. As editors we hope that the volume serves as a rich source book to explore and understand these issues.

REFERENCES

Apple, M. (1996). *Cultural politics and education*. New York: Teachers College Press.

Banks, J. (1994). *An introduction to multicultural education*. Boston: Allyn & Bacon.

Barth, F. (Ed.). (1969). *Ethnic groups and boundaries: The social organization of culture difference*. Boston: Little, Brown.

Bourdieu, P., & Passeron, P. (1977). *Reproduction in education, society, and culture*. Beverly Hills, CA: Sage Publications.

Brown, M. (1997). Internal conflict and international action. In M. Brown, W. Cote, Jr., S. Lynn-Jones, & S. E. Miller (Eds.), *Nationalism and ethnic conflict* (pp. 265-304). Cambridge, MA: MIT Press.

Bulmer, M., & Solomos, J. (1999). Introduction. In M. Bulmer & J. Solomos (Eds.), *Ethnic and racial studies today* (pp. 1-12). New York: Routledge.

Christiansen, I., & Slammert, L. (1999). *Historically black universities at the crossroads*. Belleville, South Africa: Centre for Educational Development in University, University of the Western Cape.

Geertz, C. (1973). *The interpretation of cultures: Selected essays*. New York: Basic Books.

Glazer, N., & Moynihan, D. P. (Eds.). (1975). *Ethnicity: Theory and experience*. Cambridge, MA: Harvard University Press.

Herrnstein, R. J., & Murray, C. (1994). *The bell curve: Intelligence and class structure in American life*. New York: The Free Press.

Hirsch, E.D. (1987). *Cultural literacy: What every American needs to know*. Boston: Houghton Mifflin.

Jenkins, R. (1999). Ethnicity etcetera: Social anthropological points of view. In M. Bulmer and J. Solomos (Eds.), *Ethnic and racial studies today* (pp. 85-97). New York: Routledge.

Jensen, A. (1969). How much can we boost IQ and scholastic achievement? *Harvard Educational Review, 39*, 1-123.

Lazarus, N. (1999). *Nationalism and cultural practice in the postcolonial world*. Cambridge, England: Cambridge University Press.

Levinson, B. A., Foley, D. E., & Holland, D. G. (Eds.). (1996). *The cultural production of the educated person: Critical ethnographies of schooling and local practice*. Albany: State University of New York Press.

Martin, J. R., & Noddings, N. (1997, March). *Civic education and cultural citizenship: A return call for conversation with Jane R. Martin and Nel Noddings*. Paper presented at the meeting of the American Educational Research Association, Chicago.

Ogbu, J. (1991). Immigrant and involuntary minorities in comparative perspective. In M. Gibson & J. Obgu (Eds.), *Minority status and schooling: A comparative study of immigrantion and involuntary minorities* (pp. 3-36). New York: Garland.

Omi, M., & Winant, H. (1994). *Race formation in the United States*. New York: Routledge.

Rodriguez, C., & Trueba, E. (1998). Leadership, education, and political action: The emergence of new Latino ethnic identities. In Y. Zou & E. Trueba (Eds.), *Ethnic identity and power: Cultural contexts of political action in school and society* (pp. 43-66). Albany: State University of New York Press.

Sharp, J. (1988). Introduction: Constructing social reality. In E. Boonzaaier & J. Sharp (Eds.), *South African Keywords: The uses and abuses of political concepts*. Cape Town, South Africa: David Philip.

Wilson, W. J. (1978). *The declining significance of race*. Chicago: University of Chicago Press.

I

Ethnicity, Race, and Academic Achievement

1

Reconceptualizing Ethnicity
and Educational Achievement

Douglas E. Foley
University of Texas at Austin

When I entered the field in the late 1960s, educational anthropologists/sociologists were mostly White middle-class males. One of the most exciting new developments in educational research is the emergence of the "ethnic educational ethnographer." Noted anthropological historian Marcus (1998) cited this rise of "native anthropologists" as the single most important development in anthropology. It signals the end of anthropology as a colonial/neocolonial enterprise and acknowledges that "insiders" studying their own culture elevates the quality of ethnographic fieldwork. Insiders have obvious political, linguistic, and cultural advantages. On the other hand, neither Marcus nor I would argue that "insider ethnography" is without problems. Nor would we argue that insiders can and should replace outsiders completely. I do not explore the pros and cons of insider versus outsider ethnographers in this chapter.

The story I tell highlights the contribution of ethnic ethnographers to changing the way we all think about the school achievement of ethnic youth. I start by making two qualifications. First, my story may leave the impression that all ethnic ethnographers are creative, unconventional thinkers. Such is not the case. Some ethnic scholars have done little more than conform to the conventional views of ethnicity and ethnic school achievement. Second, my story may also leave the impression that the educational establishment has welcomed the new ethnic ethnographers with open arms. Again, such is probably not the case. A recent set of reflections by ethnic ethnographers suggests that not everyone hails their arrival in the academy (Jacobs, Cintron, Canton, & Trueba, n.d.). Having made those qualifications, let us explore how ethnic scholars have transformed our explanations of ethnic school achievement.

The whole issue of the educational achievement gap between Whites and ethnic minorities surfaced in the 1960s. The exhaustive Coleman et al. report (1966), a national survey of school achievement, reported the lagging scores of African Americans, Mexican Americans, and Native Americans. The Coleman study and most subsequent studies have measured school achievement with standardized achievement tests and/or grades. During this era, liberal educational reformers blamed the "achievement gap" on the segregated, dual nature of the U.S. public education. They reasoned that mixing the races would both improve the decrepit physical facilities of "colored schools" and inspire these children to work up to the level of their White counterparts. Other liberal reformers of the 1960s championed a host of early childhood compensatory education programs like Head Start. Such programs emphasized early literacy experiences and teaching good student behaviors.

Undergirding both of these liberal reform programs was a fundamental set of beliefs and assumptions about the culture of all low-achieving non-White ethnic minority groups (Foley, 1997). In the 1960s, many liberals and conservatives subscribed to Lewis' (1965) "culture of poverty" view of the poor. According to Lewis, the urban poor, regardless of their ethnicity, lived in disintegrating, chaotic family and community structures. Each generation passed on a way of life marked by fatalistic, violent, cynical, and unproductive attitudes and values. The liberal-minded Lewis never intended to provide grist for moralizing policymakers, but social historian Katz (1989) said that is precisely what he did. He confirmed fears that the growing urban underclass needed to be resocialized into psychologically stable, optimistic, hard-working citizens.

Lewis' sweeping, negative portrait of the poor provided the cultural foundation for post-World War II educational researchers writing about low-income minority youth. A University of Texas colleague, educational psychologist Valencia (1997), reconstructed these developments in some detail. He contended that Social Darwinist theories of White racial superiority gradually shifted from a generic to a cultural difference perspective. Post-World War II educational researchers invented what Valencia called a "cultural deficit discourse" that "blamed the victim." According to deficit thinkers, low-achieving minority youth have parents who do not teach them to be assertive problem solvers and knowledge seekers (Ginsberg, 1972). Moreover, they use a "restricted language code" that lacks elaborate grammatical, lexical, and logical functions (Bernstein, 1975). Such deficient language development was thought to stunt cognitive development. Consequently these ethnic youth often lacked a "field-independent" style of learning and were less adept at the linear, higher order abstract thinking. When combined with the culture of poverty thesis, deficit thinking was a sweeping portrayal of the motivational, linguistic, and cognitive deficiencies of poor ethnic minorities.

Thirty years later, the current right-wing "backlash" against feminism and multiculturalism has reawakened this deadly culture of poverty-deficit discourse. Urban educational sociologists Fine and Weis (1998) underscored the rise of a moralistic, right-wing conservative policy discourse that blames what

Katz (1989) aptly dubbed the "undeserving poor." Herrnstein and Murray's *The Bell Curve* (1994) turns the social science clock back by explaining the failure of poor ethnic minorities as a sign of genetic inferiority. Once more, White racial superiority rears its ugly head in educational debates over affirmative action, bilingual education, ebonics, phonics, and childhood education, to mention a few. The backlash's impact on earlier liberal reform efforts has been devastating. Orfield's (1997) massive study of school segregation documents that U.S. public schools remain a dual system based on race-class differences. The system provides relatively high-quality suburban schools for the White majority and middle class of minorities, and low-quality urban schools for the predominately non-White underclasses. The difference in funding, facilities, curriculum, and instruction between these two systems of education preserves what social critic Kozol (1991) called a "savage inequality." So despite 50 years of educational reform, the educational achievement gap has joined death and taxes as a fundamental certainty in American life.

EARLY EXPLANATIONS OF THE SCHOOL ACHIEVEMENT GAP

But let us not become too gloomy. Progressive educational scholars have not rolled over and played dead. Since the 1960s, many scholars have been busy demolishing the theoretical and empirical foundations of the deficit discourse (Foley, 1997). I recap briefly the three main critiques of nonethnic scholars before presenting the contribution of the new ethnic ethnographers.

The first major school of thought emanates from various Marxist and cultural reproduction theorists (Bourdieu & Passeron, 1977; Bowles & Gintis, 1976). They generally emphasized that schools were structured to reproduce class inequality through various formal institutional mechanisms such as tracking (Oaks, 1985), distinct curriculum and instructional strategies, teacher class bias, and informal peer group life (Willis, 1981). As many critics have pointed out (Davies, 1996; Liston, 1988), the early Marxist critique concentrated mainly on class inequality, and thus had relatively little to say about how racial and gender articulates with class. Consequently the initial Marxist critique did little to challenge the notion of culture and ethnicity that underpins deficit thinking.

There were, however, several unconventional Marxist thinkers who helped reshape the way anthropologists conceptualize culture and ethnicity (Foley & Moss, 2000). This new "post-Marxist" perspective is known in educational circles as a "cultural production" and/or "practice" perspective (Levinson & Holland, 1996). It generally emphasizes the multiple struggles of cultural identity groups against race, ethnic, class, and gender dominance. McCarthy's (1998) recent reconstruction of cultural theory is a particularly good example of a multiple-dominance perspective. As is seen here, some ethnic ethnographers have built on post-Marxist production and practice perspectives to help explain minority school achievement.

In this regard, the writings of Frenchmen Bourdieu and Passeron (1977) and Englishman Willis (1981) have been particularly influential. Bourdieu emphasized the cultural and linguistic differences between middle- and working-class youths. He generally argued that youth from privileged-class backgrounds have an enormous advantage over working-class youth because they come to school already equipped with the proper etiquette, demeanor, taste, speech, and literacy styles. Bourdieu noted that possessing the "right" or preferred speech and literacy styles are a form of power or "cultural capital" that wins over teachers and leads to school success. Students from the "right classes" with the right cultural and linguistic style are expected to do better, and their speech and literary styles fit into the school's middle-class culture better.

Willis' (1981) study of British working-class youth shows us the other side of the class culture coin. He emphasized how middle-class schools and teachers systematically devalue the linguistic and cultural practices of working-class youth. When faced with teachers and a curriculum that disrespect their aesthetics and manner of speaking and acting, working-class youth rebel against the bourgeois norms of the school. They valorize their working-class ways of speaking and acting. Unfortunately their rebellion often consigns them to school failure. In the end, both Bourdieu and Willis demonstrated that the academic failure of poor students has more to do with institutional bias or a mismatch between the culture of the school and the class culture of the students than some inherent cultural and linguistic deficiency. From the post-Marxist view, deficit-culture of poverty explanations of school achievement are nothing more than ideological, pseudoscientific theories. They actually obscure formidable institutional bias that works against working-class minorities and for middle-class students.

Ironically, the best early ethnographic studies of the Marxist perspective were actually done by educational sociologists called ethnomethodologists (Cicourel et al., 1974). They produced a number of fine-grained studies of "micro" or "ethno" practices of counselors, testers, teachers, and administrators. These studies demonstrated that the failure of low-income students had little to do with deficit cultural backgrounds. In their view, schooling institutions literally constructed school failure (McDermott, 1974; Mehan, Hertweck, & Meihls, 1986). Like post-Marxists, ethnomethodologists shifted the blame for failure from the victim to the institution and its practitioners. But in the end they, too, had relatively little to say about the complex interplay of racial, ethnic, and gender factors.

A second major critique of deficit thinking emerged in the late 1960s from the seminal work of U.S. sociologists Hymes and Gumpertz. Sociolinguistically oriented educational ethnographers like Heath (1983) and

Phillips (1983) sought to directly attack the underlying culture concept of deficit theory. Being good cultural relativists, they pointed out that all allegedly "deficit minority languages" were functional in their home context. They argued that minority youth had historically different, not deficient, speech and literacy styles. The speech style of African Americans and bilingual Mexican-American and Native-American students only became "dysfunctional" when used in the middle-class culture of schools.

The sociolinguistic perspective generally "explained" the school failure of minority youth as the effect of everyday miscommunications and cultural misunderstandings. Their microethnographic studies of seemingly minor speech events revealed who got to speak, who received praise, and who was expected to succeed. More often than not, minority youth who deployed a different speech style were at a disadvantage. Curriculum materials that lacked cultural and linguistic sensitivity and diversity were also indicated. Here again, we see these scholars shifting the blame from the victim to the schooling institution, which is characterized as preferential toward the language and culture of middle-class youth. But like the Marxists, sociolinguists rarely explored how race and gender factors articulated with class factors.

A third and final critique of the deficit discourse was the cultural ecological theory of Nigerian anthropologist Ogbu (Ogbu & Simons, 1998). Unlike the Marxists and sociolinguists, he reintroduced the race factor in a serious way. Ogbu stressed that ethnic minorities are incorporated/assimilated into American society in very different ways. He makes a key distinction between minorities of color such as Asian Americans, who came to the United States freely or "voluntarily," and minorities such as African Americans, Mexican Americans, and Native Americans, who were "involuntarily" or forcibly incorporated as slaves and indentured servants.

Ogbu generally argues that forcibly incorporated "involuntary minorities" lack what he calls the "dual frame of reference" of voluntary minorities. Put simply, voluntary minorities see the United States as a land of opportunity compared to their situation "back home." They are generally optimistic and trusting of U.S. society, and work hard in school and in their jobs to succeed. Consequently, the parents of voluntary immigrants generally hold their youth, not the schools, accountable for school success and failure. They see what they are learning as additive to their own cultural and linguistic traditions, so to use Gibson's (1988) apt phrase, they feel they are "accommodating without assimilating" or losing their home culture.

In sharp contrast, Ogbu contended that many native-born "involuntary minorities" have grown up in an oppressive American racial system. Consequently they compare their social and economic status to working-class white Americans and resent the disparities. The parents of involuntary minorities believe their schools are worse than White suburban schools, and they often are ambivalent, critical, and distrustful of the school curriculum and teachers.

Unlike the optimistic, accommodating, hard-working voluntary minority, the involuntary minority develops what Ogbu called an "oppositional" collective identity and antischool peer groups. They view the requirements for school success-mastering the school curriculum and speaking and writing standard English-as "acting "White" and losing their ethnic culture. Like the rebellious working-class youth in Willis' (1981) study, they become inattentive and openly defiant and do not work hard, thus failing in school.

ETHNIC ETHNOGRAPHERS BUILD ON EARLIER CRITIQUES OF DEFICIT THINKING

The new ethnic scholars have built on these three schools of thought in a variety of complex ways. The intellectual debate surrounding Ogbu's cultural ecological theory has been particularly intense (Erickson, 1987; Foley, 1991; Levinson, 1992; Trueba, 1987). Many ethnic scholars acknowledge that new immigrants do have the positive attitudes that Ogbu subscribes to them. Nevertheless, recent studies (Gibson, 1997) have documented considerably more low-achieving "voluntary minorities" and high-achieving native-born "involuntary minorities" than Ogbu's model predicts. Moreover, some ethnic scholars fault Ogbu for not breaking sufficiently with the project of the deficit theorists. Like the deficit theorists, Ogbu remains preoccupied with developing a universalistic, scientific theory of why poor minority youth fail.

The new ethnic ethnographers, in sharp contrast, are not guided by Ogbu's cultural relativist notions of research and theory building. Many contemporary ethnic scholars are deeply influenced by the antifoundational theories of science that are characteristic of critical race, postmodern, post-Marxist, and feminist perspectives. Many come from working-class backgrounds and are what Gramsci (1971) called the "organic intellectuals" of their people. They are often deeply committed to producing knowledge that changes the world, and thus helps their own oppressed ethnic group. They generally eschew the positivist dream of a universal, "scientific" explanation of ethnic school failure. Instead, they do policy-relevant studies often labeled "critical ethnography" and "action research." They are primarily interested in document and producing ethnic school success.

University of Texas colleague Trueba (1999), following the lead of Friere, aptly dubbed these new trends a "pedagogy of hope." On the one hand, the new ethnic scholars are deconstructing the philosophical foundations of deficit thinking even more thoroughly than earlier radical White scholars did. On the other hand, they are searching for educational practices and programs that actually narrow the academic achievement gap (Ernst, Statzner, & Trueba, 1994; Mehan, Villuanueva, Hubbard, & Lintz, 1996). As is shown here, these two preoccupations, one highly theoretical and the other highly practical, represent a fundamental shift in the old deficit-based research paradigm on minority school achievement.

On the philosophical front, ethnic scholars are now doing what my poststructuralist University of Texas colleague Scheurich called "archeological excavations" of educational thought. One of my favorite archeological excavations is a book by Maori scholar Tuhami Smith (1999). She chronicled how Western scientific studies of her people have been an integral part of economic and cultural colonization. Arab anthropologist Asad and literary critic Said have made similar critiques, but they never articulated a new set of ground rules for outside, Western researchers. Tuhami Smith contends that the only self-respecting, sensible thing for Maoris to do is stop collaborating with outside White researchers-unless they demonstrate a real respect for indigenous ways and coproduce findings that are actually useful to the Maori.

Ethical, collaborative, community-based research may sound old hat to many qualitative researchers, but few educational researchers situate their studies historically the way Smith Tuhami does. Following Foucault, she recounted the long, brutal legacy of imperialist research. Research on the Maori is portrayed as a form of surveillance through the "microtechnologies" of various new social science disciplines. She called for the exclusion of harnessing of these new disciplinary technologies for local purposes that goes well beyond what qualitative researchers usually think of as collaborative.

Tuhami Smith exhorted outsider researchers to acknowledge a distinct Maori epistemology or way of knowing. In her view, the tribal elders, the repository of traditional knowledge and spirituality, must be central to any inquiry process. Outside researchers must report back to them, debate and distribute research tasks, and give voice to different community sectors. Such cultural insiders are accorded a key role in designing and monitoring all research projects. From this perspective, one must apprehend the world through Maori language and religion rather than through formalistic, positivistic research techniques. Consequently oral tradition and narration are accorded a special epistemological status. Ultimately all projects are to weave in and out of Maori cultural beliefs and values in a much more communal manner than western science usually operates.

The seminal work of African American feminist scholar Hill-Collins (1990, 1998) is another call for indigenous epistemologies. In her view, if researchers take seriously the unique experience of African American women and their stories, they will adopt a "standpoint theory" of Afrocentric epistemology. Hill-Collins postulated that a culturally distinct African American way of knowing is rooted in four basic cultural practices: common sense and intuition, dialogue with peers, an ethic of caring, and an ethic of personal responsibility. Analogizing from Gilligan's work on a female model for moral development, she argues that the Black feminist standpoint places a greater emphasis on relationships and socioemotional ties than White males typically do. Consequently, African American women develop what she called "oppositional knowledge" and a way of knowing that is quite distinct.

Traditional philosophers of science would surely question whether Maoris or African Americans or females have distinctly different ways of knowing. They would also worry about calls to subordinate their allegedly objective, rational ways of knowing no tribal elders. Traditional scholars would be quite reluctant to replace the scientific method with epistemologies based on ancient myths, dreams, parapsychological forces, and sacred oral traditions. Having spent some time in an indigenous Native-American community (Foley, 1995), I have no doubt that Mesquaki traditionalists use very different epistemological practices to know and judge their world. On the other hand, Mesquakis also have spent years in White public schools, have read many academic studies of their culture, and have endured incessant media scrutiny. Like other partially assimilated ethnic groups, their culture has evolved into a complex, hybrid mix of Western and non-Western practices and epistemologies.

So sorting out what is precisely Maori, African American, or Mesquaki epistemology can be tricky business, and as Tuhami Smith and Hill-Collins are quick to note, they are not essentializing non-Western epistemologies as exclusive or superior. They are, however, demanding that outside researchers take such cultural differences seriously and work respectfully to design studies that do not privilege only western European ways of knowing. If nothing else, getting outsider researchers to officially acknowledge indigenous epistemologies opens up an intellectual space for reimagining ethnicity and school achievement.

ETHNIC ETHNOGRAPHERS IN SEARCH OF DIVERSITY AND COMPLEXITY

Given the rise of these radical philosophical perspectives, ethnic ethnographers are increasingly questioning the universality and neutrality of all educational discourses or theories. Their work intersects with legal scholars who use "critical race theory" to critique the legal discourse (Crenshaw, Gotanda, Peller, & Thomas, 1995; Tate, 1997). For example, Chicana ethnographer Villenas (1996, in press) reintroduced the notion of race and racial privilege to critique the research discourse. She blends critical race theory, feminism, indigenous philosophy, and post-modernism into several highly reflexive pieces that question her own complicity with anthropological epistemologies and explanations. Such reflections illustrate the insidious, pervasive influence of western notions of White superiority on even the most committed "native" ethnographers.

Other excellent examples of the deconstructive impulse among ethnic ethnographers are the literacy studies of African American Delpit (1995) and Chicana de la Luz Reyes (1992). In separate studies, both authors contend that the widely popular "whole-language literacy approach" may not work as well for black and Latino youth. Building upon the work of other ethnic scholars (Valdez, 1991), they characterize the whole-language approach as more attuned to the parenting and literacy styles of the liberal middle-class White. Using the insights of ethnic teachers, they contend that "ethnic minorities" may need a more structured, phonics-oriented approach. Such critiques underscore the need to question whether the whole-language approach is a universal, neutral theory of instruction that serves all cultural groups. Perhaps it is simply a new form of deficit theory that unconsciously champions white middle-class speech and literacy styles.

Another example of the new deconstructive impulse is Lee's (1996) critique of Asian Americans as the "good" or "model minority." She pointed out how this new educational discourse about a successful minority is anything but a neutral, objective discourse. She found far too many teachers, researchers, politicians, and community leaders using this popular racist discourse to chastise non-Asian minorities. The discourse about a "good minority" is really a revival of the old deficit discourse that blames the victim. Asian Americans allegedly have the strong families and the will to succeed that unsuccessful minorities lack. Another major educational practice that has been critiqued is the pseudoscientific procedures used to classify students as "mentally retarded" (Mehan et al., 1986; Mercer, 1974). These studies have led to numerous legal challenges of the disproportionate numbers of minority youth placed in special education programs.

Ethnic ethnographers have generally been good at producing more intimate, complex, less stereotypic, humanizing portraits of their subjects. They probe the in-group variability of ethnic groups with greater cultural and linguistic sensitivity than earlier investigators. They often focus on ethnic learners' hybrid cultural identities, complex coping strategies, and elaborate networks of support. An excellent example of this type of ethnography is Fordham's (1996) study of African American youth in a Washington, DC, high school. She portrayed how African American students "produce" their own success through psychological resilience and clever communicative practices. Rather than simply studying lower achievers, she highlights Black youths who are able to tap into a positive imagined Black community and to resist peer pressures that school success means "acting White." These high-achieving Black students play up their abilities to demanding authorities and play them down to disillusioned peers. By skillful impression management, they avoid the self-defeating "oppositional culture" that ensnares too many African American students. Moreover, girls are apparently somewhat better at managing their public images as students than boys are. Fordham's successful African American youth look very similar to successful South Texas Chicano students in my study

(Foley, 1990) and in Beattie's (2000) forthcoming study of California Chicanas. By looking carefully at how students construct their own success, such studies highlight the daily practices of students.

Latino ethnographers Valenzuela (1999), Vigil (1997), and Suarez-Orozco (1997) are also exploring in-group variation in interesting new ways. These three scholars pay particular attention to the psychological and peer group differences between Mexican immigrants and U.S. born Mexican students. They (Gibson, 1997) characterize the 1.5 generation, Latino youth born abroad but reared in the United States, as an intermediate case of achievers. Prior experiences in the homeland, transnational familial networks, peer relations, gender, and other factors complicate sweeping explanations that dichotomize immigrants as "voluntary" with a positive dual frame of reference and attitude and "involuntary" with a negative ethnic oppositional culture and attitude.

Others take more direct aim at the oppressive, colonial nature of schooling and the research process (Bartolome, 1994; Lomawaima, 1994; Stanton-Salazar, 1997; Villenas, 1996; Zou & Trueba, 1998). Native-American scholar Tsianina Lomawaima gives a particularly powerful account of how Indian boarding schools surveile and control the bodies and minds of Indian students. University of Texas colleague Valenzuela (1999) also indicted the schools as uncaring, culturally insensitive places that "subtract" the cultural and psychological resources of minority youth. A schooling process filled with uncaring teachers, culturally irrelevant curriculum, and ability-tracked groups literally produces ethnic school failure. Even the presence of achievement-oriented immigrants, whom the teachers often praise, adds to this subtractive schooling process.

Valenzuela's study tends to reaffirm that many immigrant students are models of hard-working conformity, and their proschool peer groups provide them with considerable "social capital" to succeed. But by highlighting institutional and interactional factors, Valenzuela also called the sharp distinction that Ogbu made between voluntary and involuntary immigrants into question. Like Fordham, she discovered a great deal of in-group variance and highlights gender factors. Many of the "voluntary immigrants" are only moderately successful. Moreover, there are subtle and interesting in-group acculturation and achievement differences between new immigrants, the 1.5 generation (born in Mexico but schooled in the United States), and native-born Chicanos. Finally, native-born female students achieve at higher rates. Here again, an ethnic ethnographer is providing us with a more subtle, complex account of ethnic school achievers.

Finally, some new ethnic ethnographers emphasize the liberating force of community-based ethnic identity struggles (Fordham, 1996; Trueba, 1999; Trujillo, 1998; Vigil, 1997). Vigil's longitudinal study of city and suburban youth in Los Angeles notes the importance of a broader Mexicanization process that regenerates ethnic culture and pride. A number of recent studies (Delgado-Gaitan, 1996; Diaz-Soto, 1997; Romo & Falbo, 1996; Trueba, 1999; Valdez, 1996) document the importance of parents, mothers in particular, and family-based grassroots political movements. Villenas and Deyle (1999) provided an excellent review of these studies. Families are the starting point for surviving and resisting the cultural assault on Latino communities and parents. Many Latino parents provide their youth with *consejos* (stories) that seek to instill in them a broad moral notion of being *bien educado* (well educated). The Latino concept of the educated person subscribes to family loyalty, humility, and hard work. The general cultural portrait that emerges from these studies is a far cry from the cultural misrepresentations of earlier deficit-driven studies (Foley, 1997).

The findings from the aforementioned studies dovetail nicely with the South Texas study that several ethnic colleagues and I conducted for 16 years (Foley, 1989, 1990; Trujillo, 1998). We found many cases of activist mothers, teachers, and high-achieving Chicano youth in politically active small South Texas towns. In addition, we found very large increases in the social mobility of Chicano students in a town transformed by the Chicano civil rights movement. Compared to their parents, 20% more Chicano youth were going on to postsecondary education. Such findings convinced us that genuine school reform must start with a strong local grassroots ethnic political movement based in families.

Of course, politicizing the public schools may not always lead to higher achievement rates and upward social mobility. Fordham's study suggests that ethnic social movements may also have contradictory, negative effects. The African American civil rights movement and its Black power ideology generally stimulates racial pride and leads many Black youth to equate individual success with collective group success. The strong romantic identification of many African American teachers with the 1960s civil rights movement is problematic, however. Many of these middle-class African American teachers apparently moralize about the new generation's lack of collective politics and underestimate the ways that individual African American high achievers work the system for success. Clearly, more studies of the relation of ethnic political mobilization to group and individual achievement rates are needed.

The final major focus of the new ethnic ethnographers is on pedagogical and curricular practices that really work. Unlike the earlier deficit studies, studies of "best practices" are bent on improving the school experience of minorities. In Latino intellectual circles, the work of Russian linguist and historical materialist L. S. Vygotsky has been particularly influential. Chicano anthropologists Luis Moll, Carlos Velez-Ibanez, Norma Gonzales, and others emphasize that Chicano youth have a vast "fund of knowledge." They accumulate knowledge about farming, auto mechanics, homemaking, and indigenous medicine through complex kin and neighborhood networks (Moll, Amanti, Neff, & Gonzales, 1992; Velez-Ibanez & Greenberg, 1992). These scholars emphasize the importance of building on such funds of knowledge through what Vygotsky called "proximal zones of development" or culturally relevant pedagogical and curricular practices. As Vasquez, Pease, and Shannon (1994) noted, bilingualism represents another key, untapped cultural/linguistic resource. These authors provide a fascinating portrait of ethnic children serving as cultural brokers and translators for their parents.

The work of anthropologist Trueba (1999) also extends the Vygotskian "funds of knowledge" critique in interesting ways. Trueba blends the critical pedagogy of Paulo Friere into his Vygotskian critiques of how Latinos are schooled. He highlights the importance of what Vygotsky would call "scaffolding" or building "zones of proximal development" through a culturally relevant pedagogy and curriculum. He and various Latino (Delgado-Gaitan, 1991, 1996; Vasquez, Shannon, & Pease, 1994) and African American scholars (Foster, 1994, 1995; Henry, 1998) have redefined our notion of a "culturally relevant pedagogy." In their view, the culturally and linguistically sensitive, politically conscious ethnic teacher is the key to ethnic school success. Such teachers skillfully tap into ethnic funds of knowledge and utilize the learners' bilingualism or dialect or ebonics.

Unfortunately, middle-class White teachers often have little knowledge of such cultural and linguistic resources, and they tend to see these communities and their youth through the cultural deficit lens. Consequently Moll and associates advocated making White teachers into ethnographers that directly experience the rich sociocultural environments of Latinos (Gonzales et al., 1997). These Latino researchers' emphasis on direct experience of the cultural reality of Latino families, under the careful supervision of ethnic faculty, is obviously a powerful pedagogical device. Such experience-based teacher education programs suggest a very effective way of producing antideficit, antiracist White teachers. Perhaps the only thing that will prevent the spread of such programs is the lack of political will among the professoriat to commit the money and time to such labor-intensive programs.

In the search for "best practices," other ethnic scholars have advocated various alternative educational approaches such as catholic education, single-sex academies (Streitmatter, 1999), community-based education (Comer, 1980), cooperative learning (Jacob, 1999) and detracking (Mehan, Villaneuva, Hubbard, & Lintz, 1997). The work of University of Texas colleague Reyes and others (Reyes, Scribner, & Scribner, 1999) also explores a host of promising organizational practices such as collaborative governance, cooperative learning, and parental involvement. In the past 10 or 20 years, there has been a veritable flood of useful, practical books on creating culturally pluralistic schools that, to use Valenzuela's apt phrase, are less "subtractive." Well-known multicultural educators such as Banks, Gay, Nieto, and Sleeter have written numerous books with useful advice to practitioners. Critical ethnographer McLaren (1997) reviewed the field of multicultural education extensively and highlights these "pedagogies of dissent. "

A CONCLUDING NOTE: SOME NEW VIEWS OF ETHNIC CULTURE AND SCHOOL ACHIEVEMENT

I have tried to offer a flavor of the protracted struggle that progressive scholars of all races have waged against racist educational explanations of minority school failure. The range and scope of their work is difficult to capture in this short chapter; consequently, I must apologize in advance to those left out of the story. If nothing else, I hope to leave the image of a new wave of ethnic ethnographers building on the work of earlier nonethnic scholars and making a unique contribution. The research of these scholars is as philosophically and methodologically sophisticated as it is practical and political.

One major conceptual contribution of ethnic scholars is their perspective of culture and ethnicity. The previous funds of knowledge, Afrocentric, ebonic, Vygotskian, diasporic, cultural production, and practice perspectives contest in various ways a deficit/culture of poverty view of ethnic cultures. These theorists generally postulate a dynamic notion of shared culture that emphasizes historically specific patterns of oppression and resistance. On one level, this new style of cultural studies consciously seeks to deconstruct or challenge the insidious notion of a culturally, racially, intellectually, and psychologically inferior "minority group." To this end, such studies deconstruct the dominant liberal ideology that parliamentary democracies with established judicial procedures and civil rights laws have created "race neutral," egalitarian political economies. From a critical race perspective, the cultural norms of White superiority persist and reproduce through allegedly neutral legal and market systems. A wide range of cultural institutions such as the media, public schools, and everyday popular culture also continually stigmatize or "other" or "essentialize" non-White peoples. Earlier brutal systems of legalized slavery and apartheid have been replaced by more masked, euphemized forms of racial and cultural superiority. Consequently a host of "Whiteness" studies (Frankenberg, 1997; McLaren, 1997) have sprouted to root out these new, more subtle forms of White racial superiority and privilege.

On another level, the new ethnic scholars are producing new discourses and images that counter the way earlier cultural experts have stigmatized them. By emphasizing the continuing legacy of White supremacy, ethnic scholars have generally accented what I would label a cultural struggle or "ethnogenesis" perspective (Roosens, 1989). An ethnogenetic concept of culture and ethnicity highlights how historical power relationships between so-called mainstream and minority groups shape the everyday cultural practices and shared sense of ethnicity. Such a perspective breaks with earlier liberal views of ethnic culture that openly or implicitly promote cultural and linguistic assimilation into Western, Anglo-Saxon, European norms. In sharp contrast, the new ethnic formulations of culture emphasize both the survival of traditional cultural practices and the invention of new, hybrid, creole cultural forms. In this formulation ethnic cultural practices are a dynamic mix of old and new forms being invented and reinvented within a political context that stigmatizes, appropriates, trivializes, misrepresents, and misunderstands ethnic cultural differences.

This leaves ethnic intellectuals with the daunting task of valorizing and representing the history and culture of their peoples. Their role is to combat mainstream ignorance, indifference, and hostility and to save their own people from further cultural and psychological colonization. Postcolonial scholars such as Spivak (1988) argued that scholarship that "strategically essentializes" the positive cultural attributes and political struggles of stigmatized ethnic "minorities" is essential. Hence, progressive ethnic and nonethnic scholars are beginning to rewrite the history of ethnic and race relations to valorize and preserve their invented ethnic cultural traditions. The new "native ethnographers" are faced with a difficult task of essentializing cultural differences and traditions without romanticizing and glorifying their subjects in the way some race-conscious White scholars have (Foley, 1997; Foley & Moss, in press). Ultimately, a critical multicultural perspective of culture and ethnicity acknowledges the continuing legacy of racism and colonialism in a manner that liberates both the oppressors and the oppressed. This progressive political project requires the efforts of all races, but ethnic scholars must take the lead if the academy is to be decolonized.

A final and vital aspect of the research of ethnic and progressive scholars is their emphasis on pedagogical, practical matters. These new ethnic scholars have replaced the old deficit paradigm of explaining school failure with a new paradigm dedicated to better understanding ethnic school success. This may seem like a simple shift in perspective, but we must not forget how many years and studies it has taken to put a dent in the hegemony of the racist deficit discourse of White scholars. Unfortunately, the new wave of ethnic scholars has not been able to convince national economic and political leaders to institute a comprehensive urban policy that underwrites these scholars' internal school reform efforts (Anyon, 1997; Lipman, 1998). Let us not forget, however, to situate our microstudies within larger political and policy trends. We must be careful to point out the limits of the best teaching and learning practices that we document. In-school reform efforts that lack strong community political support or a strong urban reform policy are not going to transform inferior "minority schools."

Nor have the new ethnic scholars and their progressive allies been able to produce a "silver bullet" explanation of ethnic school achievement. We still do not have a unified, coherent theory of why youth of color succeed despite the odds against them. We know that equipping ethnic students with better study and social skills helps. So does creating proximal zones of development, teaching culturally relevant curricula, hiring culturally and linguistically sensitive teachers, and partnering with politically active parents and ethnic communities. We are now aware of how to alter many historical, cultural, linguistic, organizational, pedagogical, curricular, and interactional factors.

Nevertheless, we need much more research on what is called "student agency." The new formulations of culture and ethnicity point toward studying the small everyday cultural practices of ethic students. Recent theoretical and empirical work on student identity (Beattie, 2000; Fordham, 1996; Holland, Lachicotte, Skinner, & Cain, 1998; Levinson, in press; Lukyx, 1999) suggest that we may have been overly preoccupied with institutional practices and family background factors. Following practice and cultural production notions of culture, we start with that premise that ethnic students collectively and individually construct their student identities, thus academic success. The cultural identity of ethnic students can no longer be plotted on some simplistic, subtractive acculturation scale. Ethnic cultural identity is always a work in progress, a complex mix of mainstream and ethnic attributes, a hybrid, multiple-shifting public identity.

Given these more fluid notions of ethnicity and ethnic identity, the empirical task of today's educational ethnographer is to chronicle how ethnic students utilize their communities, family networks, and peer groups as cultural resources. We must pay much more attention to how they deploy specific expressive identify practices to "get ahead" or succeed in school. We must eschew earlier static, stereotypic, racially biased formulations of ethnicity and identify and focus on what ethnic groups and their youth create. By paying more attention to ethnic student agency, we will have come full circle in the struggle against deficit thinking. In doing so, we will surely find new reasons to appreciate the cultural vitality of ethnic youth, parents, and teachers. To this end, the new wave of ethnic scholars is leading the way.

REFERENCES

Anyon, J. (1981). Social class and school knowledge. *Curriculum Inquiry, 11*(1), 3-42.

Apple, M. (1982). *Cultural and economic reproduction in American education: Essays in class, ideology and the state.* Boston: Routledge & Kegan Paul.

Bartolome, L. (1994). Beyond the methods fetish: Toward a humanizing pedagogy. *Harvard Educational Review, 64,* 173-194.

Beattie, J. (2000). *Women without class: Race and identity among White and Mexican-American youth.* Berkeley, CA: University of California Press.

Bernstein, B. (1975). *Class, codes and control*. London: Routledge & Kegan Paul.

Bourdieu, P., & Passeron, J. (1977). *Reproduction: In education, society and culture*. Beverly Hills, CA: Sage.

Bowles, S., & Gintis, H. (1976). *Schooling in capitalist America: Educational reform and the contradictions of economic life*. New York: Basic Books.

Cicourel, A., Jennings, K., Jennings, S., Leiter, K., Mackey, R., Mehan, H., & Roth, D. (Eds.). (1974). *Language use and school performance*. New York: Academic Press.

Coleman, J., Campbell, E., Hobson, C., McPartland, J., Mood, A., Wernfield, F., & York, R. (1966). *Equality of educational opportunity*. Washington, DC: U.S. Government Printing Office.

Cargar, C. L. (1996). *Of borders and dreams: A Mexican-American experience of urban education*. New York: Teachers College Press.

Comer, J. (1980). *School power*. New York: The Free Press.

Crenshaw, K., Gotanda, N., Peller, G., & Thomas, K. (Eds.). (1995). *Critical race theory: The key writings that formed the movement*. New York: New Press.

Davies, S. (1996). Leaps of faith: Shifting currents in critical sociology of education. *American Journal of Sociology, 100*(6), 1448-1478.

Delgado-Gaitan, C. (1996). *Protean literacy: Extending discourse on empowerment*. London: Falmer Press.

Delgado-Gaitan, C. (1991). Involving parents in the schools: A process of empowerment. *American Journal of Education, 100*(1), 20-47.

Delpit, L. (1995). *Other people's children: Cultural conflict in the classroom*. New York: New Press.

Diaz-Soto, L. (1997). *Language, culture, and power: Bilingual families and the struggle for quality education*. Albany: State University of New York Press.

Erickson, F. (1987). Transformation and school success: The politics and culture of educational achievement. *Anthropology and Education Quarterly, 18*(4), 335-356.

Ernst, G., Statzner, E., & Trueba, H. T. (Eds.). (1994). Alternative visions of schooling: Success stories in minority settings. *Anthropology and Education Quarterly, 25*(3).

Fine, M., & Weis, L. (1998). *The unknown city: The lives of poor and working-class young adults*. Boston: Beacon Press.

Foley, D. (1997). Deficit thinking models based on culture: The anthropological protest. In R. Valencia (Ed.), *The evolution of deficit thinking* (pp. 113-131). London: Falmer Press.

Foley, D. (1995). *The heartland chronicles*. Philadelphia: University of Pennsylvania Press.

Foley, D. (1991). Reconsidering anthropological explanations of ethnic school failure. *Anthropology and Education Quarterly, 22*(1), 60-85.

Foley, D. (1990). *Learning capitalist culture: Deep in the heart of tejas*. Philadelphia: University of Pennsylvania Press.

Foley, D. (1989). *From peones to politicos: Class and ethnicity in a south Texas town, 1900 to 1989* (Rev. ed.). Austin: University of Texas Press.

Foley, D., & Moss, K. (in press). Studying American cultural diversity: Some non-essentializing perspectives. In I. Susser (Ed.), *Studying cultural diversity in America*. American Anthropological Association Publications, London: Blackwell.

Fordham, S. (1996). *Blacked out: Dilemmas of race, identity, and success at Capital High*. Chicago: University of Chicago Press.

Foster, M. (1995). Talking that talk: The language of control, curriculum and critique. *Linguistics and Education, 7*, 120-150.

Foster, M. (1994). The role of community and culture in school reform efforts: Examining the views of African American teachers. *Educational Foundations, 8*(2), 5-26.

Gibson, M. (Ed.). (1997). Ethnicity and school performance: Complicating the immigrant/involuntary minority typology. *Anthropology and Education Quarterly, 28*(3).

Ginsberg, H. (1972). *The myth of the deprived child: Poor children's intellect and education.* Englewood Cliffs, NJ: Prentice-Hall.

Gramsci, A. (1971). *Prison notebooks.* New York: International Publishers.

Heath, S. B. (1983). *Way with words: Language, life and work in communities and classrooms.* New York: Cambridge University Press.

Henry, A. (1998). *Taking back control: African Canadian women teachers' lives and and practice.* Albany: State University of New York Press.

Herrnstein, R., & Murray, C. (1994). *The bell curve: Intelligence and class structure in American life.* New York: The Free Press.

Hill-Collins, P. (1990). *Black feminist thought: Knowledge, consciousness, and the politics of empowerment.* New York: Routledge.

Holland, D., Lachicotte, W., Jr., Skinner, D., & Cain, C. (1998). *Identity and agency in cultural worlds.* Cambridge, MA: Harvard University Press.

Jacobs, L., Cintron, J., Canton, C., & Trueba, H. E. (Eds.). (n.d.). *The politics of survival in academia: Narratives of inequality, resilience and success.* Unpublished manuscript.

Katz, M. (1989). *The undeserving poor: From the war on poverty to the war on welfare.* New York: Pantheon.

Kozol, J. (1991). *Savage inequalities.* New York. Basic Books.

Lee, S. (1996). *Unraveling the model minority stereotype: Listening to Asian-American youth.* New York: Teachers College Press.

Levinson, B. (1992). Ogbu's anthropology and the critical ethnography of education: A reciprocal interrogation. *International Journal of Qualitative Studies in Education, 5*(3), 205-225.

Levinson, B. (in press). *Todos somos inguales (We are all equal): The play of student culture at a Mexican secondary school and beyond.* Durham: Duke University Press.

Levinson, B., & Holland, D. (1996). The cultural production of the educated person: An introduction. In B. Levinson, D. Foley, & D. Holland (Eds.), *The cultural production of the educated person: Critical ethnographies of schooling and local practice* (pp. 1-56). Albany: State University of New York Press.

Lewis, O. (1965). *La Vida.* New York: Random House.

Lipman, P. (1998). *Race, class and power in school restructuring.* Albany: State University of New York Press.

Liston, D. (1988). *Capitalist schools: Explanation and ethnics in radical studies of schooling.* London: Routledge & Kegan Paul.

Lomawaima, T. (1994). *They called it prairie light: The story of Chilocco Indian school.* Lincoln: University of Nebraska Press.

Lukyx, A. (1998). *The citizen factory.* Albany: State University of New York Press.

Marcus, G. (1998). *Ethnography through thick and thin.* Princeton, NJ: Princeton University Press.

McCarthy, C. (1998). *The uses of culture: Education and the limits of ethnic affiliation.* New York: Routledge.

McDermott, R. (1974). Achieving school failure. In G. Spindler (Ed.), *Education and cultural process* (pp. 82-118). New York: Holt, Rinehart & Winston.

McLaren, P. (1997). *Revolutionary multiculturalism: Pedagogies of dissent from the new millennium.* Boulder, CO: Westview Press.

Mehan, H., Hertweck, A., & Meihls, J. L. (1986). *Handicapping the handicapped: Decision making in student's educational careers.* Stanford, CA: Stanford University Press.

Mehan, H., Villanueva, I., Hubbard, L., & Lintz, A. (1996). *Construction of school success: The consequences of untracking low-achieving students.* London: Cambridge University Press.

Mercer, J. (1974). *Labeling the mentally retarded*. Berkeley: University of California Press.

Moll, L., Amanti, C., Neff, D., & Gonzales, N. (1992). Funds of knowledge for teaching: Using a qualitative approach to connect homes and classrooms. *Theory Into Practice, 31*(2), 132-141.

Oaks, J. (1985). *Keeping track: How schools structure inequality*. New Haven, CT: Yale University Press.

Ogbu, J., & Simons, H. (1998). Voluntary and involuntary minorities: A cultural-ecological theory of school performance with some implications for education. *Anthropology and Education Quarterly, 29*(2), 155-188.

Orfield, G. (1997). *Dismantling desegregation: The quiet reversal of Brown vs. Board of Education*. New York: New Press.

Phillips, S. (1983). *The invisible culture: Communication in classroom and community on the Warm Springs Indian reservation*. New York: Longman.

Reyes, M. (1992). Challenging venerable assumptions: Literacy instruction for linguistically different students. *Harvard Educational Review, 62*(4), 427-446.

Reyes, P., Scribner, J., & Scribner, A. P. (1999). *Lessons from high-performing Hispanic schools: Creating learning communities*. New York: Teachers College Press.

Romo, H., & Falbo, T. (1996). *Latino high school graduation*. Austin: University of Texas Press.

Rossens, E. (1989). *Creating ethnicity: The process of ethnogenesis*. Newbury Park, CA: Sage.

Spivak, G. (1988). *In other worlds: Essays in cultural politics*. New York: Methuen.

Stanton-Salazar, R. (1997). A social capital framework for understanding the socialization of ethnic minority children and youths. *Harvard Educational Review, 67*, 1-39.

Streitmatter, J. (1999). *For girls only: Making a case for single-sex schools*. Albany: State University of New York Press.

Suarez-Orozco, C., & Suarez-Orozco, M. (1997). *Transformations: Immigration, family life and achievement motivation among Latino adolescents*. Stanford, CA: Stanford University Press.

Tate, W. (1997). Critical race theory and education: History, theory, and implications. In M. Apple (Ed.), *Review of research in education*, 2 (pp. 191-234). Washington, DC: American Educational Research Association.

Trueba, E. (1987). Culturally based explanations of minority students' academic achievement. *Anthropology and Education Quarterly, 19*(3), 270-287.

Trueba, E. (1999). *Latinos Unidos: From cultural diversity to the politics of solidarity*. New York: Rowman and Littlefield.

Trujillo, A. (1998). *Chicano empowerment and bilingual education: Movimento politics in Crystal City, Texas*. New York: Garland Publishers.

Tuhiwai-Smith, L. (1999). *Decolonizing methodologies: Research and indigenous peoples*. London: Zed Books.

Valdez, G. (1991, April). *Background knowledge and minority students: Some implications for literacy-based instruction*. Paper presented at the meeting of the American Education Research Association, Chicago.

Valdez, G. (1996). *Con respeto: Bridging the distances between culturally diverse families and schools*. New York: Teachers College Press.

Valencia, R. (1997). *The evolution of deficit thinking*. London: Falmer Press.

Valenzuela, A. (1999). *Subtractive schooling: US-Mexican youth and the politics of caring*. Albany: State University of New York Press.

Vasquez, O., Pease-Alvarez, L., & Shannon, L. (1994). *Pushing boundaries: Language and culture in a Mexicano community*. Cambridge: University Press.

Velez-Ibanez, C., & Greenberg, C. (1992). Formation and transformation of funds of knowledge among U.S. Mexican households. *Anthropology and Education Quarterly, 23*(4), 313-335.

Vigil, J. (1997). *Personas Mexicanas: Chicano high schoolers in a changing Los Angeles.* Fort Worth, TX: Harcourt Brace,

Villenas, S. (1996). The colonizer/colonized Chicana ethnographer: Identity, marginalization, and co-optation in the field. *Harvard Educational Review, 66*(4), 711-731.

Villenas, S. (in press). This ethnography called my back: Writings of the exotic gaze, "othering" Latina, and recuperating Xicanisma. In E. Pierre and W. Pillow (Eds.), *Working the ruins: Feminist poststructural theory and methods in education.* New York: Routledge.

Villenas, S., & Deyle, D. (1999). Critical race theory and ethnographies challenging the stereotypes: Latino families, schooling, resilience and resistance. *Curriculum Inquiry, 29*(4), 413-444.

Willis, P. (1981). *Learning to labor: How working-class kids get working-class jobs.* New York: Columbia University Press.

Zou, Y., & Trueba, E. (Eds.). (1998). *Ethnic identity and power: Cultural contexts of political action in school and society.* Albany: State University of New York Press.

2

Confucianism and the Educational Process: A Comparative Analysis of Chinese and Chinese American Identity Development in Education

Vivian Ota Wang
Arizona State University

For more than 2000 years, Confucian teachings have served as cultural guideposts governing Chinese patterns of socialization and education. Traced to its origins in the Han Dynasty, Confucian ethics have promoted the internalization of values that have facilitated relationships and socialization practices influencing individuals, groups, and institutions. Not only have essential aspects of identity formation and development been dependent upon Confucian understandings of interpersonal relationships, but filial piety has served as a guiding principle governing Chinese socialization patterns. According to Confucian teachings, relationships are hierarchical and social order is ensured through each person's compliance of role-specific expectations, responsibilities, and rules of conduct; a person does not exist independently but through his or her relationships to others. For example, filial piety has justified authority of parents over children and by extension, those senior over junior in generation and rank (e.g., *wu lun*, the Five Cardinal Relations between sovereign and subject, father and son, elder brother and younger brother, husband and wife, and friend and friend).

Ironically, Chinese students who emphasize academic achievement have been faced with incongruent educational expectations of individualistic motivations of self-reliance, competence, and achievement, on the one hand, and a collective orientation of noncompetitiveness, obedience, and passive acceptance of role expectations, on the other. The influence of traditional Confucian idealism has come increasingly discrepant with current Chinese educational reforms and practices, thus, presenting students with a dilemma between individualistic affirmation for educational success and collectivistic accommodation for life-long learning.

Chinese and Chinese American ethnic identity formation and development will be examined to better understand how recent Chinese educational reforms have affected student achievement. First, a historical overview of how Confucianism has influenced Chinese education will be presented. Next, recent changes in Chinese educational reforms will be highlighted. Personal and social responses to an evolving Chinese ethnic identity will be explored, with particular attention to indigenous Chinese and American theories of individualism, collectivism, and social expectations. Finally, the influence of Confucianism on the identity development of Chinese Americans and Chinese in other predominantly White Western countries will be examined, focusing on ethnic affirmation and cultural accommodation.

CONFUCIANISM AND SOCIAL RELATIONSHIPS

Social roles in China have been traced to the prescriptions of the Chinese scholar Confucius (551–479 B.C.). By providing an ethical rationalization, Confucius developed a framework for exercising power through social conduct codes. Within this backdrop, Confucian thinking on morality and, by extension, knowledge was viewed as a conduit for defining fundamental distinctions between right and wrong. For Confucius, "his way" meant the way of truth, objectivity, and correct thinking. To this end, he forwarded a series of theories about life, society, and government that continue to be practiced today. For example, he contended that social power and subordination to authority was to be inculcated in family systems through the *Wu lun*, behavioral codes prescribing expectations and relationships (Hu, 1960). *Wu lun*, the Confucian social code of "five relationships," defined the proper dominant/subordinate behaviors between ruler and subject, father and son, elder brother and younger brother, husband and wife, and friend and friend (Latourette, 1957).

Thus, intergenerational relationships governed by filial piety have been structural, enduring, and invariable across situations in China and other Confucian-based Asian cultures. In fact, the dictates of filial piety have been potent determinants of not only intergenerational but also superior-subordinate relationships. In this respect, Ho (1996) argued that although some of its component ideas (e.g., obedience, family honor) have been shared by other cultures, filial piety has surpassed many other social and ethical codes in its historical continuity, the proportion of humanity under its governance (more than 40% of the world population), and the encompassing nature of its precepts.

For centuries, filial piety has served as a guiding principle governing patterns of socialization. Using specific codes of conduct throughout the length of a person's life span, the continuity of authoritarian moralism was established and maintained by the following five social codes: (1) obeying and honoring one's parents; (2) providing for the material and mental well-being of one's aged parents; (3) performing the ceremonial duties of ancestral worship; (4) taking care to avoid harm to one's body; (4) conducting oneself so as to bring honor and not disgrace to the family name; and (5) ensuring the continuity of the family line (Ding, 1997; Ho, 1987, 1996). Filial obligations, both material and spiritual, were overriding in importance, and rigidly prescribed from the time one was considered old enough to be disciplined to the end of one's life. For example, filial piety justified absolute authority of adults over children, veneration for the aged, and the authority of those senior in generation and gender over those junior in rank. Not so surprisingly, when examining themes related to continuities and discontinuities, authoritarian moralism and collectivism have been traced to the Confucian ethic of filial piety. Ho (1989) suggested that:

> Authoritarian moralism versus a democratic orientation and collectivism versus individualism captures succinctly the distinctive character of Chinese socialization patterns. The former entails impulse control (versus expression); the latter entail interdependence (versus autonomy) and conformism (versus unique individuation). Authoritarian moralism and collectivism underlie both the traditional and the contemporary ideologies governing socialization, and thus, preserve its continuity. (p. 154)

CONFUCIANISM AND EDUCATION

In China, Confucius was one of the first people to suggest educational access to all people as a way of dissolving the nobility class' governmental monopoly. Thus, his first principle of education was based upon the belief that *all* men (literally) had the right to be educated (Ding, 1997). Not only did he believe education was the means of achieving higher social status, he viewed learning as training toward the overall betterment of human development (Mordkowitz & Ginsburg, 1987). By studying the classics (knowledge), moral conducts (the relationships between knowledge and practice), loyalty (an aspect of humanity), and trustworthiness (based upon interpersonal relations), he envisioned educated people understanding man and society through knowledge of the past as a means of providing a clear vision of the future.

Other Confucian teachings were also selectively valued as a means to maintain social order. For example, through filial piety, social order based on obligatory roles for members in a hierarchy was maintained. In the family, the children were obliged to obey their parents, the wife was obligated to obey her husband, and the younger brother to respect his elder. Socially, as an extension of the family, all officials and citizens were expected to obey the will of the supreme authority (the emperor), and absolute loyalty was the political standard of quality.

Confucius' advocacy of providing education without regard to social class ideally made knowledge accessible not only to the ruling class but also to the broad masses. Unfortunately, while social class, family background, nation/state, geographic regions, and age barriers were eliminated, education for girls and women faced differential role strains. While Confucius advocated that all men (literally) were educable, this position created a significant barrier for girls and women. For women, he considered education endangering feminine virtue because a woman's prescribed life status was to be a devoted helper to her future mother-in-law and a bearer of preferably male children. It was only in the 19th century, with the influence of Western religious missionaries, that Chinese women had access to education primarily through Christian schools and colleges. As late as 1910, these schools provided women with educational opportunities similar to men. Although their educational ambitions have grown, Chinese women continue to experience educational inequity in Chinese society.

Guided by filial piety, Ho (1994) argued that Chinese socialization and education have embodied two salient aspects of authoritarian moralism: hierarchical ranking of authority in the family, educational, and sociopolitical institutions and a pervasive application of moral precepts that serve as a primary barometer against which people are judged. To this end, absolute authority of parents and educators has been both a symptom and a cause of the overriding emphasis in education on the development of a moral character. The consequence of these orientations has been children judging themselves in terms of whether their conduct meets some external moral criteria (e.g., school achievement) rather than internal needs, feelings, and aspirations. These children have been expected to transform into adults who exercise impulse control, behave properly, and fulfill filial obligations (Ho, 1987).

CHINESE EDUCATION REFORMS

Chinese intellectuals and government officials have repeatedly initiated and promoted movements for national revitalization at different points in Chinese history. For example, in the late Qing dynasty (1644-1911), two major national movements of modernization-the Self-Strengthening Movement (1860-1894) and the Political Reform Movement (1906-1911)-were organized. The first movement's goals were the initiation and implementation of programs involving founding schools, translating books, establishing factories, constructing railroads, and opening mines. The second, while endorsing the efforts of the first, proposed the modernization of the central political system by introducing basic institutional changes.

In 1911 China switched central political structures from an imperial to a republican system after the overthrow of the Qing dynasty. However, an effort at modernization through national reforms was not successful and a large-scale political protest, later referred to as the May Fourth Movement, occurred in

1919. This protest transformed itself into the New Culture Movement, which proposed a rejection of Chinese traditions (especially those emanating from Confucianism) and advocation of total acceptance and adoption of Western science and democracy. In 1949, in the founding of the People's Republic, all Western European teachings were brought to a halt and Russian educationalists ushered in dialectical materialism and collectivism as the central philosophy for education.

Thus, up until the mid-1980s, following the Russian model, the Chinese educational system had been centralized and politicized in terms of its administration and financing (Kwong, 1997; Mok, 1997). Then, with the success of agricultural and economic reforms, increased financial resources became available for education initiatives (Paine, 1991; Riskin, 1993; Tsang, 1996). To this end, a series of educational reforms beginning in 1985 were implemented when the Communist Party of China's Central Committee enacted the *Decision of the CPC Central Committee on the Reform of China's Education Structure*. The Compulsory Education Act, the first education law since 1949, was promulgated in 1986, marking a turning point in the universalization of education. The most important features of this fundamental reform were the legalization of a 9-year compulsory universal education, decentralization of educational administration, and diversification of educational financing (Lewin, 1994; Zhu & Lan, 1996). (It should be noted that the State Education Commission was renamed the Ministry of Education in 1998.)

The current national focus on establishing a socialist market-driven economy has generally informed China's fundamental educational policy reforms. One result has been an increase in both access and quality of education at all levels (Zhao, 1998). Additionally, whereas the 1980s was a decade of educational reforms focused on expansion and restructuring (specifically in vocational education at upper secondary and undergraduate levels), the 1990s has been one meeting the diversifying needs of a market-driven economy and sustainable social development. Ideally, although the intention of the recent educational reforms has been aimed to address the students' overall development in moral, intellectual, physical, aesthetics appreciation, and work skills, the most significant changes have been in the central governments, decreasing its financial responsibilities and encouraging lower level governments and communities to finance education. Unfortunately, despite these reforms, the investment of national and local governments in basic education has remained inadequate, much below the average level of developing countries (Tsang, 1996; Zhao, 1998).

EDUCATION FOR LIFE-LONG LEARNING AND DEVELOPMENT

Although progress has been made in access and quality of education at all levels, problems have continued to exist in educational structures, content administration, admission, and graduate placement. Palpable tensions between equal access and quality improvement, examination-driven practices and learning for overall development, institutional autonomy and state macro-level regulation, and limitations of educational supply due to financial constraints and the increasingly diversified demands of market forces have been felt by educators and students alike. Nevertheless, current educational reform ideology has held fast to the following ideals:

1.   Compulsory 9-Year Education. A major educational policy goal has been to implement a universal 9-year education plan for all students by the year 2000. Within this context, poverty has been identified as the major contributing factor and greatest barrier to universal basic education. Despite high economic growth rate and progress, in 1966, 650 million people have remained in poverty (which is defined as a person's annual income level of less than 540 RM, equivalent to less than US $70), or 87%. Thus, policy reforms have emphasized the relevance of basic education in communities as a means to poverty alleviation and capacity building by: (1) increasing access to primary education; (2) improving teachers' qualifications and teacher education programs, and (3) providing basic facilities for all schools.

2.   Education for girls and women. Before the founding of the New Republic of China in 1949, girls accounted for less than 25.5% of primary school students. Within a span of 40 plus years, the 1990 enrollment rate for girls 7 to 11 years old had risen to 96.8%. Although educational programs focusing on girls and women have been attributed to the more than 45% increase in professional and technical positions held by women in 1990, the illiteracy rates for women during the same time remained more than twice as high (44.5%) as men (18.45%). So, what may account for this inequality between women and men in terms of educational rights? Among the causes may be traditional Confucian values that have suggested uneducated women as possessing better moral character. Providing a justification for many parents to invest differentially in their son's education over their daughter, this notion has been

reinforced in the intermittent implementation and enforcement of constitutional regulations stipulating equal educational equality for boys and girls.

3. Education for the disabled. Legislative, administrative, economic, and social means have been employed to develop educational programs for the disabled not only as an integral part of but also as a precondition to the general human rights. Both the 1986 *Compulsory Education Act of the People's Republic of China* and the *Act on the Protection of the Handicapped* have described the legal rights and duties to the disabled, including the development and implementation of special education programs in integrated schools and classrooms.

4. Transformation of Examination/Testing and University Admissions. Deng Xiaoping's college-entrance examination initiative reinstituted in 1977 was the first of a series of fundamental reforms in Chinese higher education. During the 20 years thereafter, Chinese universities and colleges have enrolled 11 million students; 8 million have graduated using a national unified college-entrance examination as the essential instrument in selecting qualified freshmen.

5. Standardized Testing and Humanistic Evaluations. In response to using standardized examinations as the only means of measuring student academic achievement, national advocacy and reform efforts have shifted educational policy away from examination-driven practices toward a more humanistic evaluation of a student's overall cognitive, intellectual, and affective development in education (e.g., systematic programs have been created to develop individual student interests, talents, and aspirations). Entrance examinations have been eliminated from junior high school education, thus allowing direct enrollment of primary school students. Additionally, new theoretical frameworks, standards, indicators, and learning achievement grading alternatives have been developed in (1) raising academic achievement while reducing student workloads; (2) increasing creativity through arts education; (3) identifying and remediating noncognitive, affective factors that may contribute to low scholastic achievement; and (4) applying *situation instruction* and student *observation* in teaching primary school courses.

6. Diversification of Education Institutions. Targeting private and non-governmental education programs have encouraged

education reforms to better respond to labor market needs for school and college-aged children and working adults. For example, the passing of the Vocational Education Act in 1996 signaled a new phase of vocational education development in China by expanding vocational and technical training at the post-primary, post-junior high school, and post-upper secondary levels.

7. Curriculum Changes. The curriculum has been changed to meet demands of local socioeconomic development and to cater to individual student interests and aptitudes. Students are now required to develop employable work skills and personal talents while learning fundamental school subjects. Although the general guidelines remain under the control of the Ministry of Education, textbook compilation has become more decentralized.

8. Strengthening Education-Business Partnership for Economic Development. For example, in 1995 the Council on Education-Business Partnership was established at the Ministry of Civil Affairs. The use of information technology under the Ministry of Education's Center for Research on Computer Educational Secondary and Primary Schools has increased linkages between educational institutions and businesses (e.g., IBM, AST, Apple Computers, and Intel).

9. Internationalization of education. From 1978 to 1997, nearly 270,000 Chinese students and scholars have traveled abroad to 103 countries and regions for advanced study, making China the largest country of origin and the United States the largest receiving country for these international students. Reforms have been developed and implemented to support those who study abroad and to encourage their return through lenient professional-entry policies. In 1995 the State Study-Abroad Fund Administration Committee was founded. It developed policies for screening qualified candidates, improving the return rate of study-abroad students/scholars, developing equitable policies for ethnic minority candidates, diversifying funding sources, and balancing the distribution of candidates sent to developed and developing countries (Zhou, 1997).

Like the 1919 May Fourth Movement, Chinese educational reforms have shifted from a fundamentally Confucian, social, and collectivist orientation to the direction of a more person-centered, individualistic, market-driven orientation. Against the background of negative social reactions to this shift, recent educational reforms have rebounded with a renewed stress on Confucian ideology, moral values, and social expectations.

EDUCATION AND SOCIAL EXPECTATIONS

By encompassing a society's view of knowledge, way of becoming, and goals of existence, what a person holds as essential, valuable, and desirable is developed, shaped, and reinforced. Although cultures have often reflected slow processes of value transformations and long-range moral, spiritual, and epistemological changes, sudden shifts can accelerate cultural transfigurations and abruptly disrupt a seemingly tranquil equilibrium. Sadar (1993) proposed that the influence of Western culture on Asia is but one example of many of such accelerated cultural changes. Thus, with the recent Chinese educational reforms from a Confucianistic orientation to a diametrically opposed individualistic Western perspective, one must wonder about the impact these changes have had on student, parent, and teacher attitudes and expectations about education.

In Chen's study of Chinese and American children as reported by Stevenson and Lee (1996), he showed Chinese children having incorporated more traditional Confucianistic education-based beliefs (e.g., on a wishing task, they mentioned education-related items more often, such as books, stationery, grades, future educational aspirations) than American students who listed a more diverse range of items (e.g., money, toys, pets). These Chinese students also reported liking school more than their Western counterparts did and perceived education as their most pressing task.

In a longitudinal study of a tertiary-level student cohort, Balla, Stokes, and Stafford (1991) reported Chinese students having a greater receptivity towards education, filial piety, obedience to authority, and approval seeking from their teachers. Similarly, in a separate study, Houghton (1991) reported students tending to seek approval and confirmation from their teachers, paying particular attention to what should be reproduced.

The importance of education and scholarship has persisted in Chinese public service today. While competition for advancement to successively higher levels of schooling is present for contemporary Chinese students, parents, and teachers, Stevenson and Lee (1996) reported strong student educational motivation even when students have been aware that their probability of gaining such an education is relatively low. For example, they noted that in Beijing, 86% of the high school students studied said they would like to graduate from college or have a graduate degree, despite the fact that only about 40% of junior high school graduates enter high school. Among these students, about 20% are able to gain admission to institutions of higher education. No more than 3% of the students from any one cohort are admitted to colleges and universities (State Education Commission, 1992).

The Chinese social orientation of academic achievement and consequences of failure are manifested by the person's identification with their families and the larger society. Thus, underlying a student's striving for academic success is the recognition and increase of social status of his or her family. Just as successes enhance family status, the consequences of poor performance may include not only a loss of status and prestige for the individual, but also a far more critical loss of family face. Within this cultural context, Stigler, Smith, and Mao (1985) found students actively avoiding this stigma and shame of failure. Hsu (1985) described this phenomenon as *da wo* (the greater self) that is family and society oriented and viewed as the dominant face in the motivation of Chinese students for academic success rather than the individual *xiao wo* (the smaller self). Yang and Yu (1989, July) reported similar distinctions of socially oriented and individually motivated achievement. They suggested that in Chinese culture where the orientation may be assumed to be toward the larger group, students' motivation to do well in school might be based on societal values or parental expectations, rather than simply for self-advancement.

In a study examining Chinese parental child-rearing attitudes and practices, Ho and Kang (1984) reported parental expectations of the children as adults. The most frequently mentioned personal characteristics were concerns with competence and achievement followed by those of moral character, sociability, and controlled temperament. In related studies, researchers examined efforts to foster development of independence and achievement motivation in Chinese children (Chang, 1979; Lewis, 1965; McClelland, 1963; Solomon, 1965). Overall, they found discontinuity between the educational socialization of children that stressed individualistic achievement and the ideology of their political cadres, who emphasized noncompetitive and collectivistic orientations. For example, Lewis' content analysis study of selected teachers' kindergarten manuals showed a sophisticated program of training conducive to individual achievement motivation by directing children to become active, self-reliant, competent, intellectually critical, and achievement oriented. McClelland (1963) compared three sets of Chinese stories used to teach children in public schools and discovered the content was low in need for achievement, very low in need for affiliation, and very low in need for power. When Solomon (1965) analyzed two sets of Chinese children's texts, he found an increase in achievement-oriented activities.

INDIVIDUALISM, COLLECTIVISM, AND SOCIAL EXPECTATIONS

Analyzing the Western notions of individualism and collectivism, Triandis (1988) suggested collectivism as promotive of interdependence where the self and group have shared compatible goals, as contrasted with individualism where a relationship between personal and collective goals may not be congruent. Ho and Chu (1994) contrasted a Chinese perspective with the Western view that regards individualism as affirming uniqueness, autonomy, freedom, personal responsibility, well-being, and intrinsic worth of the individual. They proposed that Chinese collectivism appear in varied forms emphasizing interdependence and group interests superseding those of the individual. They add that the meaning of individualism within a Chinese cultural context connotes selfishness, lack of concern for others, and aversion to group discipline. Within this cultural context, collectivism has more positive connotations as group affirmation and solidarity. They suggested that based upon Confucian precepts, collectivists have organized Chinese reality on the basis of a dialectic view in which the individual and the group derive meaning from coexistence with each other that include (1) the priority of collective interests governing the vertical individual-collective relationship; and (2) the reciprocity of responsibilities and obligations governing both vertical and horizontal interpersonal relationships within the collective.

Hwang (1987) and others (Wheeler, Reis, & Bond, 1989) showed that a person's individual personality is less evident in collectivist than individualist cultures. For example, they reported collectivists shifting their behavior depending on the context more than individualists, behaving differently and communicating less with outgroup or strangers, and interacting more uniformly and frequently with ingroup people (e.g., relatives, colleagues, neighbors). Similarly, others reported Chinese making more distinctions between ingroup and outgroup members than people in the United States (Bond, 1986; Triandis, McCusker, & Hui, 1990). They reported Chinese showing more intimacy within in-groups, exhibiting higher needs for abasement and socially oriented achievement, and having more formality and superordination toward outgroups than other Western people.

CHINESE ETHNIC IDENTITY AND CULTURAL ACCOMMODATION

Given the historical repetition of educational reforms, a growing impetus exists to better understand how modernization has influenced Chinese ethnic identity. By examining modernization as a transformative process, insight can be gained into its effects on ethnic affirmation and cultural accommodation of Chinese people who live outside China. To understand how people accommodate and adapt to unfamiliar cultures, researchers frequently have focused on demographic indicators, including length of time in the country of residence; vocation; years of schooling; age, time, and length of immigration; and immigrant status (e.g., Hong Kong-born Chinese versus PRC-born Chinese or native-born members of other ethnic groups). Unfortunately, such demographic indicators have not been sufficient when understanding individual identity development because they only indirectly measure the nature and extent of the acculturation process. Furthermore, demographic indicators such as length of residence or generation status have been confounded with other variables such as citizenship status, occupation, and education.

In a cross-cultural study comparing reported child-rearing practices of Chinese parents from Taiwan, immigrant Chinese parents originally from Taiwan who reside in the United States, and White Americans, differences were found on measures of parental control, parental encouragement of the child's independence, and parental emphasis on achievement (Lin & Fu, 1990). As expected, Chinese and immigrant Chinese parents reported greater parental control and emphasis on achievement compared to their White American counterparts. However, contrary to expectations, Chinese parents showed greater encouragement of independence in kindergarten and early primary school-age children than the White American parents. Lin and Fu (1990) suggested that although interdependence within the family has been stressed in Chinese families, independence beyond the family is also encouraged to facilitate achievement within the larger society.

In another study, Ho and Hills (1992, October) compared individual differences in cultural identity development among three groups of Hong Kong Chinese youth in different phases of migration to New Zealand: premigration (less than 2 years after migration) and 2 and 4 years after migration. Four styles of cultural adaptation and accommodation were found in these students: assimilation to the host society; integration with the host society while maintaining Chinese identity; retention of the Chinese identity (separation); and identification with neither one's native culture nor the host society (marginalization). The proportion of adolescents in the assimilation and integration categories increased with length of time since immigration. However, even after 2 to 4 years in New Zealand, about half of the adolescents (52.6%) were categorized as maintaining a predominant traditional Chinese cultural identity.

Wolfgang and Josefowitz (1978) explored possible value conflicts of Chinese immigrants in Toronto by assessing Chinese and North American values among 109 high school students, including China-born Chinese, Canadian-born Chinese, and Canadian non-Chinese individuals. Although shared similarities among all three groups were found in the domains of family, nonverbal behavior, sex, and marriage, Canadian non-Chinese students valued individualism and openness to change more than the other Chinese groups, who valued community and education as a means to achieve respect.

Using Western-derived research instruments, Ho (1990) showed value orientations of Chinese students shifting toward individualism, materialism, less ambition, and less obedience after exposure and adaptation to Westernization. Yang and Cheng (1987) found similar results using a Chinese indigenous instrument that measured the following five value factors: Chinese familism (including the values of loyalty to family, filial piety, and mutual help among family members); modesty and contentment (moderation, noncompetition with others, and self-sacrifice for group); face and relationship orientation (face protection, wealth pursuit, and relationship based on favor); solidarity and harmoniousness (harmony with others, spirit of solidarity, and honesty and faithfulness); and capacity for hardship and perseverance (bearing risks and difficulty, tolerating hardship, and accepting the unavoidable). They concluded that during the process of societal modernization, Chinese people have become more individually oriented, as seen in their familism and other focused relationships decreasing in magnitude and their self-independent, competitive, and egalitarian orientations increasing in importance.

Yang (1992) questioned whether Confucian and Western values and/or attitudes were able to coexist peacefully in society and should show that filial piety and self-reliance were able to exist together during a process of social change in college students. Yang's findings were supported by Brindley's (1989/1990) interview data, which suggested traditional values such as relationship orientation and filial piety were able to coexist along with utilitarianism, materialism, and independence in Chinese academics. These findings have been in agreement with Lee's (1985) observations that traditional beliefs and practices like *feng shui* (geomancy) and *yuan fen* (predestined affinity) are still observed and serve important functions for many Chinese to explain social and psychological stresses.

CHINESE AMERICAN ETHNIC IDENTITY AND CULTURAL ACCOMMODATION

In the United States, Chinese Americans and Asian Americans more broadly defined have been mythologized as a highly successful "model" minority. Superficial economic, social, and educational indicators of success have often overshadowed the discrimination that has been directed at them (e.g., denial of citizenship rights, ownership of land, personal and properly assaults). For example, beginning in the 1840s, Chinese men arrived in the United States in large numbers because of the high demand for cheap labor (the discovery of gold in the Sacramento Valley and building of the transcontinental railroad) and the political unrest in China. However, given the U.S. economic recession in the

1860s, the Chinese were eventually viewed as an economic threat. Systematic harassment resulted in legal discrimination, including exclusionist legislation at all levels of government that culminated in the 1882 Chinese Exclusion Act (which was eventually repealed in 1943).

The mythical image of Asian or Chinese Americans as a "model minority" has been especially visible in education. Although a perception of high educational attainment has been attributed to a Confucian remnant of the importance of education and academic success, educational success has not been experienced equally among all Asian groups. Within the context of the United States, this high-achieving "model minority" label for Asian Americans has not been supported because their educational success has followed a bimodal distribution, weighted on one end with extraordinary high educational achievements and the other with a large undereducated mass. Thus, how has Confucianism influenced students at both ends of this educational achievement spectrum in terms of cultural expectations?

As Chinese in America have been faced with value conflicts when sojourning to countries outside of China, Chinese Americans have been affected by the U.S. White American culture. Faced with issues of cultural adaptation and accommodation, Chinese Americans have experienced varying degrees of acculturation, a process of accumulating and incorporating the beliefs and customs of an alternate culture (Fong, 1965; Sue & Kitano, 1973; Sue & Morishima, 1982). As a means of coping with differing cultural expectations, Sue and Sue (1971) developed a conceptual scheme for understanding how Asian Americans adjust to cultural conflicts generated by differing racial-ethnic values and acculturation processes within the context of oppression found in U.S. society. They observed that Asian Americans resolve cultural conflicts by (1) remaining loyal to their own ethnic group by retaining their version of traditional Asian values (e.g., living up to family expectations); (2) rejecting their ethnic group and attempting to identify with White dominant cultural values and expectations; or (3) developing a new identity that incorporates ethnic and White American values, resulting in a bicultural orientation. Unfortunately, research about Chinese American ethnic identity is blended into studies about intrapersonal processes (e.g., Asian American racial-cultural identity) and interpersonal processes (acculturation theories). Nevertheless, the framework of locus of control and racial identity can be informative in understanding the process of Chinese American identity formation and accommodation.

Researchers on racial identity have argued that different identity statuses reflect an internal or external locus of control as one means of an individual's effort to integrate his or her understanding of self with the implications of his or her membership in an ethnic group in the United States (Carter, 1995; Helms, 1990). To this end, Rotter's notion of control being internal or external has been informative to the degree that an individual feels he or she can shape or control his or her own destiny. Rotter (1966) formulated the concept of internal-external control as a personality trait operating across situations where experiences rest either within the individual (internal locus of control) or by chance and luck (external locus of control). For example, researchers have found that Chinese, American-born Chinese, and White Americans varied in the degree of internal control, with the Chinese reporting internal control the least, followed by the American-born Chinese and White Americans (Hsieh, Shybut, & Lotsof, 1969; Leong, 1985). They concluded that the "individual-centered" White American culture has emphasized an internally driven locus of control fostering independence and self-reliance, and the "situation-centered" Chinese culture placed importance on the group, tradition, and social role expectations of individuals.

CONCLUSION

One of the difficulties in approaching the topics of Confucianism, education, and identity is the vastness of the topic. Although researchers have reported studies from many parts of the world, varying aspects of achievement employing different research methods and theoretical paradigms have been used. One explanation of why a more coherent literature does not exist is in the very complex nature of understanding the bases and consequences of identity formation and education in a world that is consistently changing. As China and the United States strive to maintain or improve global status, the need for knowledge about how to improve education assumes growing economic, social, and personal importance.

To this end, the resiliency of how and what Chinese cultural traditions have been maintained and transformed in changing social, cultural, and political conditions needs to be understood in terms of the process of adaptation and accommodation. In some domains, Confucian values and behaviors have had enduring historical and cultural continuity despite geographic separation, generation status, and ideological differences. Education and the socialization of Chinese children play a central role in developing and maintaining Chinese identity. However, a personal construction of Chinese identity is a complex process involving acculturation and accommodation into the society where Chinese live. Either way, as the Chinese idiom *Cang Hai Sang Tian* (the blue seas and the mulberry orchard) describes the constant changes in world events (Zhang, 1996), educators and policymakers must keep abreast of these changes or be forever lost in a world of ineffective educational efforts that will leave both educators and students without any identity to ground them.

REFERENCES

Balla, J. R., Stokes, M. J., & Stafford, K. J. (1991). Changes in student approaches to study at CPHK: A 3-year longitudinal study. *AAIR Conference refereed proceedings* (pp. 7-31). Melbourne: Melbourne Australasian Association for Institutional Research.

Bond, M. H. (1988). Finding universal dimensions of individual variation in multicultural studies of values: Rokeach and Chinese value surveys. *Journal of Personality and Social Psychology, 55*, 1009-1015.

Brindley, T. A. (1989/1990). Socio-psychological values in the Republic of China. *Asian Thought and Society, 14*, 980-115, and *15*, 1-15.

Carter, R. T. (1995). *The influence of race and racial identity in psychotherapy: Toward a racially inclusive model.* New York: John Wiley & Sons.

Chang, P. H. (1979). Children's literature and political socialization. In G. C. Chu and F. L. K. Hsu (Eds.), *Moving a mountain: Cultural change in China* (pp. 237-256). Honolulu: University of Hawaii Press.

Ding, W. (1997). *Understanding Confucius.* Beijing, China: Chinese Literature Press.

Fong, S. L. M. (1965). Assimilation of Chinese in America. Changes in orientation and social perception. *American Journal of Sociology, 71*, 265-273.

Helms, J. E. (Ed.). (1990). *Black and White racial identity: Theory, research, and practice.* New York: Greenwood.

Ho, D. Y. F. (1987). *Family therapies with minorities.* Newbury Park, CA: Sage.

Ho, D. Y. F. (1989). Continuity and variation in Chinese patterns of socialization. *Journal of Marriage and the Family, 51*, 149-163.

Ho, D. Y. F. (1990). *Chinese values and behavior: A psychological study.* Unpublished manuscript, University of Hong Kong.

Ho, D. Y. F. (1994). Filial piety, authoritarian moralism, and cognitive conservatism in Chinese societies. *Genetic, Social, and General Psychology Monographs, 120*, 347-365.

Ho, D. Y. F. (1996). Filial piety and its psychological consequences. In M. H. Bond (Ed.), *The handbook of Chinese psychology* (pp. 143-154). Hong Kong: Oxford University Press.

Ho, D. Y. F., & Chu, C. Y. (1994). Components of individualism, collectivism, and, social organization: An application in the study of Chinese culture. In U. Kim, H. C. Triandis, C. Kagitcibasi, S. C. Choi, and G. Yoon (Eds.), *Individualism and collectivism: Theory, method, and applications* (pp. 137-156). London: Sage.

Ho, D. Y. F., & Kang, T. K. (1984). Intergenerational comparisons of child-rearing attitudes and practices in Hong Kong. *Developmental Psychology, 20*(6), 1004-1016.

Ho, E. S., & Hills, M. (1992, October). *The challenge of cultural change: Hong Kong Chinese adolescent immigrants in New Zealand.* Paper presented at the Asian Conference of Psychology, Singapore.

Houghton, D. (1991). Mr. Chong: A case study of a dependent learner of English for academic purposes. *System, 19*(1-2), 75-90.

Hseih, T., Shybut, J., & Lotsof, E. (1969). Internal versus external control and ethnic group membership: A cross-cultural comparison. *Journal of Consulting and Counseling Psychology, 33*, 122-124.

Hsu, F. L. K. (1985). The Chinese family: Relations, problems, and therapy. In W. Tseng and D. Wu (Eds.), *Chinese culture and mental health* (pp. 95-112). New York: Academic Press.

Hu, S. M. (1960). *China.* New Haven, CT: HRAG Press.

Hwang, K. K. (1987). Face and favor: The Chinese-power game. *American Journal of Sociology, 92*, 944-974.

Kwong, J. (1997). The reemergence of private schools in socialist China. *Comparative Education Review, 8*, 244-259.

Latourette, K. S. (1957). *A short history of the Far East*. New York: Macmillan.

Lee, R. P. I. (1985). Social stress and coping behavior in Hong Kong. In W. S. Tseng and D. Y. H. Wu (Eds.), *Chinese culture and mental health* (pp. 361-380). Taipei, Taiwan: Institute of Ethnology, Academia Sinica.

Leong, F. T. (1985). Career development of Asian Americans. *Journal of College Student Personnel, 26,* 539-546.

Lewin, M. K. (1994). *Educational innovation in China: Tracing the impact of the 1985 reforms*. Essex, England: Longman Group Limited.

Lewis, J. W. (1965). Education and political development: A study of preschool training programs in mainland China. In J. S. Coleman (Ed.), *Education and political development* (pp. 423-429). Princeton, NJ: Princeton University Press.

Lin, C. Y. C., & Fu, V. R. (1990). A comparison of child rearing practices among Chinese, immigrant Chinese, and Caucasian-American parents. *Child Development, 61,* 429-433.

McClelland, D. C. (1963). Motivation patterns in Southeast Asians with special reference to the Chinese case. *Social Issues, 19,* 6-19.

Mok, K. (1997). Private challenges to public dominance: The resurgence of private education in the Pearl River Delta. *Comparative Education, 33*(1), 43-60.

Mordkowitz, E. R., & Ginsburg, H. P. (1987). Early academic socialization of successful Asian-American college students. *The Quarterly Newsletter of the Laboratory of Comparative Human Cognition, 9*(2), 85-91.

Paine, L. (1991). Reforming teachers. In I. Epstein (Ed.), *Chinese education: Problems, policies and prospects* (pp. 217-254). New York: Garland Publishing.

Riskin, C. (1993). *China's political economy: The quest for development since 1949.* London: Oxford University Press.

Rotter, J. (1966). Generalized expectancies for internal versus external control of reinforcement. *Psychological Monographs, 80,* 1-28.

Sadar, Z. (1993). Asian cultures: Between programmed and desired futures. In E. B. Masini and Y. Atal (Eds.), *Perspectives on Asia's futures III: The futures of Asian cultures* (pp. 37-56). Bangkok, Thailand: UNESCO-Principal Regional Office for Asia and the Pacific.

Solomon, R. H. (1965). Educational themes in China's changing culture. *China Quarterly, 22,* 154-170.

State Education Commission (PRC). (1992). *Educational statistics yearbook of China 1991/1992*. Beijing, China: People's Education Press.

Stevenson, H. W., & Lee, S. Y. (1996). The academic achievement of Chinese students. In M. H. Bond (Ed.), *The handbook of Chinese psychology* (pp. 124-142). Hong Kong: Oxford University Press.

Stigler, J. W., Smith, S., & Mao, L. W. (1985). The self-perception of competence by Chinese children. *Child Development, 56*(5), 1259-1270.

Sue, S., & Kitano, H. H. L. (1973). Stereotypes as a measure of success. *Journal of Social Issues, 29,* 83-98.

Sue, S., & Morishima, J. K. (1982). *The mental health of Asian Americans*. San Francisco, CA: Jossey-Bass.

Sue, S., & Sue, D. W. (1971). Chinese-American personality and mental health. *Amerasia Journal, 1,* 36-49.

Triandis, H. C. (1988). Cross-cultural contributions to theory in social psychology. In M. H. Bond (Ed.), *The cross-cultural challenge to social psychology* (pp. 122-140). Newbury Park, CA: Sage.

Triandis, H. C., McCusker, C., & Hui, C. H. (1990). Multimethod probes of individualism and collectivism. *Journal of Personality and Social Psychology, 59,* 1006-1020.

Tsang, M. C. (1996). Financial reform of basic education in China. *Economics of Education Review, 15,* 423-444.

54   OTA WANG

Wheeler, L., Reis, H. T., & Bond, M. H. (1989). Collectivism-individualism in everyday social life: The middle kingdom and the melting pot. *Journal of Personality and Social Psychology, 57,* 79-86.

Wolfgang, A., & Josefowitz, N. (1978). A comparative study of assimilation of the Chinese in New York City and Lima, Peru. *Canadian Ethnic Studies, 2,* 130-135.

Yang, K. S. (1992). Do traditional and modern values coexist in a modern Chinese society? *Proceedings of the conference on Chinese perspectives on values* (pp. 117-158). Taipei, Taiwan: Center for Sinological Studies (Chinese).

Yang, K. S., & Cheng, B. S. (1987). Confucianized values, individual modernity, and organizational behavior: An empirical test of the post-Confucian hypothesis [in Chinese]. *Bulletin of the Institute of Ethnology, Academia Sinica (Taiwan), 64,* 1-49.

Yang, K. S., & Yu, A. B. (1989, July). *Social- and individual-oriented achievement motivation: An attributional analysis of their cognitive, affective, motivational, and behavioral consequences.* Paper presented at the July 10th Biennial meeting of the International Society for the Study of Behavioral Development, Jyvaskyla, Finland.

Zhang, C. (1996). *Chinese idioms and their stories.* Beijing, China: Foreign Languages Press.

Zhao, F. (1998). A remarkable move of restructuring: Chinese higher education. *Education Policy Analysis Archives, 6*(5), 1-14.

Zhou, N. Z. (1997, April). *Education reforms in China for the 1990's: Strengthening links with educational research: An overview and some illustrations.* Paper presented at the annual meeting of the American Educational Research Association, Chicago.

Zhu, Y., & Lan, J. (1996). Educational reform in China since 1978. In H. Hong & Starvou (Eds.), *In search of a Chinese road towards modernization: Economic and educational issues in China's reform process.* Wales: The Edwin Mellen Press.

II

Ethnic and Racial Identities in National Contexts

3

Multicultural Identities and Adaptation of Young Immigrants in Israel

Gabriel Horenczyk
Uzi Ben-Shalom
Hebrew University of Jerusalem

A foreign visitor looking at Israeli society would probably be impressed by its diversity, by its complex tapestry of groups and cultures: Arabs and Jews-religious and secular; Ashkenazi and Sephardic Jews; Arabs with different religious and ethnic backgrounds-Muslims, Christians, Druze, Bedouins; and immigrants and tourists from many parts of the world. It has a large variety of languages, traditions, worldviews, customs, and norms, out of which a rich multicultural society could emerge and flourish. Israeli society, at this stage of its development, however, can at best be described as plural with certain multicultural features, for it lacks much of the ideology, ethos, and institutional support needed to transform it onto one that "promotes the value of diversity" (Fowers & Richardson, 1996, p. 609) and that strives "to enhance the dignity, rights, and worth of marginalized groups" (p. 609).

One of the areas in which this pattern of plurality without multiculturalism is most clearly reflected is in Israel's educational system. Multicultural education, broadly speaking, is based on two major prerequisites: intercultural contact and cultural recognition (using Taylor's [1994] influential term). Although Israeli education is almost totally "public" (in the sense that there are almost no "private" K-12 schools), the educational system is divided largely along national and religious lines. Arabs and Jews, for the most part, attend different schools; within the Jewish sector, there are separate "state-religious" and "state" (secular) schools. Within the Arab sector, most of the Muslim children are enrolled in "state" Arab schools and Christian children generally attend church-run educational institutions. In contrast to this national and religious segregation, the educational integration of Jewish immigrants traditionally has been described as reflecting a "melting pot" approach, although in practice it has basically followed assimilationist policies and strategies. (We will elaborate on this topic later in this chapter.)

Walzer (1998) related these institutional and ideological patterns to the fact that, for historical reasons, Israel is triply divided. First of all, it has retained the millet system imposed by the Ottoman Empire, which allows and encourages the various religious communities to run their own courts and to develop and maintain partially differentiated educational programs. Secondly, Israel is a modern nation-state, established by a nationalist movement and incorporating a substantial national minority whose members are citizens of the state, but do not necessarily find their culture or history mirrored in its public life. Thirdly, Israel's Jewish population is a society of immigrants "drawn from every part of a widely scattered Diaspora, an ingathering of men and women who have in fact, despite their common Jewishness (itself sometimes subject to dispute), very different histories and cultures" (p. 155). These historical legacies have resulted, according to Walzer, in complex educational arrangements, so that institutions have different and not entirely consistent aims: sustaining and legitimizing differences and divisions, both religious and national; fostering a single national (Zionist or Israeli) consciousness; and assimilating Jewish immigrants.

The segregated school system, with separate schools for different national and religious groups teaching particular histories, cultures, religions, and values, is not likely to provide the optimal bases for multicultural education. Israeli schools can, and often do, deal with issues of tolerance and coexistence. Some educational institutions also send their students to intergroup encounters, where youngsters from different national and/or religious sectors can explore their mutual perceptions and attitudes (see, e.g., Weiner, 1998). But improving intergroup relations is only one of the aims of multicultural education (Banks, 1995). A more genuine and courageous multicultural education needs a broader common educational ground, or at least the possibility-both institutional and ideological-that a common, although not uniform, educational space can be created by means of proper educational strategies and interventions. Issues related to multicultural education are being raised in those arenas of the Israeli educational system where cultures come together, where cultural identities are debated and negotiated. In Israeli society today, multicultural educational discourse-or rather discourse about multicultural education and multicultural identities-is confined primarily to the education of immigrants, particularly that of recent newcomers from the former Soviet Union.

Since 1989, approximately 900,000 immigrants from the former Soviet Union arrived in Israel[1]; during this decade, Israel also received more than 40,000 Ethiopian immigrants and approximately 90,000 immigrants from other parts of the world. (These figures do not include temporary foreign workers not automatically granted Israeli citizenship by the Law of Return.) The newcomers from the former Soviet Union today make up about 15% of the total Israeli population. Such a big wave of immigration within a relatively short period of time has posed serious challenges to Israel's economic, social and educational infrastructure. The sudden influx of large numbers of immigrants into the educational system has also inevitably led to changes in the discourse about multicultural identities and multicultural education. It is important to note that cultural identity issues have always been particularly salient in the public rhetoric about immigration in modern Israel. Israel is formally committed to the "ingathering of exiles"; Israelis see Jews worldwide as members of its "imagined community" (Anderson, 1991) and Jewish immigrants as returning to their historical homeland. Thus, immigrants are expected to rapidly redefine their cultural identities, both in relation to their affiliations with their society of origin and their new receiving society.

This chapter examines the role of cultural identity in the psychological and school adaptation of young Israeli newcomers from the former Soviet Union. We will first conceptualize the theoretical constructs, and review briefly research related to cultural identity and to psychological adjustment among immigrants in general, and among Israeli immigrants from the former Soviet Union in particular. This will lead to the formulation of a "cultural identity accumulation hypothesis," according to which the more cultural groups the immigrant individual identifies with, the higher his or her level of adaptation--both in the psychological and educational spheres. Support for this hypothesis will be provided by findings from a study recently conducted among young immigrants residing in Israeli boarding schools. We will then discuss the educational implications of the "cultural identity accumulation" notion in light of the research literature on multicultural education and on the educational approaches toward the integration of immigrant students.

CULTURAL IDENTITY

One of the central notions in the discourse on multicultural education is cultural identity (Ogbu, 1995). Education is often perceived as a powerful tool for the development-or transformation-of cultural identities, and, in turn, cultural

---

[1]According to the Central Bureau of Statistics and the Ministry of Immigrant Absorption, Israel received 847,890 immigrants from the former Soviet Union between the years 1989 and 1997.

identity is regarded as an important factor in school adaptation and achievement, especially among immigrant and minority youth. The idea of cultural identity, in spite of its elusiveness, seems to be essential for the understanding of the psychological processes involved in cultural transition. Various concepts are being used in the psychological and sociological literature to describe the individual's connection to his or her cultural group-social identity (e.g., Tajfel & Turner, 1986), national identity (e.g., Smith, 1991), ethnic identity (e.g., Phinney, 1990; Weinrich, 1989), basic group identity (Isaacs, 1989), cultural identity (Collier & Thomas, 1988; Ferdman & Horenczyk, in press), and others. Although many of these terms are meant to refer to cultural identification in different areas, the distinctions are not always clear and consensually accepted (Hutnik, 1991). Because identification with a cultural group involves social, personal, and cultural aspects, no single conceptualization and definition is likely to encompass the richness and complexity of the construct. As we are focusing in this chapter on individuals undergoing cultural transition, it seems to us that the term "cultural identity" is most appropriate. Generally speaking, cultural identity refers to cognitive, affective, and behavioral aspects that reflect the nature of the individual's attitude toward his or her ethnic, national, or cultural group (Hutnik, 1991). Following Tajfel's (1981) widely accepted definition of social identity, we conceptualize cultural identity as "that part of the self-perception of the individual derived from his or her membership in a cultural group (or cultural groups) together with the emotional significance attached to this (these) memberships."[2]

The migration process involves almost inevitably a redefinition of cultural identities. As Maines (1978) pointed out "identities migrate every bit as much as bodies" (p. 242). During all phases of the intercultural migration process, newcomers must continuously reorganize the delicate structure of their various subidentities-those related to their membership in the new host society and those involving their attachment to the values of their former culture (Horenczyk, 1996).

Two general orientations have guided the study of identity change among immigrants (Sayegh & Lasry, 1993), with very different and far-reaching psychological and educational implications. For many decades, theory and research on the adaptation of newcomers was characterized by the adoption and development of *linear* models of acculturation. Influential sociologists, such as Gordon (1964), proposed a unidirectional process of assimilation: In order to gain access to cultural and social resources in the new society, they suggested,

---

[2]A slight different conceptualization of "cultural identity," grounded in a social constructivist orientation (Ferdman & Horenczyk, in press), will be presented in a later section of this chapter.

immigrants have to give up their traditional culture. In Gordon's (1964) words: "The price of such assimilation . . . is the disappearance of the ethnic group as a separate entity and the evaporation of its distinctive values" (p. 81). Such an unidimensional and bipolar model clearly implied that the adoption of a new identity requires the relinquishment of the previous one. This theoretical approach reflected-and also contributed to-the general assimilationist attitudes that guided immigration policies in various parts of the world, particularly in the United States.

Such an assimilationist strategy was also implemented by the Israeli establishment during the mass Jewish immigration from the Arab countries in the 1950s (Smooha, 1978). One of the underlying assumptions of these policies suggested that the quick adoption of an Israeli identity by the newcomers is beneficial not only from an ideological point of view but also for the immigrants' successful adaptation because it was seen as a way of reducing possible conflict among identities, values, and norms. In other words, the assimilationist approach to immigrant absorption was also based on a psychological rationale: The replacement of the original culture by the new Israeli culture will prevent identity conflict and will ease the immigrant's adaptation to the new society.

During the past two decades, new bidimensional models have been increasingly replacing these unidirectional conceptualizations. One of the most widely used models was developed by Berry (1990, Berry & Sam, 1997). According to Berry, minority members of plural societies (such as immigrants) must confront two important issues-the extent to which they wish to maintain their minority cultural identity, and the degree of intercultural contact with majority members they desire. For the sake of conceptual simplicity, the model assumes dichotomous decisions on each of the issues: "yes" or "no" to the maintenance of minority identity, and "yes" or "no" to intercultural contact.

Posing the two issues simultaneously generates a framework that defines four types of acculturation attitudes: integration, assimilation, separation, and marginalization. The *assimilation* attitude reflects a strong orientation toward, and adoption of, the majority culture with a relinquishing of ties to the former (and now minority) culture. The opposite orientation is that of *separation, which represents a strong allegiance to the minority culture, together with a detachment from the new culture. Integration* involves the identification with, and adoption of, components of both the minority and majority cultures. Finally, the *marginalization* attitude is characterized by a rejection of, and/or lack of involvement in, one's own minority culture, as well as in the culture of the larger society. Berry's model of acculturation attitudes is not worded in terms of identity; we prefer, however, to conceptualize the four options as distinct immigrant's *identity orientations*, each representing a different possible "combination" of old and new identities.

Numerous studies have been conducted to assess the acculturation attitudes of various immigrant groups worldwide (Berry, 1997). Results generally show integration--the bicultural identity orientation--to be the preferred mode of acculturation, followed either by assimilation or separation, while marginalization has always been the least favored mode of acculturation. The high endorsement of the bicultural orientation was also found consistently in a series of studies conducted in Israel with young immigrants from the former Soviet Union (Ben-Shalom, 1997; Horenczyk, 1996; Horenczyk, in press). In these studies, immigrant respondents were also asked about the acculturation expectations that they attribute to their host peers. Results showed that integration was also perceived by the newcomers as the acculturation ideology of the receiving society, although immigrants felt relatively strong expectations of assimilation, as compared to their own less willingness to relinquish their culture of origin.

ADAPTATION

The primary objective of social and cross-cultural psychologists interested in identity processes and acculturation among newcomers is to identify variables that may help predict, and eventually improve, the adaptation of the immigrants during the various phases of their cultural transition. Searle and Ward (1990) make the distinction between psychological and sociocultural adaptation. At the psychological level, they focus on personal and cultural identity, mental health, and quality of life. Sociocultural adaptation refers to the interaction between the individual and social institutions and norms of their new society; its primary components are work, family life, education, and the acquisition of communicative skills. According to Ward (1996), psychological and sociocultural adjustment are interrelated, but they are predicated largely by different types of variables and show different patterns of variations over time.

The evidence related to the psychological adaptation of immigrants is inconclusive, and this state of affairs can be attributed to different conceptualizations and operationalizations of *adaptation*, *adjustment*, and mental health used in the various studies. It is evident that migrant individuals have to face drastic changes in a wide range of areas. Cultural transition is a stressful life event, and it has been argued that such a powerful experience is likely to lead to psychological distress during certain periods in the migration process. The term "culture shock" (Oberg, 1960) suggests such an inevitability of psychological problems among immigrants. Some researchers, however, have pointed to potential beneficial psychological outcomes of cultural transition (Adler, 1975). Berry (1990) introduced the term *acculturative stress*, which, unlike culture shock, does not imply a positive or a negative resolution of the stressful situation, and he calls for research aimed at identifying the moderating and mediating variables that intervene in the relationship between acculturation and mental health. One review of the literature (Berry & Kim, 1988) concluded that mental health problems clearly often arise during migration; however, these problems are not inevitable and seem to depend on a variety of group and individual characteristics that enter into the acculturation process.

Psychiatric epidemiological studies conducted in Israel during recent years tend to show relatively high levels of psychological distress among immigrants from the former Soviet Union as compared to similar samples from the host population (Mirsky, 1998). Psychological disturbances were found to be more prevalent among immigrants from different age groups. In samples of high school and university students, for example, new comers from the former Soviet Union reported levels of psychological distress higher than those that characterize their Israel-born counterparts (Mirsky, 1997).

CULTURAL IDENTITY AND ADAPTATION

As indicated earlier, sociopsychological research can contribute to the understanding of migration processes and outcomes by exploring variables that might be related to the newcomers' adaptation to the new society. This study focuses on one major factor, namely, cultural identity, and examines its role in the psychological and school adjustment of immigrant adolescents.

Bidimensional models of immigrant's identity allow for the conceptualization and measurement not only of monocultural identities (such as maintenance of identity of origin or adoption of host identity), but also of bicultural identities (positive attitudes both to identity of origin and to new host identity).[3] But the model itself does not endorse nor recommend any of the identity orientations. A certain identity orientation can be preferred on a variety of grounds: ideological, moral, legal, and others. Quite often, however, arguments for or against multiculturalism and multicultural identities are phrased in psychological or educational terms: They suggest that multicultural identities are beneficial (or detrimental) to psychological or school adjustment.

Opposing predictions can be, and have been, formulated for the relationship between biculturalism (or multiculturalism) at the individual level and psychological adaptation. On one hand, norms, values, and expected behaviors of different cultures are sometimes incompatible with one another, and they are likely to exert conflicting demands on the bicultural individual. Within

---

[3]It should be noted that within the framework of unidimensional models, biculturalism is seen as a transitory phase, as the model assumes that successful assimilation inevitably involves a shift from maintenance of the immigrant culture to full adoption of the host culture (Bourhis, Moise, Perreault, & Senecal, 1997).

the sociological literature, leading theorists and researchers have claimed that role strain and role conflict are normal consequences of multiple identities (Goode, 1960; Sarbin & Allen, 1968). It can be assumed that when these multiple identities are all in the same realm, such as ethnic and cultural identification, the likelihood of strain and conflict is even greater. This line of thought is reflected in the psychological rationale for assimilation policies toward immigration mentioned earlier.

During recent years, it has been increasingly argued that the benefits of a multicultural orientation tend to outweigh its costs. According to Berry (1998), "personal diversity" gives a person flexibility and choice in daily life that those who hold monocultural identities do not have. A multicultural orientation often also entails a positive attitude and an openness toward diverse cultural groups, increasing the extent and variety of available social support. At a more existential level, the availability of multiple cultural resources can provide immigrants with additional sources for meaning-making, especially during critical periods of their cultural transition. In her analysis of the advantages of "identity accumulation," Thoits (1983) suggested that "[t]he greater the number of identities held, the stronger one's sense of meaningful, guided existence. The more identities, the more 'existential security' . . . A sense of meaningful existence and purposeful, ordered behavior are crucial to psychological health . . ." (p. 175).

Research conducted within Berry's conceptual framework tends to support this latter position (Berry & Sam, 1997). Many investigations have shown that individuals who prefer and in fact attain some degree of integration (the bicultural identity orientation) report less psychological distress. Among South Asians in the United States, for example, integration scores predicted lower overall acculturative stress (Krishnan & Berry, 1992). In a study of immigrants in Germany, Schmitz (1992) found that integration was associated with reduced levels of both neuroticism and psychoticism.

Our study examined the role of cultural identity and adjustment among adolescent students who recently immigrated to Israel from the former Soviet Union. Although based on the sociopsychological framework outlined earlier, our approach to the relationship between multiculturalism (at the individual level) and adaptation rests on a broader perspective. First, we examined adaptation in two separate, although interrelated, areas: We measured both immigrants' psychological adaptation and their adjustment to the education context. School adjustment is generally regarded as the primary sociocultural and developmental task for adolescents attending school. Within most immigrant communities, the importance attributed to school adjustment and achievement is particularly high: Newcomers tend to see schools as welcome avenues to participation and mobility (Gibson, 1991). The high emphasis placed on education seems to be even more accentuated among immigrants from the former Soviet Union. Due mainly to anti-Semitism, Jewish children tend to excel at schools in order to enter Soviet universities, and educational achievement was therefore very high on the normative and economic priority lists of Soviet Jews; this cultural pattern is clearly reflected in the very positive attitudes toward education and schooling held by immigrant parents and children after their transition to Israel.

Second, in our study, we examined multicultural identities, rather than bicultural identities conceptualized and operationalized within Berry's (1990) methodological framework. The particular identity configuration of Jewish immigration to Israel from the former Soviet Union allowed us to measure three ethnic and cultural identities of the newcomers: the Israeli (host), the Jewish, and the identity of origin (transformed-or rather reconstructed and redefined--as a minority identity in the new society). We put forward a cultural identity accumulation hypothesis: The more positive cultural identities held by the immigrant individual, the higher will be his or her levels of psychological and educational adjustment.

METHOD

Participants

Our sample consisted of 270 immigrants from the former Soviet Union, residing in four boarding schools for immigrant youngsters. Fifty-eight percent of the respondents were males and 42% females; their ages ranged from 15 to 18 years (mean = 16.6 years). Eighty-six percent of the participants were born in European republics of the former Soviet Union, and 14% arrived from former Soviet Asian countries. Length of stay in Israel ranged from 4 to 31 months (mean = 13 months).

Questionnaires and Procedure

The research questionnaire consisted of several sections of dealing with identity and adjustment. In this chapter we will focus on results obtained from two major sections, one dealing with cultural identity and the other with psychological and school adjustment.

Cultural Identity. Respondents were first presented with 12 statements related to 4 dimensions of 3 different cultural identities. The statements referred to the Jewish identity of the respondent, to his or her Israeli identity, and to the identity of origin (reformulated as a minority identity within Israeli society, e.g., "Russian"). For each of the identities, we measured its centrality, valence, the respondent's feelings of pride toward that identity, and his or her sense of closeness to members of the cultural group. The centrality and valence items were derived from Herman's (1989) conceptualization and methodology. The item assessing the centrality of Jewish identity, for example, read as follows: "I feel that my being Jewish affects many areas in my life," and the *valence* of the Israeli identity, for example, was measured by the item: "If I were born again, I would like to be born Israeli." The third item of cultural identification assessed the respondent's sense of pride in the group membership; Phinney (1992) included this component in her measure of ethnic identity on the grounds that the term "pride" is increasingly used to refer to positive feelings toward one's group. The last component, closeness to members of the cultural group, reflects identification with the "imagined community" (Anderson, 1991) and seems especially relevant to the sense of group membership among individuals in cultural and geographic transition. Respondents were asked to indicate their extent of agreement with each of the statements in this section, on a 5-point sale (high values reflecting high levels of cultural identification).

The internal structure of the identity questionnaire was examined using factor analysis (with varimax rotation). Results showed a clear differentiation between the three cultural identities-Jewish, Israeli, and identity of origin-with three of the four components (valence, pride, and closeness) loading strongly on each of the factors. Taken together, the three factors-representing the three cultural identities-explained 49% of the variance. A fourth factor emerged from the analysis that consisted of the three centrality items. This factor was not included in subsequent analyses. Three identification scales were then computed, one for each cultural identity, as the mean of the three components (valence, pride, and closeness). Values of Cronbach alpha ranged between 0.60 and 0.72, suggesting a satisfactory reliability of the scales based on the number of items included (Cortina, 1993).

We then created a new *cultural identity accumulation* variable. We first computed dichotomous dummy variables for each cultural identity (1 for high cultural identification, 0 for low identification) using the median of each distribution as the cutoff criterion. The new accumulation variable was then computed as the sum of the three dummy variables, ranging from 0 (no high identity) to 3 (high values on all three cultural identities).

Adaptation. Following Searle and Ward's (1990) important distinction between psychological and sociocultural adaptation of immigrants and minorities, we decided to examine in our study the respondents' self-reported adaptation in both the psychological and the educational areas. Three aspects of psychological adjustment were measured in this section of the questionnaire: life satisfaction, loneliness, and mastery. The life satisfaction score was computed as the mean of the immigrant's extent of agreement with four items taken from the Life

Satisfaction Index A (Neugarten, Havighurst, & Tonin, 1961). This measure uses the individual's own evaluations as the point of reference and is relatively independent of level of activity or social participation. The immigrant's sense of loneliness was assessed using five items from the UCLA Loneliness Scale-Version 3 (Russell & Cutrona, 1988). This measure conceptualizes loneliness as an emotional response to a discrepancy between desired and achieved levels of social contact. Mastery scores were computed based on the immigrants' responses to the seven-item Mastery Scale developed by Pearlin, Schooler, Menaghan, and Mullan (1981), which measures the extent to which the individual regards his or her life-chances as being under his or her control in contrast to being determined fatalistically. Internal reliability of the psychological adaptation scales was found to be satisfactory (.65, .72, and .75 for the Life Satisfaction, Loneliness, and Mastery scales, respectively).

Respondents were also presented with eight items related to various aspects of their adaptation to the educational setting. A factor analysis yielded three clearly distinguished factors accounting for 51% of the variance: The first factor included three statements related to satisfaction with the studies at school, the second factor is related to three items which measure satisfaction with the living conditions at the boarding school, and the third factor consisted of two statements dealing with satisfaction with the schoolmates in the educational institution. Alpha reliability values for the resulting three scales were .70, .60, and .68. In addition, three questions measured the immigrants' general satisfaction with the educational program; the alpha value for this scale was .68.

Respondents received a Russian version of the questionnaire, carefully produced by the method of back-translation.[4] Participants responded anonymously. Fifteen questionnaires (approximately 16%) were discarded due to very high rates of missing data.

RESULTS AND DISCUSSION

Preliminary analyses revealed almost no differences between male and female respondents, both on the cultural identity and on the adaptation variables. Moreover, there were no gender differences in the patterns of relationship between cultural identity and adaptation. We therefore present our results for immigrant boys and girls together.

---

[4]Questionnaires were first written in Hebrew (some of the measures translated and adapted from their English original versions), then translated into Russian by a fully bilingual research assistant, and later translated back into Hebrew by another assistant. The very few discrepancies were resolved by the research team.

We first examined the strength of identification with the three different cultural groups. Results show that the immigrants' high identification was with their Jewish identity (mean = 3.94, *sd* = 0.7), followed by the identity of origin (mean = 3.67, *sd* = 0.9), with the Israeli identity receiving the lowest scores (mean = 3.02, *sd* = .83). These findings resemble closely the patterns of cultural identification obtained consistently in recent studies conducted with Israeli immigrants from the former Soviet Union (Gittelman, 1994; Horowitz & Leshem, 1998).

Two of these results called for further examination and clarification. First, the relatively low scores on Israeli identity could be understood as a rejection of Israeli culture and as an expression of a separatist attitude. But this is not necessarily the case: The mean score obtained in this study is close to the scale midpoint, and this can be interpreted-although with caution-as reflecting a rather moderate level of Israeli identification. Moreover, the immigrants' responses to acculturation items included in another section of the questionnaire clearly showed a preference for the bicultural orientation; integration scores were significantly higher than those on the separation scale (Ben-Shalom, 1997). This finding reflects a willingness by the immigrant to enter Israeli society, and to adopt aspects of its norms and culture, without relinquishing their former identity.

Second, the high levels of Jewish identification reported by the immigrants can come as a surprise to many Israelis and scholars of Israeli immigration. Whereas religious and national beliefs and behaviors are seen by most Israelis as the two major-and almost only possible-expressions of Jewish identity (Herman, 1989; Horenczyk & Bekerman, 1993, February), as a group immigrants from the former Soviet Union do not tend to be involved in Jewish religious activities nor to exhibit particularly strong national attitudes (Horowitz & Leshem, 1998). It would seem, thus, that the immigrant adolescents see their Jewishness in a markedly different way from the common conceptions held by most Israelis.

Recently, Ferdman and Horenczyk (in press) suggested that our understanding and measuring of acculturation processes during immigration should take into account the individual and group constructions of old and new group memberships. Their analysis and methodology is based on Ferdman's (1990) conceptualization of cultural identity as one's individual image of the behaviors, beliefs, values, and norms-in short, the cultural features-that characterizes one's group(s), together with one's feelings about those features and one's understanding of how they are (or are not) reflected in oneself.

Two of the idiographic examples provided by Ferdman and Horenczyk can illustrate the nonnormative nature (at least, in the Israeli sense) of some constructions of Jewishness among immigrants from the former Soviet Union. Ana, a newcomer from Russia who reported strong Jewish identification, described "the Jew" as one that helps people, achieves goals, thinks first about others and later about self, is moral, and has good manners. The image of the Jew depicted by Boris, a 18-year-old student born in Leningrad, is that of the *Russian Jew*, characterized (primarily by Jews in Russia themselves) by intelligence, high culture, high respect for parents, and attraction to knowledge. Both Ana and Boris did not think about Jewishness either in religious or in national terms. These two participants in Ferdman and Horenczyk's study exhibit relatively high levels of Jewish identification: In their responses to other questions, they reported a strong sense of belonging to the Jewish group, pride in this membership, and a feeling that Jewishness is a positive and essential component of themselves. It would seem that they hold these positive attitudes toward an identity constructed, as shown above, in a relatively idiosyncratic way.

Our main interest in this study is on the relationship between cultural identity and adaptation. The results are presented in Table 3.1. It should be noted that scores on some adaptation measures were reversed so that, for all indices, high values reflect better psychological or school adjustment.

Results show that each of the cultural identities is positively related to some aspects of psychological adaptation. As to adaptation to the educational environment, it is the Israeli identity that is most consistently related to immigrant's adjustment. The other two cultural identities are related to some facets of school adjustment and not to others. An interesting finding is the negative correlation between identity of origin and general satisfaction from the boarding school. Those scoring high on identity of origin, however, show greater satisfaction with their schoolmates, and this may explain their lower levels of loneliness.

Table 3.1 also shows positive relationships between the identity accumulation variable and all measures of adaptation both in the psychological and educational realms. In other words, the greater the number of positive cultural identities reported by the immigrant adolescents, the higher his or her level of adjustment. This relationship between identity accumulation and the various measures of immigrant's adaptation is consistently linear, as shown in Table 3.2 and graphically in Figure 3.1.

This pattern was also examined by means of two Multivariate Analyses of Variance (MANOVA) with the identity accumulation score as independent variable: The first MANOVA was performed on the three variables of psychological adaptation, and the second on the four indices of adaptation to the educational environment. Results showed significant differences between the various levels of the identity accumulation variable on the linear combinations both of the psychological adaptation measures (Wilk's Lambda = 0.90, F [9,567], = 2.68, $p < 0.005$) and the school adjustment variables (Wilk's Lambda = 0.88, F [12,632] = 2.58, $p < 0.005$). Univariate ANOVAs yielded significant

TABLE 3.1

Pearson Correlations Between Cultural Identity Measures and
Adaptation Indices

	Identity of Origin	Israeli Identity	Jewish Identity	Cultural Identity Accumulation
Psychological adjustment				
Life satisfaction	-.03	.34**	.18**	.22**
Loneliness	.24**	.21**	.11	.21**
Mastery	.13*	.14*	.22**	.21**
School adjustment				
Satisfaction with studies	-.01	.23**	.24**	.28**
Satisfaction with living conditions	-.01	.17*	.09	.14*
Satisfaction with school mates	.19**	.14*	.07	.17*
General satisfaction	-.16*	.31**	.21**	.17*

*$p < .05$.
**$p < .01$.

F values for all the psychological adaptation measures and for three out of the four indices of adaptation to the educational environment (see Table 3.2).

In sum, our findings suggest that holding multiple cultural identities may lead to better adaptation among immigrants. Positive cultural identities can provide individuals in general, and immigrants in particular, with valuable social, cultural, and educational resources. The sense of being "grounded" (LaFromboise, Coleman, & Gerton, 1993) in multiple social and cultural networks is likely to enhance the individual's ability to cope with the stresses

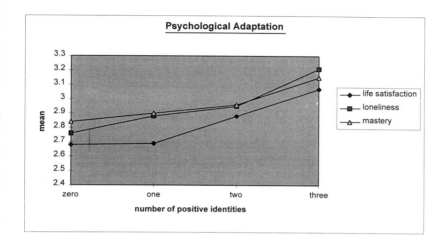

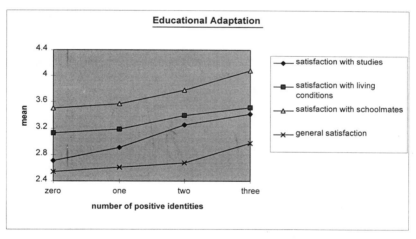

Fig. 3.1. Graphic display of linear relationships between cultural identity accumulation and measures of psychological and school adjustment.

TABLE 3.2

Means, Standard Deviations, F (One-way ANOVA) and T (Linearity) Values of
Adaptation Variables by Levels of Cultural Identity Accumulation ($N = 235$)

| | | Number of Positive Identities | | | | | |
		0	1	2	3	F	T
Psychological adjustment							
Life satisfaction	M	2.68	2.69	2.88	3.07	4.6**	3.24**
	SD	0.48	0.39	0.55	0.39		
Loneliness	M	2.76	2.88	2.95	3.21	3.7*	3.47**
	SD	0.60	0.41	0.60	0.39		
Mastery	M	2.84	2.90	2.96	3.15	3.6*	3.48**
	SD	0.47	0.39	0.48	0.48		
School adjustment							
Satisfaction with studies	M	2.71	2.91	3.25	3.42	6.48*	4.02**
	SD	0.89	0.79	0.70	0.84		
Satisfaction with living conditions	M	3.50	3.18	3.39	3.52	1.68	1.89
	SD	0.99	0.98	0.83	0.91		
Satisfaction with schoolmates	M	3.50	3.57	3.78	4.08	3.17*	2.45*
	SD	1.02	0.96	0.86	0.87		
General satisfaction	M	2.54	2.61	2.68	2.98	3.30*	3.02**
	SD	0.59	0.62	0.55	0.47		

*$p < .05$.
**$p < .01$.

and difficulties involved in cultural transition. On the other hand, it has been noted that different groups may often pose incompatible demands on the multicultural immigrant and that tension could result from his or her allegiance to--and identification with--multiple cultural groups. According to the results from our study, the benefits derived from a multicultural orientation seem to outweigh these possible costs.

In our research, we proposed a conceptualization and methodology for examining the hypothesis linking multicultural identification with psychological and school adjustment in terms of cultural identity accumulation. The variable used, however, does not distinguish between the different cultural identities; it simply counts the number of the individual's positive identifications. Therefore, among the respondents scoring "1" on the identity accumulation variable, there are immigrants whose only positive identity is the Jewish, together with those who report only a positive Israeli identity and those who showed relatively strong identification with their identity of origin only. Likewise, category "2" (two positive cultural identities) lumps together three combinations of two strong cultural identities: Jewish/Israeli, Israeli/Origin, and Jewish/Origin. This raises the important question about the relative adaptive advantage of one identity, or of one specific combination of positive identities. Among those who reported only one positive identity, for example, do those who score high on the Israeli identity fare better than those who hold strong attachments to their identity of origin only, as some assimilationist theoreticians would predict? Or is the identification with both Israeli and Jewish society and culture more adaptive than the combination of positive Israeli identity with the identity of origin, assuming that the former pair involves less conflict than the latter?

Two sets of one-way ANOVAs, with post-hoc pairwise multiple comparisons (using Tukey's HSD test), were conducted. We first selected those respondents with only one high cultural identity, and examined possible differences among those holding different positive identities (Jewish, Israeli, and identity of origin) on all the indices of adaptation--both psychological and educational. We then chose those participants who reported two positive cultural identities and compared the adaptation scores of individuals with different identity combinations. Out of 21 tests, only 1 of the comparisons was found statistically significant. It would seem that it is the *extent* of resources available to the immigrant individual that contributes to his or her adaptation, rather than the specific origin or nature of these resources. In other words, the more positive identities the better the immigrant's adaptation, as our identity accumulation hypothesis asserts, quite irrespective of the particular cultural groups with which the immigrant identifies.

It is important to note, however, that findings from our study point to the particular importance of the host identity to immigrant's school adjustment. This can be attributed to the immigrants' learning environment, which--as we will see later--is largely *assimilationist* and where Hebrew is the primary language in most of the educational and social activities. This context seems to confer certain advantage to those immigrants holding more favorable attitudes toward Israeli culture and Hebrew language. But we should still remember that the primary findings from our study suggest that a multicultural orientation on the part of the immigrant has the highest adaptive value not only in the personal but also in the educational realm.

We have proposed a causal interpretation for our correlational findings by claiming that identity accumulation contributes to psychological and school adjustment and even suggested mediating variables, in terms of resource availability and groundedness. We are aware, however, of alternative interpretations to our findings. We cannot rule out, for example, the possibility that individuals who are better adjusted tend to relate positively and warmly to many of their personal and social identities, including their cultural affiliations. It may be also the case that multiple positive identities and adaptation are both simultaneously affected by other factors. One of these variables could be length of stay in the new society. It has been widely suggested that levels of adaptation to the new society change during the various phases of the migration and acculturation process (e.g., Berry, 1997), although research evidence is rather inconclusive and the relationship between time and adaptation is not necessarily linear. Some studies conducted among Israeli immigrants from the former Soviet Union have also found that time since immigration is related to strength of cultural identification (see, e.g., Farago, 1979), but this pattern has not been found consistently across studies and populations. Results from our study showed no significant correlations between length of stay in the new country and any of the adaptation variables (psychological or educational), nor between time and any of the cultural identities or the identity accumulation variable. We believe that the relationship between cultural identity and adaptation is indeed a complex and multidirectional phenomenon, as is the widely documented link between the integration attitude and psychological adjustment among immigrants and members of minority groups (for a review, see Berry, 1997). The question of causality remains open, and it seems that only longitudinal studies that will follow immigrants during the various phases of their transition process will be able to clarify this important issue.

Implications: Multicultural Identities and Multicultural Education

We Are All Multiculturalists Now--this is the title of a recent book by Glazer (1997) that critically analyzes the intense contemporary debate on multiculturalism and multicultural education. If all of us are indeed multiculturalists, then our study--and most of the research showing the benefits of multiculturalism--can be seen as trivial, if not completely redundant.

To some extent, educational leaders all over the world have adopted some components of the multicultural discourse. The titles of the other chapters in this book reflect worthy multicultural efforts in various parts of the globe to deal in a pluralist way with cultural diversity in their educational systems. But, in many countries, a close examination of actual educational policies and practices reveals that multicultural education has not fully permeated the layer of public and professional rhetoric. Olneck (1995), for example, reviewed ethnographic research conducted in the United States and concluded that schools continue to seek to integrate immigrant children into an assumed American mainstream.

Israel has undoubtedly moved, to a significant extent, away from the strong assimilationist policies implemented during the mass Jewish immigration from the Arab countries in the 1950s. During that period, newcomers were expected to leave behind much of their cultural baggage, and to adopt the "Israeli way of life," portrayed in rhetoric as the new blend just produced in the cultural "melting pot" although, in fact, remarkably similar to the normative and religious outlook of the first immigrants to modern Israel, the majority of whom came from European countries. Nowadays, pluralistic tunes are increasingly heard in the public discourse on the education of immigrants, although the boundaries of such a discourse are still delimited by strong ideological constraints, reflected even in the use of the term *klitah* (absorption) for the official and social treatment of immigrants.[5]

Horowitz (1999) argues that the educational policies for immigrants from the former Soviet Union were implicitly guided by the principle that "new immigrants should be absorbed according to the assimilationist model, on the one hand, and the ethnic additive model, on the other" (p. 35). In other words, education should strive to absorb the new immigrants into the mainstream of Israeli society, while allowing for the expression of traditions brought with them from their countries of origin. This ideological position clearly departs from the previous approach in that it incorporates elements of cultural recognition into the educational discourse.

It should be noted that, although some degree of cultural maintenance is accepted and even encouraged, the nature of intergroup cultural influence is seen as absolutely unidirectional: Israeli society is not supposed to learn from the immigrants nor to adopt element of their traditions, norms, or values. Acculturation is still conceived almost solely as the extent to which the immigrant learns the roles, norms, and customs of the receiving society (Eisenstadt, 1955). In the social sciences, this approach has been gradually replaced by a perspective that conceptualizes acculturation as the process of

---

[5]The name of the Israeli authority in charge of immigration is the Ministry of Immigrant Absorption.

bidirectional change that takes place when two ethnocultural groups come into contact with one another (Bourhis, Moise, Perreault, & Senecal, 1997). Quite often, however, the notion of mutual influence is not more than "lip service" paid to the prevalent multiculturalist Zeitgeist. In Berry's (1990) model of the acculturation process, for example, arrows in two directions are drawn connecting majority and minority cultures. When describing this acculturation framework, Berry (1990) asserts that ". . . [i]n principle each [of the two cultures] could influence the other equally . . ." (p. 462), but his subsequent analyses focus only on the minority or immigrant groups. "This is not to say that changes in the dominant culture are uninteresting or unimportant . . . . But these changes, however significant, have generally fallen outside the competence of cross-cultural psychology" (pp. 462–463).

The acculturative effects of immigration on the host society are thus generally overlooked by researchers as well as by educators and policymakers. This neglect can be attributed, in most cases, to the small size of the immigrant group relative to the general population, which makes changes in the receiving society very unlikely and unnoticeable. But the large wave of immigration from the former Soviet Union to Israel seems to have reached a critical mass, and the presence and potential contribution of this minority culture to the host society can no longer be ignored. Both Israeli and the immigrant societies and cultures will be inevitably transformed and enriched, and it is imperative that educators and researchers begin to recognize and legitimize these bidirectional processes.

Language education policies in Israel seem to be more resistant to multiculturalist influences. According to Horowitz (1999), the main task in the education of immigrant students was seen to be Hebrew-language instruction. " . . . [I]t was assumed that whoever succeeds in acquiring and mastering the language would integrate into society, adopt its values, and adjust socially" (p. 36). The ideology of monolingualism (Hebrew) in the educational system was therefore considered to be justified and hence it continued, with resorting to Russian strongly discouraged. Sever (1999) strongly criticizes these policies. Pressures to give up the Russian language, she contends, can have negative effects on immigrants' development and adaptation: They may leave recently arrived children without adequate linguistic skills, deprive them of valuable communicative tools in the minority language, and thus, negatively affect vital intergenerational relations within the family, in addition to conveying an indirect message of disrespect toward the original culture and tradition of the newcomers and their families.

Without clearcut and explicit guidelines, Israeli schools have to develop their own strategies for dealing with the education of new immigrants. These approaches can be characterized on the basis of four parameters (Tatar, Kfir, Sever, Adler, & Regev, 1994): (1) the basic attitude of the school toward the integration of immigrants—assimilation to pluralism; (2) the priority given by the school to immigrant integration—high to low; (3) the school's perception of the change it is undergoing-a first-order additive change or a second-order metamorphic change; and (4) the school's methods of coping-habitual (more-of-the-same) or creative and entrepreneurial. These dimensions are largely interrelated allowing two "pure" types of schools to be portrayed. In schools with an assimilationist orientation, the immigrant integration task is usually seen as marginal, no major structural or pedagogical changes are considered necessary, and routine coping strategies are maintained. On the other end of the scale, schools that have adopted a multiculturalist philosophy assign a central place to the education of their immigrant students, and tend to perceive the new composition of their student body as a turning point calling for qualitative chance and the development and implementation of new coping strategies.

In the absence of new coherent and comprehensive policies of immigrant integration, assimilation continues to be the common "acculturation ideology" (Horenczyk, 1996) of Israeli schools and educators (Sever, 1999). In his study of the strategies used by Israeli school counselors with their immigrant students, Tatar (1998) characterized most of his interviewees as "culturally encapsulated assimilators": They tend to emphasize the first enthusiastic stage following the arrival of the new immigrants, while minimizing the legitimization of a long period of adaptation; they stress the importance of Hebrew language acquisition and conceive of the school as a powerful agent for the transmission of cultural values (national, traditional, or religious). Finally, they see their primary counseling goal as one of helping the immigrants to adapt their needs and expectations to the reality of the school.

Our final conclusions are tentative and based on still scare research evidence. Studies cited in an earlier section of this chapter report relatively low levels of psychological adjustment among adolescent newcomers from the former Soviet Union. Findings from other studies dealing with the approach of schools and school staff to immigrant integration show assimilation to be the prevailing educational orientation. With great caution, we suggest that this insufficient cultural and linguistic recognition and tolerance is responsible, at least partially, for the adaptation problems of immigrant youth. Sever (1999) warns that assimilationist school orientations are likely to contribute to the transformation of temporary marginality-which is seen as an almost inevitable phase in the cultural transition process-into permanent nonvolitional marginality among immigrant adolescents.

Our study provides additional support for the multicultural educational ideology by showing that cultural identity accumulation is related to psychological and school adjustment. We are aware that our research findings cannot serve either as sufficient or as necessary arguments for the adoption of multicultural policies in education: not sufficient, because much more research is needed to establish the cross-situational, and eventually cross-cultural, validity of our claims, and not even necessary, because there are plenty of other valid and convincing arguments-moral, social, and legal-for being, and allowing others to be, truly multicultural.

REFERENCES

Adler, P. S. (1975). The transitional experience: An alternative view of culture shock. *Journal of Humanistic Psychology, 15*(4), 13-23.

Anderson, B. (1991). *Imagined communities*. London: Verso.

Banks, J. A. (1995). Multicultural education; historical development, dimensions, and practice. In J. A. Banks & C. A. M. Banks (Eds.), *Handbook of research on multicultural education* (pp. 3-24). New York: Macmillan.

Ben-Shalom, U. (1997). *Attitudes toward acculturation, ethnic identity, and well-being among adolescents from the former Soviet Union participating in the Naael--16 project*. Unpublished master's thesis, The Hebrew University, Jerusalem.

Berry, J. W. (1990). Psychology of acculturation: Understanding individuals moving between cultures. In R. W. Brislin (Ed.), *Applied cross-cultural psychology* (pp. 232-253). Newbury Park, CA: Sage.

Berry, J. W. (1998). Social psychological costs and benefits of multiculturalism: A view from Canada. *Trames: A Journal of the Humanities and Social Sciences, 3*, 209-233.

Berry, J. W., & Kim, U. (1988). Acculturation and mental health. In P. R. Dasen, J. W. Berry, & N. Sartorius (Eds.), *Health and cross-cultural psychology* (pp. 207-237). Newbury Park, CA: Sage.

Berry, J. W., & Sam, D. L. (1997). Acculturation and adaptation. In J. W. Berry, Y. H. Poortinga, & J. Pandey (Eds.), *Handbook of cross-cultural psychology* (2nd ed., Vol. 3, pp. 291-326) Boston: Allyn & Bacon.

Bourhis, R. Y., Moise, L. C., Perreault, S., & Senecal, S. (1997). Towards an interactive acculturation model: A social psychological approach. *International Journal of Psychology, 32*, 369-386.

Collier, M. J., & Thomas, M. (1988). Cultural identity: An interpretive perspective. In Y. Y. Kim & W. B. Gudykunst (Eds.), *Theories in intercultural communication* (pp. 99-120). Thousand Oaks, CA: Sage.

Cortina, J. M. (1993). What is coefficient alpha? An examination of theory and applications. *Journal of Applied Psychology, 78*, 98-114.

Eisenstadt, S. N. (1955). *The absorption of immigrants*. Glencoe, IL: The Free Press.

Farago, U. (1979). Changes in the ethnic identity of Russian immigrant students in Israel (1973--75). *Jewish Journal of Sociology, 21*(1), 37-52.

Ferdman, B. M. (1990). Literacy and cultural identity. *Harvard Educational Review, 60*(2), 181-204.

Ferdman, B. M., & Horenczyk, G. (in press). Cultural identity and immigration: Reconstructing the group during cultural transition. In E. Olshtain & G. Horenczyk (Eds.), *Language, identity, and immigration*. Jerusalem: Magnes Press.

Fowers, B. J., & Richardson, F. C. (1996). Why is multiculturalism good? *American Psychologist, 51*, 609-621.

Gibson, M. (1991). Minorities and schooling: Some implications. In M. A. Gibson & J. U. Ogbu (Eds.), *Minority status and schooling: A comparative study of immigrant and involuntary minorities* (pp. 357-381). New York: Garland.

Gittelman, Z. (1994). Jewish-Soviet identity in a transition period. *Soviet Jews in Transition, 1*, 148-165 (Hebrew).

Glazer, N. (1997). *We are all multiculturalists now*. Cambridge, MA: Harvard University Press.

Goode, W. J. (1960). A theory of role strain. *American Sociological Review, 25,*483-496.

Gordon, M. M. (1964). *Assimilation in American life*. New York: Oxford University Press.

Herman, S. N. (1989). *Jewish identity: A social psychological perspective* (2nd ed.). New Brunswick, NJ: Transaction Books.

Horenczyk, G. (1996). Migrating selves in conflict. In G. Breakwell & E.Lyons (Eds.), *Changing European identities*. London: Pergamon.

Horenczyk, G. (in press). Conflicted identities: Acculturation attitudes and the immigrants' construction of their social worlds. In E. Olstein & G. Horenczyk (Eds.), *Language, identity, and immigration*. Jerusalem: Magnes Press.

Horenczyk, G., & Berkerman, Z. (1993, February). *Directions in Jewish-Israeli identity research*. Paper presented at the Ayala (Israel Association for Educational Research) Conference, Haifa, Israel.

Horowitz, T. (1999). Assimilation, monolingualism, unidirectionality, and stereotyping. In T. Horowitz (Ed.), *Children of perestroika in Israel* (pp. 22-71). Lanham, MD: University Press of America.

Horowitz, T., & Leshem, E. (1998). The immigrants from the FSU in the Israeli cultural sphere. In M. Sicron & E. Leshem (Eds.), *Profile of an immigration wave* (pp. 291-333). Jerusalem: Magnes Press (Hebrew).

Hutnik, N. (1991). *Ethnic minority identity: A social psychological perspective*. Oxford, England: Clarendon.

Isaacs, H. (1989). *Idols of the tribe: Group identity and political change*. Cambridge, MA: Harvard University Press.

Krishnan, A., & Berry, J. W. (1992). Acculturative stress and acculturation attitudes among Indian immigrants to the United States. *Psychology and Developing Societies, 4,* 187-212.

LaFromboise, T., Coleman, H. L. K., & Gerton, J. (1993). Psychological impact of biculturalism: Evidence and theory. *Psychological Bulletin, 114,* 395-412.

Maines, D. R. (1978). Bodies and selves: Notes on a fundamental dilemma in demography. *Studies in Symbolic Interaction, 1,* 241-265.

Mirsky, J. (1997). Psychological distress among immigrant adolescents: Culture specific factors in the case of immigrant adolescents from the former Soviet Union. *International Journal of Psychology, 32,* 221-230.

Mirsky, J. (1998). Psychological aspects of immigration and absorption of immigrants from the Soviet Union. In M. Sicron & E. Leshem (Eds.), *Profile of an immigration wave* (pp. 334--367). Jerusalem: Magnes Press (Hebrew).

Neugarten, B. L., Havighurst, R. J., & Tonon, S. (1961). The measurement of life satisfaction. *Journal of Gerontology, 16,* 134-143.

Oberg, K. (1960). Culture shock: Adjustment to new cultural environments. *Practical Anthropology, 7,* 177-182.

Ogbu, J. U. (1995). Understanding cultural diversity and learning. In J. A. Banks & C. A. M. Banks (Eds.), *Handbook of research on multicultural education* (pp. 582-593). New York: Macmillan.

Olneck, M. R. (1995). Immigrants and education. In J. A. Banks & C. A. M. Banks (Eds.), *Handbook of research on multicultural education* (pp. 310-327). New York: Macmillan.

Pearlin, L., Schooler, C., Menaghan, E., & Mullan, J. (1981). The stress process. *Journal of Health and Social Behaviour, 19,* 2-21.

Phinney, J. S. (1990). Ethnic identity in adolescents and adults: Review of research. *Psychological Bulletin, 108,* 499-515.

Phinney, J. S. (1992). The Multigroup Ethnic Identity Measure: A new scale for use with diverse groups. *Journal of Adolescent Research, 7,* 156-176.

Russell, D. W., & Cutrona, C. E. (1988). *Development and evolution of the UCLA Loneliness Scale*. Unpublished manuscript, University of Iowa, Center for Health Services Research, College of Medicine.

Sarbin, T. R., & Allen, V. L. (1968). Role theory. In G. Lindsey & E. Aronson (Eds.), *The handbook of social psychology* (wnd ed., Vol. 1, pp. 488-567). Reading, MA: Addison-Wesley.

Sayegh, L., & Lasry, J. C. (1993). Immigrants' adaptation in Canada: Assimilation, acculturation, and orthogonal cultural identification. *Canadian Psychology, 34,* 98-109.

Schmitz, P. (1992). Immigrant mental and physical health. *Psychology and Developing Societies, 4,* 117-131.

Searle, W., & Ward, C. (1990). The prediction of psychological and sociocultural adjustment during corss-cultural transition. *IJIR, 14,* 449-464.

Sever, R. (1999). Patterns of coping with the task at schools. In T. Horowitz (Ed.), *Children of perestroika in Israel* (pp. 178-189). Landham, MD: University Press of America.

Smith, A. D. (1991). *National identity*. Reno: University of Nevada Press.

Smooha, S. (1978). *Israel: Pluralism and conflict*. Berkeley: University of California Press.

Tajfel, H. (1981). *Human groups and social categories*. Cambridge, England: Cambridge University Press.

Tajfel, H., & Turner, J. C. (1986). The social identity theory of intergroup relations. In S. Worchel & W. Austin (Eds.), *Psychology of intergroup relations* (pp. 7-24). Chicago: Nelson-Hall.

Tatar, M. (1998). Counselling immigrants: School contexts and emerging strategies. *British Journal of Guidance and Counselling, 26,* 337-352.

Tatar, M., Kfir, D., Sever, R., Adler, C., & Regev, H. (1994). *Integration of immigrant studends into Israeli elementary and secondary schools: A pilot study*. Jerusalem: The NCJW Institute for Innovation in Education, School of Education, The Hebrew University (Hebrew).

Taylor, C. (1994). The politics of recognition. In D. T. Goldberg (Ed.), *Multiculturalism: A critical reader* (pp. 75-106). Oxford, England: Blackwell.

Thoits, P. A. (1983). Multiple identities and psychological well-being: A reformulation and test of the social isolation hypothesis. *American Sociological Review, 48,* 174-187.

Walzer, M. (1998). Education, democratic citizenship, and multiculturalism. In E. Weiner (Ed.), *The handbook of interethnic coexistence* (pp. 153-161). New York: Continuum Press.

Ward, C. (1996). Acculturation. In D. Landia & R. S. Bhagat (Eds.), *Handbook of intercultural training* (2nd ed., pp. 124-147). Thousand Oaks, CA: Sage.

Weiner, E. (Ed.). (1998). *The handbook of interethnic coexistence*. New York: Continuum Press.

Weinreich, P. (1989). Variations in ethnic identity: Identity structure analysis. In K. Liebkind (Ed.), *New identities in Europe* (pp. 41-76). London: Grover.

4

Buraku Students and Cultural Identity: The Case of a Japanese Minority

Hiroshi Ikeda
Osaka University

Student resistance to school authority is a popular theme with some researchers (e.g., Giroux, 1983; Ogbu, 1978; Willis, 1977). According to one line of thinking, identified as resistance theory, an oppositional culture shared by minority students originates from a common cultural position of subordination. In contrast to resistance theory, I will present what I call a "reinvention theory" to explain the relationship between student identities and the oppositional culture in which students participate. "Reinvention theory" is a theory of social contingency that emphasizes the unpredictable and interactive aspects of identity formation of minority youth. Their identities are not mere reflections of a parental or community culture. Rather they are relatively autonomous, created through interaction in their encounters with school culture. School life can be seen as a mirror in which they look at themselves. However, in that mirror they may not find real or authentic images of themselves, for the figures they see are to some extent *refracted* by the way school authorities and other students perceive them, and also by how minority students represent their school life and themselves.

In this chapter I will discuss the significance of school life in the formation of minority youth identities. In their encounters with school culture, minority students reinvent their identities in their own ways. I will emphasize the concept of multivoiced identity instead of that of monological identity. Multivoiced identity consists of both dissonant and consonant voices that contradict and conform and sympathize. Reinvention theory emphasizes the relative autonomy of the culture of minority, youth and their subjective forms of coping and modes of interaction in the social contexts of oppression. Although many negative voices interpellate them, they manage to defend their self-esteem by reinventing ways of representing the self and the situation of confronting them.

BURAKUMIN: DISCRIMINATION AND SELF-CONCEPT

In Japan, more than a million people are called Burakumin. They have been an outcaste group since the beginning of the Tokugawa period (1603-1868). DeVos (DeVos & Suarez-Orozco, 1990) described the Burakumin and their situation as follows: "First, the Burakumin are not physically distinct or visible discernible in any way. Second, a major collectively exercised coping technique of contemporary Japanese society in respect to members of this group is avoidance or direct denial that any such group continues to exist, or that there is any problem" (p. 149). The attitudes of exclusion or direct rejection are disappearing these days, but avoidance of the Burakumin is still persistent among ordinary Japanese.

The most distinct characteristic of Burakumin is that they are *not* different from other Japanese in skin color, language, or religion. Since they literally look like most majority Japanese, it is nearly impossible to identify a Burakumin if the person does not make explicit his or her identity, or unless an investigation of social background is conducted and citizens' registers are reviewed. But even though there are no physical or visible differences between the Burakumin and other Japanese, as DeVos (DeVos & Suarez-Orozco, 1990) described: "Various visibly different physical characteristics may be suggested as necessary criteria for differentiation, but nonvisible features can be used with equal force to segregate off a portion of a society as essentially inferior, or in religious terms, impure (p. 171)." The stigma of birth has been inflicted on them and along with it discrimination against them by other majority Japanese.

The self-image of the minority is burdened by the majority's prejudice against it, which forms a maligned ego. The majority is likely to stereotype the minority based on its perceptions of the minority's cultural degradation, physical inferiority, spiritual impurity, innate violence, and so forth. Such stereotyping often overlooks individual differences within a minority group, and characterizes the minority group as genetically inferior. Unconscious and suppressed negative self-images are likely to develop in the minority, and minority individuals may become subject to self-hate. How to deal with vulnerability of this situation is a tremendous social burden for the minority member who is placed in the negative category of "unwanted outsider" or "illegitimate Japanese," not unlike the experience of foreign immigrants in Japan.

Because of the invisibility of their identity and the severe discrimination inflicted on them, a number of Burakumin have been tempted to assume a majority Japanese identity and thereby get along in a majority world. "Passing" has been a common pattern among the Burakumin, and was the central theme presented in *Broken Commandment*, written by the novelist Tohson Shimasaki (1905) nearly a century ago.

Nowadays the social and psychological vulnerability experienced by minorities, often in the form of an internalized sense of inferiority, is believed to be related to the low level of school achievement among minority youth. The low school achievement level of Buraku children is considered both the result and the cause of their vulnerability. Many majority Japanese believed that most Buraku youths are low achievers because of their inherent inferiority. In turn, if Buraku youths see their low achievement as a proof of their inferiority, the fact of low achievement brings about and increases their vulnerability. The self-concept of Buraku youth is, thus, immensely influenced by majority Japanese's perceptions of Burakumin.

The gap in school achievement between Buraku and majority students is significant today. As students go through the school system, the discrepancy in academic performance becomes greater. This leads to a lower rate of minority youth enrollment in high school and a higher high school dropout rate. But the achievement gap has been closing more recently. According to a report by Mori (1984), who studied the records of children's achievement in several schools, nearly all Buraku children displayed extremely how school performance in the 1960s. The Burakumin school performance distribution curve in those days showed two peeks-one representing extremely low achievers and the other representing those performing slightly above average. The typically lower scores of Buraku children were attributed to the fact that those who came from Buraku communities often suffered from serious disadvantages such as poverty, broken families, and a lack of cultural capital. This legacy is still evident in Buraku communities today.

Social diversification in the Buraku population is under way, however. In spite of the fact that discrimination against them persists, we commit the error of oversimplifying the present state of Buraku children and youth if we do not take social diversification into account.

IMPROVEMENT IN THE BURAKU COMMUNITIES

In the feudal period (1603-1868), four major social classes were established in Japan: the warrior, the peasant, the artisan, and the merchant. Below these categories was an outcaste status called "Eta," a designation for people who had been cast out of a village and worked with what were considered to be "impure" materials, such as leather. Since the term Eta (literally meaning "defilement abundant") had discriminatory implications, with its reference to this group's supposedly subhuman attributes and polluted nature, the more descriptive terms "Buraku" ("special communities" or "unliberated communities") and

"Burakumin" (people who live in Buraku communities) are in common use today to refer to this minority group. The Meiji government proclaimed the emancipation of the Burakumin from the outcaste status in 1871. After their emancipation, the Burakumin were officially defined as commoners, and thereafter, discrimination against them was supposed to disappear under the law. However, their past outcaste status continued to be inscribed in official registers, and prejudice and discrimination against them persisted. Their life opportunities are no longer limited by the Constitution, which guarantees human rights for everyone. But even now overt discrimination against them persists in marriage and employment, and subtle discrimination in other arenas.

Before 1960, Buraku communities were typified by poor housing and crowded living conditions in disorganized neighborhoods, as well as economic deprivation. But, since special measures regarding Buraku communities were implemented by the national government beginning in 1969, the physical and social conditions of Buraku communities, which had not received any of the benefits of rapid economic growth in the 1960s, have changed significantly. Housing, roads, drainage systems, health care, welfare provisions, educational subsidies, and the other aspects of life in Buraku communities were markedly improved. *Dowa Education*, that is, education for the liberation of Buraku children, became a major concern among many teachers. This state of affairs coincided with the rise of the Buraku Liberation Movement.

The Buraku Liberation Movement peaked in the early 1970s. Similar to the civil rights movement in the United States, the liberation movement in Japan found wide support in the 1960s. Some organizations have increased their vigor ever since, continuing to mobilize Buraku people. Among them, the Buraku Liberation league is well know for its extensive and well-run organization, with a branch in each Buraku community. Its members are concerned with education for the young as well as betterment of community life and elimination of prejudice and discrimination. In each community, a children's group for liberation, called Kodomokai, is organized, and through its activities children learn the history of the Burakumin and the principles of the liberation movement.

In the communities where the liberation movements flourish, children can find respectable role models offered by youth and adults. Dowa Education puts a priority on the consciousness raising of children and the formation of their identity as Burakumin, aimed at enhancing their self-esteem and academic motivation. The devastating effects of their often poor academic performance on self-concept seem to be mitigated by the efforts of the liberation movements. Indeed, it is not uncommon to find Buraku children and youth who, having joined the liberation movements, construct positive self-concepts as Burakumin.

But we can hardly suggest that Buraku children's vulnerability and negative self-images have been eradicated and that they can now see themselves completely positively. I will describe in detail actual cases of how Buraku children construct their identities, to show the complexities and contradictions of the Burakumin self-concept.

The people in the liberation movement have considered it reasonable so far to instill Burakumin identity into children because the Burakumin have been discriminated against for a long time and remain destined to struggle with discrimination by majority Japanese. When the various Buraku liberation movements became popular in the 1970s, Buraku children used to confess their identity in the presence of their classmates at the beginning of a school year. Teachers believed Buraku children's identity should be revealed rather than concealed. they often discussed with their students the difficulties and suffering Burakumin had experienced, expecting that both Buraku and majority students would become more aware of the Burakumin's historical identity. However, that approach had to be reconsidered in the 1990s, because the teachers' efforts were not, for the most part, generating significant results.

Hence it has once again become difficult and inappropriate for someone to reveal Burakumin identity. Why is this so? It is by no means easy to answer this question because many factors are involved. Although discrimination persists against marriage between Burakumin and majority Japanese, a sense of persecution is largely missing among younger Burakumin. They are seldom exposed to the blatant prejudicial attitudes and discriminatory behaviors of majority Japanese that were common in the past. It is difficult to explain to Buraku children the stigmas attached to Burakumin identity that led to the terrible social experiences of the past generations. Today Buraku children are more often than not unaware of overt prejudice and discrimination. For these reasons, schools are giving up the practice of encouraging Buraku children to reveal their Burakumin identity.

FOUR TYPES OF BURAKU YOUTH

Ogbu (1978) classified the Burakumin as "the caste-like minority" in his typology. As mentioned above, the Burakumin were denigrated as outcastes and discriminated against by the majority for centuries. As a consequence, Buraku families' social outlook, including attitudes toward children's academic work, often differs from majority families'. School is one of the most prominent social institutions with which the Burakumin have trouble. However, it is not proper to characterize the whole minority culture as having an antischool orientation, to use Ogbu's terms. Nevertheless, Buraku children and youth often disagree with formal authority concerning educational interventions imposed on them by teachers. In respect to Buraku students' commitment to community culture and to school culture, we can distinguish between several types of Buraku boys. These types of boys reveal differential constructions of their identity in which subjectivity plays a critical role, illuminating a reinvention of their cultural identity.

We have conducted research on the school achievement and self-concept of Buraku students in ninth grade at a middle school (Nan-chu) and their relation to the community culture of Toda (a pseudonym for the Buraku community located in the north part of Osaka prefecture). The Buraku population of Today in 1996 was 796, one of the largest Buraku communities in the Osaka area. The local branch of the Buraku Liberation League has been well organized in the community, and the government's minority assistance projects have been implemented extensively, encompassing housing, employment, education, community facilities, health care, and so on. Today the average household income of the community is still a little lower than that of the surrounding majority communities, but more Burakumin are engaged in public service and more than half of the residents live in public housing. There is no external differences between the Buraku and the surrounding communities, except for the presence of Buraku community facilities and the public display of large banners connected with the Buraku liberation movement. As the minority's economic conditions and social environment have changed, including the appearance of class stratification based on income, solidarity within the Buraku community has gradually broken down. Social consciousness among Buraku people has accordingly begun to diverge, and likewise, the response of the Buraku youth to school culture has varied as well.

Let us look at four types of boys closely. We call the first three types "delinquent boys," "college boys," and "corner boys," following Cohen's (1956) typology of working-class boys, and we add another type called "liberatory boys" who identify themselves with liberation ideas and movements. At the time of observation, these four types of boys were in ninth grade at the same middle school. They had been brought up in the same community and attended the same nursery and elementary schools from infancy.

Shige represents the delinquent boy, and is a member of a motorcycle gang, driving recklessly on the road with other members every weekend. As he is often absent from school, teachers are concerned about him. Because of his frequent truancy, he is not expected to go to senior high school. Incidentally, high school education is not compulsory in Japan, and students must pass entrance examinations to be enrolled in high school.

Yuta typifies the corner boy, who is an average student and moderate in school performance. He has been on a soccer team since elementary school, and, unlike other Buraku children, went to *Juka*, a cram school. His parents have discouraged him from participating in the activities of the Buraku community youth center, and have prevented him so far from discussing discrimination against Burakumin with them. His parents are changing their attitudes, however, as they perceive Yuta's growing awareness of Buraku history.

Kenji epitomizes the college boy, who performs well in school and intends to go to college. His family belongs to the most affluent group in the community and, unlike many other Buraku boys who live in publicly subsidized apartments, he lives in a single-family dwelling. He does not keep company with other Buraku youth in school and in the community.

Senji represents the liberatory boy; he is a son of a leader of the local branch of the Buraku Liberation League. As his parents are working for the local government, his family is better off than average families. He has been a pivotal member of the children's group at the Buraku community youth center. Although he is poor in school performance, he seldom stays away from school. He is now involved in practicing Japanese drums, which is one of the activities of the Buraku center's children's group.

The four boys diverge distinctly in terms of their attitudes toward school authority. Kenji, the "college boy," is the most adaptive to school life. He concentrates his attention on every lesson in school, and ranks high in academic achievement. His teachers expect him to attend one of the highest ranked senior high schools. His parents are enthusiastic about his education and expect much of him. He goes to Juku, a cram school, after school three times a week. Although he is not on good terms with every teacher, his attitudes toward his teachers are usually not hostile. He can see his own future as full of potential and success. The fact that he receives high grades makes him confident in himself, and his social behavior is outstanding. This, beyond a doubt, results in his adaptation to school life. In his elementary school years he readily associated with other Buraku children, but in middle school he does not.

Yuta and Senji are in between in regard to their adaptation to school life and attitudes toward school authority. Yuta, the "corner boy," gets moderate scores on achievement tests because he has attended Juka and a language school since his elementary school years. Although he occasionally harbors ill feelings toward his teachers, he never openly rebels against them. Because he can actualize himself in sports, he is secure and his self-esteem is relatively high.

Senji, "the liberatory boy," who is placed in the lowest group in academic achievement, attends special classes for some subjects, which separates him from his classmates. Attending special classes publicly reveals the fact that he is a low achiever, yet he does not hesitate to go. He likes the more intimate contact with some teachers there then in the regular classes, and he feels it is the right of a Buraku student to attend the special classes because it is the right of the Buraku students to attend special classes. He sometimes expressed distrustful attitudes toward school authority-attitudes created by the Buraku liberation movement. But, contrary to his apparent expressions of discontent and defiance, he has, to a certain extent, committed himself to school life.

Compared to the other three boys, Shige, "the delinquent boy," is the most maladapted to school life. Shige's mother died when he was 7 years old. Since then his father has brought up Shige and his elder brother and sister. His father favors Shige, but he has by no means enjoyed a nurturing upbringing partly because, besides the death of his mother, his father has been hospitalized several times because of his alcoholism. Because his father has not been able to hold a steady job, his family is the poorest in the community and depends on welfare. Soon after entering middle school, Shige began to socialize with members of a motorcycle gang. Now that he has become a leader of the gang, his frequent truancy is resulting in very low academic achievement. Although most of his friends go to senior high schools, he has little hope of doing so because of his low achievement and delinquent behavior.

However, Shige was not always behind the other students. While teaching him in a short summer session in 1996, I found him to be an able boy. The summer session was held at the community youth center when he was in sixth grade. Although I taught him for a brief time, I soon realized he was very smart. But, it was impossible to direct him to engage in schoolwork because he saw himself as a drifter and an outsider.

He rebelled occasionally against his teachers when he was in the higher grades of elementary school. Recalling that time, he told me how he felt: "In the third or fourth grade I gradually lost interest in learning because I could not understand lessons. I began to feel myself left behind the classmates in the higher grades. And I became hostile to my teachers. I hate Mr. Kondo (his homeroom teacher) because he forced me to obey classroom rules."

Some Buraku students, including Shige, Kenji, an Yuta, collectively defied their teachers, and led the whole class into chaos when they were in fifth grade. That chaotic classroom continued over months, forcing Mr. Kondo to turn over his class to another teacher halfway through that year. Indeed, some poor achievers, like Shige, had intense conflicts with their teacher, and those confrontations resulted in the teacher's attempt to control their behavior in the classroom. that defiant attitude was to some extent shared by other students, but most who contributed to the chaos in the classroom did not seem to do it intentionally. They were simply getting along with the "problem students" at that particular moment. Buraku children are inclined to behave collectively because they have been together since infancy. In a different situation in a different teacher's classroom, Buraku students were likely to follow another type of students and their behavior would change accordingly. As Shige and Senji had already fallen far behind academically and were not able to follow the lessons, they lost interest in classroom work and became annoyed by the teacher's interventions. Although Kenji had been a member of an oppositional group at one time, he stopped disrupting lessons as he began to receive good grades.

All things considered, we come to the conclusion that Buraku students' disruptive behavior and their resistance to the teachers at the elementary school cannot be interpreted as opposition to school authority in general or as stemming from the oppositional Buraku culture. Most of the resistant students were Buraku children and low achievers. Some Buraku students who have done poorly in school are, more or less, committed to an antischool youth culture, particularly in middle school. This youth culture plays a critical role in forming and distinguishing its participants' identities during adolescence, when academic difficulties often aggravate. As Buraku students advance to middle school, they develop feelings of inferiority, which, in part, stem from their homes' poor cultural capital. Eventually, their feelings of being ill suited to school life overwhelm them, discouraging them from enhancing their self-concepts as students. Such a defeatist posture is transformed into a hostile stance to school authority in adolescence.

But after advancing to middle school, Buraku boys become involved in a broader range of peers, although they sometimes meet other Burakumin in school or on the street. Yuta, for example, explained who his friends are: "I sometimes talk with Senji in school, but not with other Toda youths. My most favorite friend is now someone else; he comes from another area. I have quite a few friends. But most of them are not Toda youths. I have joined the soccer team since I was in elementary school, so I get along well with members of the team." Even if an oppositional group forms an anti school culture in middle school, its members are not limited to Buraku students. The graduate student who participated in my research at Nan-chu observed the process of group formation: Several separate peer groups were formed among students based on different academic achievement levels. In the middle school, we seldom see Buraku students collectively oppose teachers or lead classes in disruptive behavior.

In the peer groups consisting of both majority and Buraku students, many Buraku children seem to recover from injured self-esteem. However, each group is often characterized by an oppositional posture against school culture. They make a mockery of formal school activities and reject the models of success and educational objectives articulated by the school. Thus, by inverting the school values, they protect their identity from being injured by what they perceive to be oppressive school life.

According to Ogbu's formulation, the oppositional culture of minority students in school draws its vigor from the community oppositional culture (Ogbu, 1978, 1987; Ogbu & Simons, 1997). But his formulation largely fails to explain the group formation of Buraku students in middle school. Furthermore, his view dismisses the subjective aspect of the students who struggle daily to defend their self-esteem against various assaults and attempt to reconstruct their identities in contingent circumstances. Their identities are not a direct product of the community or parent culture, but are reflectively constructed in contingent social circumstances. The group formation of minority students may be viewed as a realization of self-defense against the pressure imposed by mainstream culture, represented by school authority. The point I stress here is that the oppositional peer culture to which Buraku students subscribe is organized in reaction to school authority and their perception of oppression. They develop attitudes that subvert school values in their group, thereby enhancing otherwise smothered and debilitated self-concepts. Their self-concept emerges in response to the attitudes that people such as teachers, classmates, or families take toward them. If the school culture were not oppressive or coercive, the culture that minority students develop might be different.

As teachers have altered oppressive and coercive attitudes toward minority students in the 1990s, oppositional students have become accommodating to them and developed more friendly relations with them. In fact, although committed to delinquent behavior outside of school, Shige has not always been in trouble with teachers; he keeps on good terms with some teachers who have often visited his home to maintain close contact with him. He can find secure and relaxed space in school through such interpersonal relations with teachers. Likewise, other Buraku students have developed similar relationships with some teachers. Yuta described: "I sometimes get mad at teachers when they do not understand what I mean. But some teachers understand how I feel; particularly I like one of the language teachers, who sometimes talks to me and understands my feelings. I disliked other language classes so far, but his class is interesting to me."

ACADEMIC ACHIEVEMENT AND THE BURAKU STUDENT'S SELF

Except for Shige, who will not attend high school and frequently ignores school work, the other three boys are committed to school life. Senji, "the liberatory boy," despite his low school achievement and related problems with teachers, manages to find a degree of satisfaction in the classroom or other places in school. He is also aware that leaving school means closing the door on a future career. While recognizing school as a place to learn, low achievers have to find alternative meanings in school life to survive in school. But staying in school, on the other hand, causes another crisis for them. Subscribing to the idea that school is a place to learn increases the possibility of injuring their self-esteem because of their low academic achievement.

Next I turn to the school achievement of Buraku students. The number of ninth graders at Nan-chu is 130, among whom 25 boys and girls are from the Buraku community. The latest test scores of students at Nan-chu show that of the 25 ninth-grade Buraku students, 7 students (28%) are in the lowest decile and 15 students (60%) are in the lowest two deciles. Only one student is in the highest decile. The number of ninth-grade students who fall into the lowest decile and thus cannot be admitted into high school is 12; the 7 Buraku students make up nearly 60% of this lowest ranked tier, though they are only 19% of the whole ninth-grade class.

Most Buraku students, suffering from such low achievement, do not feel confident in themselves and, once in a while, are caught up in feelings of alienation or desperation. While Buraku students seldom express their anxiety about competence, they have deep-seated feelings of inferiority. Several years ago, a female Buraku student expressed her feelings of inferiority as follows: "You know, I am poor in school performance. Because my grandpa and grandma didn't go to school, and my pa and ma barely graduated middle school. I am their child. So, I can't be smart in school." To defend their self-esteem, they invent various strategies to prevent a sense of inferiority from intensifying. The development of oppositional groups in an antischool culture, in which the values and meanings imposed on them by the school are reversed, is not so much a reflection of some oppositional community culture as the resistance theorists would have it as it is the elaborate effort of individual students or groups to reinvent themselves to defend their self-esteem and protect their self-concept.

There is an enigmatic relationship between minority students' self-esteem and their academic achievement. Generally speaking, self-esteem and academic achievement have some correlation; a person with high self-esteem tends to attain high achievement. But it is not necessarily the case for minority students.

I conducted and supervised three large-scale research projects in the Osaka area in the 1990s. The purpose of our work was to determine the level of Buraku students' academic achievement and to examine why their performance is generally lower than majority students'. We looked at various possible factors to find relationships between school achievement and family life and between school adaptation and students' attitudes toward academic work. We also conducted interviews with parents, community workers, and schoolteachers in the Buraku communities. I will discuss some results focusing on achievement and self-esteem.

Past research indicated there is a significant gap in academic achievement between Black and White students in the United States. A positive relationship between achievement and self-esteem has been shown in a number of students (Brookover, Thomas, & Patterson, 1964; Coleman et al., 1964; Coopersmith, 1967). Nevertheless, the fact that there is little difference between Blacks and Whites in self-esteem was noted in the reports of Rosenberg and Simmons (1971; Rosenberg, 1989) and other researchers in the 1970s. this puzzle has never been resolved in a conclusive way.

Our research findings are similar to those in the United States. Although there was a significant gap between Buraku and majority students in school achievement, we did not find a difference in self-esteem based on our middle school data. Table 4.1 indicates the results of achievement tests in Sennan city, showing the average score of both Buraku and majority students. (The scores in the table represent composite standardized scores for math and language in grade 5 and 6, and math, language, and English in grades 7 and 8.) In all grades except for fifth-grade Buraku students' scores were lower than majority children's. However, fifth-grade Buraku children performed better on the tests than majority children did. According to teachers, this grade was exceptional because there were more academically talented Buraku children

TABLE 4.1

The Distribution of Test Scores (Sennan)

Level/Group	Low	Low Medium	High Medium	High	Total
Elementary school					
5th grade majority N(%)	102(25.2)	101(25.5)	100(25.1)	94(24.1)	398(100.0)
Buraku N(%)	7(17.5)	9(22.5)	9(22.5)	15(37.5)	40(100.0)
6th grade majority N(%)	110(24.0)	113(24.6)	115(25.1)	121(26.3)	459(100.0)
Buraku N(%)	13(39.6)	10(30.3)	7(22.2)	3(9.1)	33(100.0)
Middle school					
7th grade majority N(%)	101(24.0)	108(25.8)	105(25.0)	106(25.2)	420(100.0)
Buraku N(%)	11(38.0)	4(13.8)	7(24.1)	7(24.1)	29(100.0)
8th grade majority N(%)	109(23.8)	116(25.3)	115(25.1)	118(25.8)	458(100.0)
Buraku N(%)	15(38.5)	8(20.5)	9(23.1)	7(17.9)	39(100.0)

Note. Survey conducted by Sennan City Board of Education in 1992.

enrolled in fifth grade in the year when the tests were administered than in normal years. To indicate a general pattern, therefore, I will also draw on the results of an Osaka Prefectural research project, which was concluded on the prefectural level, including samples of Buraku children (see Table 4.2).

TABLE 4.2

The Distribution of Test Scores (Osaka Prefecture)

Level/Group	Low	Low Medium	Medium	High Medium	High	Total
Elementary school						
Buraku %	28.2	23.5	20.1	16.6	11.6	100.0
Majority %	18.0	18.5	20.1	21.0	22.4	100.0
Middle school						
Buraku %	32.2	26.5	16.7	15.3	9.3	100.0
Majority %	18.0	18.4	20.6	20.9	22.1	100.0

Note. Survey conducted by Osaka Prefectural Board of Education in 1989.

We point out the tendency that the higher the grade, the greater the gap in test scores between Buraku and majority students. This gap leads to a lower rate of enrollment in high schools and a higher high school dropout rate among Buraku students. As mentioned before, the achievement gap between Buraku and majority children has been somewhat reduced over the past several years. Nevertheless, a substantial discrepancy between the two groups is still present.

Table 4.3 indicates the results on self-esteem. This table represents the aggregated data for fifth and sixth graders and for seventh and eighth graders, respectively, because the two groups attend different schools in the Japanese educational system. At the elementary school level, there is a significant difference in self-esteem between Buraku and majority children. Yet, in contrast, the middle school data show no significant difference.

TABLE 4.3

The Distribution of Self-esteem Ratings

School/Group	Low	Low Medium	High Medium	High	Total
Elementary school					
Buraku %	50.0	21.6	21.6	6.8	100.0
Majority %	24.3	25.0	26.0	24.7	100.0
Middle school					
Buraku %	31.9	24.6	17.4	26.1	100.0
Others %	25.6	27.2	22.4	24.8	100.0

Note. Survey conducted by Sennan City Board of Education in 1992.

As shown above, Buraku students display low achievement, and the gap between Buraku and majority adolescents is greater at the middle school level than at the elementary school level. There is also a substantial correlation between self-esteem and academic achievement at the elementary level. Judging from these data, one would expect that Buraku adolescents' self-esteem would be lower than majority adolescents' at the middle school level. But the data do not support such an expectation.

Data show that elementary Buraku children reveal indications of negative relationships with teachers and classmates as well as anxieties and troubles in their lives. But these negative indicators become less evident at the middle school level. It looks as if Buraku adolescents have largely overcome their disadvantages.

To understand our data, I draw on Rosenberg and Simmons' (1971) findings of the self-esteem of minorities in the United States. Against a general belief that Black self-esteem must be lower than that of Whites, Rosenberg and Simmons found that Black students' self-esteem is actually higher than that of their White counterparts. They interpreted their findings by applying reference group theory. Their findings provide us with a relevant clue to interpret our data. Employing Rosenberg and Simmons' formulation, we propose that Buraku adolescents' maintenance of relatively high self-esteem is attributable to the fact that their peer groups, which are oppositional to school authority and nullify the negative effects of their school experiences, help to mediate in the construction of self-esteem. Their low academic achievement insignificantly influences the process in which self-esteem is developed.

However, although the influence of peers as a reference group should be noted as a significant factor, the role that school plays in shaping minority adolescents' self-concepts should be take into account as well. In the past, resistance theory, promoted by Willis (1978) and Ogbu (1978), has been used to support the argument that an oppositional culture in school originates from the community culture of subordinate people. I will introduce an alternative theory, reinvention theory, to explain Buraku adolescents' behavior and the development of their self-esteem. It emphasizes the relative autonomy of the culture in which minority adolescents are involved and their subjective choice in defense of their identity against injuries and oppressions stemming from school and social life.

SELF-CONCEPT: COMPETENCE AND VULNERABILITY

Recently Steele (1992) called attention to the relationship between achievement and self-esteem for minority youth. His theory of "disidentification" suggests that Black youth are disinclined to identity their self-esteem with their academic achievement. Rather, there is a tendency for Black youth to protect their self-esteem by actively disassociating their academic achievement from it. Using Steele's (1992) point of view, Osborne (1995) analyzed data from a large-scale research project and concluded that Black children and youth certainly illustrate this disidentification pattern. As for why, Steele points out that Blacks have a strong sense of vulnerability in terms of academic competence. Various types of failure, such as low test scores, can provide a clue or a ground for the majority to stigmatize Blacks as inferior. Blacks are vulnerable to such attributions to them by the majority; thus, they make a deliberate effort to deny a relationship between their self-esteem and their academic performance.

This disidentification process is evident elsewhere in both Japanese and U.S. school contexts. Minorities such as Blacks and Burakumin are often devalued in school, and this devalued status in school leads to their devaluation of their work in the classroom. As Steele observed: "Unable to entrust his sense of himself to this place, he [a Black] resists measuring himself against its values and goals. He languishes there, but not allowing achievement to affect his view of himself. The psychic alienation-the act of not caring-makes him less vulnerable to the specter of devaluation that haunts him" (p. 74). Likewise, although Buraku students, especially boys, had lower test scores than majority classmates, their overall self-esteem was just as high. As Steele (1992) discussed: "This stunning imperviousness to poor academic performance was accomplished by their deemphasizing school achievement as a basis of self-esteem and giving preference to peer-group relations-a domain in which their esteem prospects were better. They went where they had to go to feel good about themselves" (p. 72).

Although Buraku students hope to go to high school, they avoid the topic of school achievement when they receive career guidance from their teacher, and they evade it in a strategic way in social conversations. Their deemphasis on academic work is evident elsewhere. The Buraku community youth center has provided an evening special session every week in cooperation with teachers of Nan-chu Middle School, aiming to improve students' academic achievement. Few students participate in the special session, however, and boys who are slow achievers do not show up for lessons. Although Shige and Senji occasionally pay enthusiastic attention to their teachers, they usually do not open their textbooks and, what is worse, they sometimes do not even bring their textbooks to school. They often chat with other boys or pretend to nap during class. In contrast to them, Kenji and Yuta pay close attention to teachers and take notes on the lessons. Certainly the differences in their attitudes and behavior result from differences in their academic achievement.

THE CHANGING CULTURAL IDENTITY OF BURAKU YOUTH

Buraku youths' cultural identities are changing as society's once discrimination has become benign and very covert, if remaining. A few comments are in order on these changes.

In urban Buraku communities, adolescents whom Ogbu or Willis would characterize as committed to the community culture and oppositional to school culture have become fewer. Even when they are oppositional to school culture, such students seem to be unable to find support from within their own community culture for sustaining opposition. Nowadays, most Buraku parents, along with the leaders of the Buraku community youth center and teachers, encourage Buraku children to adapt to school life and strive for good grades in school. Against this background, "delinquent" older boys, like Shige, have more difficulty finding peers with similar problems within their Buraku community. In the Toda Elementary School, where Buraku children make up one third of the total students and only two classrooms make up each grade, Buraku children flock together in the classroom or school grounds and resist teachers collectively. After entering middle school, however, they are divided into four classrooms, and school authority, except for extracurricular activities, deliberately controls student social groupings outside of the classroom. Further, as their interests change over time, each adolescent seeks out non-Buraku peers. Likewise, Shige sought out peers outside of his school and joined a motorcycle gang.

In contrast, the "liberatory" Buraku students whom Senji represents are committed to both community culture and school culture. Nowadays they can commit to both because some schools with Buraku youth have adopted active Dowa Education in collaboration with the liberation movements in the Buraku community. Dowa Education is offered in schools where Buraku youth attend. Dowa Education is characterized by the following educational emphases: to be on the side of the discriminated and learn from the reality of discrimination; to foster capabilities to understand critically and eliminate discrimination and poverty; to encourage recognition and awareness of one's own social position; and to establish collectively and democratically oriented children's groups.

Reflecting on his school days and the positive effects of Dowa Education, a Buraku youth of Toda, who graduated from university and is working for the local branch of the Buraku Liberation League commented:

> I had not felt the same anxiety and distrust toward the classmates
> in Nan-chu as I did after entering high school, where many class-
> mates, I felt, held prejudice against Burakumin. I always had to
> hide my identity. In contrast, even if discrimination occurred
> in Nan-chu, both teachers and the classmates assumed an affirmative
> antidiscriminatory stance. Under the circumstances, I was not isolated
> or alienated.

As part of Dowa Education, teachers and classmates support Buraku students at the middle school (also at the elementary school), and as a result, some of Buraku students actively play leadership roles in the classroom. Some Buraku students are convinced of the liberation beliefs in Burakumin equality and thereby maintain high self-esteem.

We characterized Senji as a "liberatory boy." However, in a strict sense, such a characterization does not hold entirely true. He has been involved in the activities of the community children's group supported by staff of the Buraku community youth center, and his father is one of the leaders of the local branch of BLL. But he seems oddly unaware of the harsh realities Burakumin encountered in the past. He appears more willing to fight against discrimination than other Buraku students, but he seems to believe that such discrimination against Burakumin is a past phenomenon. Consequently he looks like a puppet simply parroting the liberation mottoes used by his father and BLL leaders.

In terms of Burakumin identity, the four boys all became aware of their minority status in Japanese society in their elementary school years. In the activities at the community youth center, staff discussed the Buraku identity and the creeds of the liberation movement, referring to, for example, the Sayama trial case, a notorious trial in which, BLL argued, a Buraku defendant was arrested with false charges. When Yuta, the "corner boy," learned of the Sayama trial for the first time, he was interested and read a book about it. Although it might be difficult for such children to understand the complex nature of the Sayama trial, learning about such events helps them realize that "we are different from others." Such an awareness of discrimination may cause a suppressed anxiety that they themselves will suffer discrimination in their adolescent years. However, most of Buraku youths, except for Senji, do not want to talk about such a possibility, pretending not to care about it. Some turn their backs on the liberation movement, and take a typical attitude toward discrimination against burakumin as is evident in this Japanese metaphor: "Let's keep quiet and let sleeping dogs lie." Such attitudes persist among Buraku "college" boys. Kenji is uninterested in talking about Burakumin status and identity, as if mentioning such issues threatens his self-esteem. He studies hard to pass into majority society. He believes that he need not carry the burden of his Burakumin identity. Thus, for him, attending high academic achievement is a denial of his identity, in a sense. He is the Japanese counterpart of the Black students who assume "racelessness" in the interest of pursuing academic success, as noted in Fordham's (1988) ethnographic work.

Yuta, a "corner boy," has been at times oppositional to school culture, yet he is not entirely committed to community culture. He oscillates and drifts between community and mainstream culture. He wants to be a professional soccer player. If he cannot realize this dream, he wants to become a movie makeup artist. He does not seem to be concerned about his Burakumin identity, believing that his future will not be restricted by past discrimination.

A recent episode transformed him, however. Although his parents had not thought it important to discuss with their son his minority identity, they recently changed their mind. Yuta was worried about telling his Burakumin identity to his non-Buraku girlfriend. His parents capitalized on the occasion to talk with Yuta about the history of discrimination against Buraku and how they felt about Burakumin identity. After a few months, Yuta confessed to his girlfriend that he is a Burakumin and told her what he thought of his identity and discrimination against the Burakumin. She did not respond negatively to the revelation; instead, she was empathetic. After that, Yuta began to talk more openly about Buraku problems with his parents and friends.

In summary, Buraku youths do not subscribe to a single identity and a single social reality, because their views of the social situations in which they cope with personal and collective problems differ. Further, their cultural identities are gradually changing as Buraku youth resort to different strategies to secure their self-esteem. They need protective walls and a security basis to guard the self against various injuries and oppression from the outside.

CONCLUSION

Burakumin have been discriminated against by majority Japanese for nearly four centuries. Against this historical background, the minority group launched a liberation movement to emancipate its people from the ascribed status, poverty, and other social disabilities they have suffered. The central government's special legislative measures, dating from the late 1960s, have contributed immensely to improving Burakumin communities and education for Buraku students. At present, many past forms of prejudice against Burakumin have disappeared; some have become subtle and covert; marriage and employment discrimination against them, however, is still evident. As a result of improved economic conditions in the Buraku neighborhoods, social differentiation has occurred within their communities. Consequently, Burakumin no longer perceive their social reality in a unitary frame.

Likewise, in their social encounters buraku students see themselves represented in multiple realities and voices, which reflect their varied strategies to adapt to school. I discussed four types of Buraku boys, using Cohen's (1956) typology of working-class boys and adding one type of my own, that epitomize diversity in defining their identities. Buraku identity is a common denominator for all Buraku youth, stemming from their history of discriminated status, but it is only one of the essential attributes that influence their social perspectives. Their identities are not mere reflections of their history and their community culture. Instead, their self-concepts are relatively autonomous, created through their encounters with school culture. Minority youth reinvent themselves in their own ways. The reinvention theory I suggest underscores the relative autonomy of the culture of minority youth and their subjective forms of coping in the social context of oppression. I emphasize that minority adolescents' identities are far from predetermined; they are fluid in their development, always under construction. The process of identity formation is the process of seeking a security basis in which they feel secure and fulfilled.

One invariable source of oppression in the process of identity formation is the history of discrimination and the majority's devaluation of the minority as inferior. Moreover, most Buraku students feel vulnerable when they are measured against their generally low school achievement. Many Buraku youth cope with a sense of vulnerability by dissociating their academic work from their self-esteem. Consequently, their is little correlation between the two variables. "Disidentification" of self-esteem and academic performance is a strategy often used by Buraku youths. Their cultural identities are changing as they reinvent them in changing social situations in and out of school. The extent to which Buraku youth can choose to fulfill their desires is expanding, mediated by class differentiation within the community, the development of the liberation movements, and growing social mobility beyond the Buraku community.

Nonetheless, their alternatives are still limited.

It is important to examine further the aspirations and needs of Buraku children and adolescents, the difficulties they face in everyday life, and their definition of the situations in which they are positioned. To understand the multiple realities confronting them, we should shy away from deterministic views about their lies and pay attention to the contingencies that influence the construction of their cultural identities and the role that reference groups play in social interaction. And, most importantly, while recognizing the contradictory relationships between social factors such as school, family, and the liberation movements, we must connect these to the process of identity formation among children and youth.

REFERENCES

Brookover, W. B., Thomas, S., & Patterson, A. (1964). Self-concept and school achievement. *Sociology of Education, 37,* 271-278.

Cohen, A. K. (1956). *Delinquent boys: The culture of the gang*. Glencoe, IL: The Free Press.

Coleman, J. S., Campbell, E. R., Hobson, C. J., McPartland, J., Mood, A. M., Wernfirld, F. D., & York, R. L. (1964). *Equality of educational opportunity*. Washington, DC: Office of Education, Department of Health, Education and Welfare.

Coopersmith, S. (1967). *Antecedents of self-esteem*. San Francisco: Freeman.

DeVos, G. A., & Suarez-Orozco, M. (1990). *Status inequality: The self in culture*. Newbury Park, CA: Sage.

Fordham, S. (1988). Racelessness as a factor in Black students' school success: Pragmatic strategy or pyrrhic victory? *Harvard Educational Review, 58*(1), 54-84.

Giroux, H. A. (1983). *Theory and resistance in education: A pedagogy for the opposition*. Westport, CT: Bergin and Garvey.

Mori, M. (1984). *The improvement of school achievement in Katsura Elementary School: Interim report*. Osaka, Japan: Faculty of Human Sciences, Osaka University.

Ogbu, J. U. (1978). *Minority education and caste: The American system in cross-cultural perspective*. New York: Academic Press.

Ogbu, J. U. (1987). Variability in minority school performance: A problem in search of an explanation. *Anthropology & Education Quarterly, 18,* 312-334.

Ogbu, J. U., & Simons, H. (1997). Voluntary and involuntary minorities: A cultural-ecological theory of school performance with some implications for education. *Anthropology & Education Quarterly, 29,* 155-188.

Osborne, J. W. (1995). Academics, self-esteem, and race: A look at the underlying assumptions of the disidentification hypothesis. *Personality and Social Psychology Bulletin, 21,* 449-455.

Rosenberg, M. (1979). *Conceiving the self*. New York: Basic Books.

Rosenberg, M., & Simmons, R. G. (1971). *Black and White self-esteem: The urban child*. Washington, DC: American Sociological Association.

Steele, C. (1992). Race and the schooling of Black Americans. *The Atlantic Monthly, 269*(4), 68-78.

Willis, P. (1977). *Learning to labour: How working-class kids get working-class jobs*. Farnborough, England: Saxon House.

5

Culture, Race, and Ethnicity in Education in South Africa

Crain Soudien
University of Cape Town

The purpose of this chapter is to examine the relationship between the formal education system of South Africa and the racial, cultural, and ethnic context within which the educational system is set. It draws on studies of two schools in Cape Town to show how these relationships play themselves out in the identities of young people.

South African education, like its health, welfare, and housing sectors, is historically embedded in the complex encounters of Black and White, European and African, and freeman and slave over and during a 350 year period of social subjugation, confrontation, accommodation, resistance, and compromise. From this encounter has emerged a violent and deeply fractured society marked by the pervasive and recurrent themes of White supremacy and economic exploitation on the one hand, and Black alienation and social dislocation on the other hand. These themes have provided the framework for the provision, organization, and experience of schooling for all South Africans. South Africans classified White, as a result, have been the beneficiaries of the system, while those classified Black have, for the most part, been its victims. Its colored (a social category of South Africans other than Whites, Blacks, and Indians) and Indian subjects have been suspended in a twilight world where they have neither been fully permitted into the system not properly shut out.

This chapter begins with the recognition that the idea of race, as an analytic device, has been deployed in both totalizing and minimalist ways in South Africa. In the former, it has come to subsume all other dimensions of social life in South Africa. In the latter, it has been reduced to a subordinate reality-as in the notion of "false consciousness"-with equal salience to other social factors. The thrust of this work is to foreground the ubiquity of race in the making of hierarchy in South Africa but also to show simultaneously that the experience of race shifts and changes over periods of time.

In relation to schooling, the essay seeks to make a similar analytic point. Education, as the groundbreaking work of Bowles and Gintis (1976) demonstrated, was central to the making of society in so far as young people were socialized for their respective places in the world of work. A problem with this work, however, was its reduction of what happened in school to the status of an epiphenomenon of the social forces that surround them. What happens inside schools, I will argue, is as important as what happens around them. Apartheid and the heritage of division in post-apartheid South Africa have been the primary conditioning experience for people inside the schools, specifying the nature of the curriculum, the racial and ethnic character of schools and preparing young White and Black people for their respective places in the economy and broader society. Teachers and their students inside of these schools have actively engaged with their history. And so, young people have emerged from schools with identities that are much more complex than the stereotypes ordained for them by apartheid. Identity, as the work will argue, is a process of making and of taking.

I will argue that the construction of the South African subject within the schools of apartheid is a profoundly contradictory process in which the vectors of race, ethnicity, and culture are, at various times, elided, brought into alignment, conflated, juxtaposed, contrasted, and hierarchalized. The subject, as a result, is accessible only through a complex reading.

This chapter is structured in three major sections. It begins with a description of the social dynamics of race, ethnicity, and culture in South Africa and attempts to show how these, as social constructions, might be approached to understand social fragmentation and division. The chapter moves on to examine the location of education within these dynamics, and pays particular attention to the notion of schooling as a vehicle for the promotion of the apartheid agenda. In a final section, the chapter draws on empirical material to show how young people are positioned and position themselves in relation to these processes.

RACE, CULTURE, AND ETHNICITY

As working frameworks for understanding division and oppression, race, culture, and ethnicity have been the watchwords of most sociologies and histories of South Africa. They have, however, been notoriously difficult to come to terms with their meaning in society. To understand their salience, Sharp (1988a), in a classic text, suggested that they have to be understood within what he called the "discourse of domination." Commonsense explanations of South

Africa invariable present South Africa as a society consisting of four major racial groups, Africans, Whites, coloreds, and Indians, each of which exists within its own cultural forms. Sharp (1988a) made the argument that these explanations have been reified and are presented as if races and/or ethnic groups have an objective reality in and of themselves. He argued that all groups are socially constituted and are representations, rather than features of the real world. As representations they consist of selected constellations of narratives that are configured in ways that help to order the world and position individuals and groups within it. These narratives, and the symbols and tropes through which they gain form, inevitably speak the world as their interlocutors wish it to be seen and reveal, therefore, the interests of those who have the power to speak.

Discourses, however, as the work of Foucault (1989) shows, are always mystified. They are seldom accessible in their own terms, but have their own specific logics of production. The interests they contain are not immediately legible or visible, but are, instead, located in what Grossberg (1997) called "regimes of power," or what Sharp would have called "discourses of domination." They produce languages and encoding practices in which reality is territorialized through the positioning of certain "facts." Meaning is thus confined within the limits of description determined by the discourse. To unlock these discourses, one has to be able to interpret the logics of their production. Toward that process it is necessary to emphasize the point that discourses are not simply articulations of the real; they are not objective descriptions of the world, but are compositions riven with fractures and illogicalities that "betray" their social constructedness. It is this social constructedness that makes them available for scrutiny, and so permits a reading of their character. Once they are understood as social constructs they can be seen for that they are, namely, regimes of power that shift and change.

THE CHANGING DISCOURSE OF DOMINATION[1]

The nature of the South African society has come under intense and repeated scrutiny over the past 40 years. Key texts include the work of Rhoodie (1972), Tabata (1960), De Kiewiet (1966), Brookes (1968), Magubane (1979), Wilson and Thompson (1969), Johnstone (1976), Adam (1971), No Sizwe (1979), Nolutshungu (1982), Comaroff (1985), O'Meara (1988), Sharp (1988a), and

---

[1]This is a heading used by John Sharp (1988b).

Dubow (1995). Most of these texts were informed by a liberalism that grew in the wake of a powerful segregationist tradition led by the Social Darwinists such as Theal (1894, 1902).

This was followed by the emergence of a liberal tradition, the most important of which include Macmillan (1927, 1929) and De Kiewiet (1966). After this start, it took nearly 20 years for a visible radical tradition to emerge in South Africa. The radicals, largely White, rejected the explanation of the liberals that South Africa was governed by economic irrationality and ideological prejudice. Prejudice, they sought to emphasize, was not a sufficient analytic vehicle to contain the complexity of White supremacy. The question that needed to be answered, they contended, was that of accounting for how the South African state had managed to accumulate and retain such extraordinary power and had managed to oversee the process of capital accumulation so successfully. Class for them was the primary factor in explaining division in South Africa (see the seminal contribution of Johnstone, 1976; Legassick, 1974; Wolpe, 1972). They in turn were critiqued for their class reductionist approaches (see Bundy, 1979; Dubow, 1995; Van Onselen, 1982).

It is against this background that Sharp's (1988a) notion-a "discourse of domination"-presents itself as a useful way of developing a reading practice for the question of race. In this reading Sharp showed, as Omi and Winant (1992) have shown for the United States of America, that race has to be approached as a shifting phenomenon. Sharp (1988a) identified three recognizable phases in racial discourse, each of which is associated with a particular rendering of the idea of race. His first phase spans the first half of the 20th century, in which the idea of "race" as biology is dominant. In this period the conventional understanding was "that the South African population was divided into separate races. Those races were conceived as natural units, and as distinct from each other in both physical and cultural terms" (p. 7).

Sharp's second phase begins in the 1950s and sees the concepts of race being supplemented by the idea of ethnicity. While references to race do not disappear, increasingly, after the advent of the National Party in 1948, discourse shifts to the disaggregation of groups like "natives" and "Blacks" into distinctive "nations" with their own ethnicities and historic cultures. The substance of this shift is prompted by the need for a rationale for providing people access to their "own" homelands. The development results in the identification of 13 distinct and separate "Bantu" nations or ethnic groups, each with their own languages, cultures, histories, and, most significantly, ancestral lands. Thus, Zulu-speaking South Africans became the Zulu nation, Xhosa speakers two separate Xhosa nations, and so on. This was the high period of culture and ethnicity in South Africa, or, as Sharp (1988a) argued, the era of social engineering on a grand scale. He commented: "Even a most cursory glance at the various historical accounts of the African population revealed the artificiality of the groups and boundaries which were constructed by fiat"(p. 8). What the concept of ethnic group provides is scope for greater ideological maneuverability for the apartheid government.

Sharp's third phase witnesses the further decentering of the idea of race and the arrival of the idea of South Africa's people being divided into first- and third-world peoples. The discourse of domination is distinctly more fragmented during the 1970s and 1980s and presents itself, in the climate of reform through which the country goes, as a political language that is consistent with development discussion taking place elsewhere in the world. As Sharp (1988a) said, "(T)his assumed co-existence of two worlds in one country provides a comfortable explanation of South Africa's current problems, and marks, by an easy analogy (to the rest of the world), both its tragedy and its challenge" (p. 9).

While Sharp's typology is not inaccurate in so far as it explains contemporary South Africa, there is need to emphasize how race enters and settles on the country's discursive landscape. In terms of this, it is important to recognize the founding myths that shape the sociological contours of what we call modern South Africa. Central in these are ideas imposed on the society by Europeans which, variously, deny indigenous people the capacity to be human (Chidester, 1996) and ascribe to indigenous people animal qualities. These ideas interpret the genealogy of indigenous people through Biblical lenses that place them-as descendants of Ham-outside of "God's grace" and reduce them to a status akin to apes and baboons. The central effect of this imposition was to construct the stereotypes of "self" and "other," which have animated South African discourse and served to justify slavery, the wars of dispossession on the Eastern Cape Frontier, the denial of the franchise to Black South Africans after Union in 1910, and the race-class political economy that sprang up around the diamond and gold mines.

In constructing this typology, it is important to recognize how flexible race and the ideas surrounding it, such as ethnicity and culture, are. The world is defined and constantly redefined as social pressures loom large and recede. Race, culture, and ethnicity present themselves as highly mobilizable concepts. Important, nonetheless, is the structuring hold that race has over the discourse of differences in South Africa. While the vocabulary and meaning of difference shifts and changes, it does so in relation to race.

At the same time, and this bears emphasizing, Sharp (1988b) reminded that these concepts are not simply abstract descriptions of the world in which South Africans live. People subscribe to them too. As he argued, "Africans have remained interested in, and concerned with, the specificities of regional or tribal practices without subscribing to the apartheid vision of primordial ethnic groups" (p. 98). The observation is salutary, and emphasizes how social constructions produce real effects as people take on ideas and defend them as if they are real.

EDUCATION IN SOUTH AFRICA

It is widely accepted that schooling, in the form of the debased and separate Bantu Education that was introduced specifically for Africans in 1953, for example, has been a major instrument in constructing the racial order in South Africa (Christie & Collins, 1984). And, indeed, as nearly 40 years of discriminatory policies have shown, schools have been instrumental in promoting the hierarchy of White, Indian, colored, and African in South Africa (Christie, 1990). As a result, most commentaries on education present schools as sites for the playing out of the apartheid agenda. Powerful as this conventional wisdom might be, the approach taken in this part of the essay is informed by the perspective that schools are not simply mirror images of the society in which they find themselves. The argument that was made above with respect to race and schooling sought to suggest that any analysis of education, if it was to make sense of the complex social relations embodied within the dyad of school and society, had to grasp the experience of schooling from both *inside* and *outside*. Education in these terms is both a site that is acted on and a terrain for action. It is influenced by the outside world and the inside world of its inhabitants. The outside world, consisting of the social structures, rules, and practices promulgated and regulated by the state, is represented by the *official curriculum*. The inside is made up of formal curricula that embody individual institutions' specific understandings of their identity and place, and, in particular, of their race, culture, and ethnicity. These understandings are mediated through a range of school practices and traditions and provide schools with the means to promote one or other understandings of their students' racial, cultural, and ethnic place within South Africa. Inside schools are also what one might call informal discourses. These are non school-based cultures that students and teachers bring into the school setting and that are often at odds with both the official and the formal curricula.

This essay seeks to show how the official apartheid discourse, the formal and the informal school discourses, exist in a complex articulation. This articulation sometimes produces a challenge to apartheid, but often provides the framework for the maintenance of domination and subordination. Very few South African studies have worked with this understanding.

Academic studies of race and education have a long lineage in South Africa that goes back to Loram's (1917) *Education of the South African Native*. Following that work, other studies, some polemicist, have appeared, the most noteworthy of which includes Brookes' (1930) *Native Education in South Africa*, Majeke's (1952) *The Role of the Missionary in Conquest*, Bernstein's (1972) *Schools for Servitude*, and in recent times, Hirson's (1979) *Year of Fire, Year of Ash*. Much of this, with the exception of the last three, falls within the liberal tradition, which, as Kallaway (1984, p. 5) remarks, was crucial, but made "no attempt to problematize the historical context" in which policy for education was made. Moreover, in neither the liberalism of the Lorams and the Brookes, nor the radicalism of the Majekes, were the subjects with which they worked people of substance. They were often stereotyped, positively or negatively as political tastes demanded, and almost never permitted an opportunity to speak in their own voices. The field was dominated, moreover, by structuralists texts that belittled the possibility, conceptually, that oppression and exploitation could arise in forms of social organization that have nothing or little to do with economics and caricatures such suprastructural approaches as idealism (see Kros, 1993, October, and Callinicos, 1992). Even Cross' (1992) excellent historical accounts of the emergence and development of countercultures in urban African communities, particularly among the youth, manifest an inability to work with subaltern voice. Seldom in these works does one encounter first-person speakers. Christie and Collins' (1984) work, for example, sought to explain the relationship between school and work, and made the point that crucial as race was as an ideological construct in apartheid schooling, the identities of young people were molded to the needs of the capitalist economy. Dube's "The Relationship Between Racism and Education in South Africa" (1985), the work of Horrell (1964, 1968), and even the authoritative Behr and MacMillan (1971) describe education for Blacks in South Africa-first missionary education and then "Bantu Education"-as "intended to make both African and White children believe that they, by nature, have different destinies" (Dube, 1985, p. 93). The thrust of much of this work is to show how schooling has been organized to produce difference, that of race or class, or, in some instances, both Macrostudies, however, still command the center stage. Du Preez's (1983) *Africana Afrikaner* is an interesting exemplar; it is an attempt to show, via a study of history textbooks in use in Afrikaans White schools, how Afrikaner racial hegemony operates through the use of Afrikaner master symbols. Like other studies in the macrogenre, however, Du Preez's explanation, based as it is on a textual analysis, has little to say about the subjects themselves, the students, and instead focuses on what is done to them.

The approach used in this analysis is informed, firstly, by the discussion above on race, ethnicity, and culture. It seeks to avoid theory, such as that of Bowles and Gintis (1976), which turned the school into a black box and reduced everybody inside it to impotent derivatives of the larger socioeconomic system. It does not wish to argue, on the other hand, that people possess the autonomy to reject, at will, the commanding influences brought to bear on them such as race, gender, and class. It, therefore, seeks to suggest that in taking on identity, people do so within a taunt dialectic of choice and compulsion. As a result, the assumption that guides the discussion is that schooling is one of the central institutions in the making and reproduction of social difference and inequality (class, race, gender), but that the idealized identities sought by the forces of domination seldom materialize because people engage with the forces of their domination (see Thompson, 1968, p. 9).

The approach adopted for the essay is also influenced by deconstructivist theory, which, broadly following Bhabha (1994), argues that subjects seldom fulfill the preassembled identities invented for them. On the contrary, they always transform the images, and so produce "an atmosphere of certain uncertainty." This approach is used to show how the subjects of apartheid engage with the stereotypes their schools present to them and emerge as the recognizable "children" (see Soudien, 1996) of apartheid, but seldom exactly as apartheid would have wanted them to be.

Two Schools in the Apartheid System

Schools in South Africa have been structurally organized to articulate racial difference. For the predominantly Afrikaner Nationalist Party, coming into power in 1948, that African people were drinking from the fountain of European knowledge as *if it were their own* (my italics) was not acceptable. The *Bantu* had to learn their own culture. School in the apartheid era was, thus, fundamentally organized to create and to validate racial difference. In this part of the essay, the discussion shifts to examine how schools, and the people inside them, manage their implicatedness inside of the apartheid system. The discussion focuses on young people and their responses to the system of apartheid. The two schools examined here are called Southern Suburbs Secondary and City Central and are located in the city of Cape Town.

Southern Suburbs Secondary and City Central, were, outwardly at least, the epitome of what the apartheid system had intended. They were racially and ethnically correct. Officially, their students were colored and so were their teachers. At the same time, however, the schools were led, for the most part, by men and women who were deeply hostile to the idea of apartheid. There were, of course, many teachers who enjoyed the benefits of and indeed supported apartheid. Of those who were against it, many, in contrast to others who had left because they were not prepared to teach in the racial environment of apartheid, *chose* to work as teachers because they believed it was necessary to challenge the racial propaganda of the apartheid system. For them, the word race had no meaning (see Jaffe, 1995; No Sizwe, 1979).

What this opposition signaled, moreover, was the presence in the schools of a culture of opposition. These teachers offered their students a means of interpreting the discursive modalities of apartheid, particularly the grand narrative of race (Chisholm, 1994). How students experienced and worked with these signals of incorporation and resistance is explored later. The discussion offers cameos of these experiences and seeks to show the complexity of being a student inside the apartheid school. Emphasized in the discussion are the experiences of students who were classified African at Southern Suburbs Secondary, and those who were classified colored at City Central. Terms such as African and colored have very specific meanings in the South African context. While I do not accept the descriptive classification implied by it, it is necessary to make clear that the term Africans stands for "indigenous" people. Colored is a residual term for people who are classified as being neither White nor African.

Fifty young people were interviewed for this study. Those who were classified African were generally from poor African ghettoes many miles distant from their school. Their colored counterparts were more local and often considerably better off economically.

The discussion below attempts to provide some insight into how these students dealt with the social and ethnic forces that circulated in their schools. The discussion begins with a brief examination of the racial experiences of African students at Southern Suburbs Secondary and then shifts to their colored counterparts at City Central. Both schools, as explained above, were formally colored before 1994. Southern Suburbs, however, during the mid-1990s, when this study was conducted, had gone much further in accepting African students into its midst than had City Central.

BEING AFRICAN AT SOUTHERN SUBURBS SECONDARY

Coming to a school that was not African was, for many students from the township, initially a distressing experience. Against the background of their apartheid-organized lives, making the social adjustment proved to be emotionally painful. This section of the essay begins by looking at how students speak generally of their experiences with their teachers and their fellow colored students.

Phyllis, an African student who had previously attended a colored school in the city of Port Elizabeth on the South-Eastern seaboard of South Africa, explained what she had felt like when she first arrived at Southern Suburbs Secondary,

Phyllis:	. . . (hesitation) . . . It's like I was a visitor here. A visitor now here. It's like the Blacks are the visitors, but the colored children are not all . . . [but the colored children are not all] . . . The colored children some of them are alright to the Black children. They are not doing funny stuff to them.
Interviewer:	But there are children that are racist?

Phyllis:　　　　　　　Ja, some of them. . . . Ja. at first it felt like
　　　　　　　　　　being a visitor.

Several other African students were to make similar remarks. Lindi, a student from the African township of Gugulethu, for example, commented that she "did not feel free" when she first arrived. It took her 3 years to arrive at the point where she had no longer felt afraid.

Several features of the school were intimidating for the students, not least of all having to speak in a language that was not their own. Another Gugulethu young woman, Naledi, found that her lack of Afrikaans, the Dutch-derived language of the Afrikaners, placed her at an immediate disadvantage. She found herself suspecting people of gossiping about her" "(s)sometimes it will happen at . . . in English class, because there we talk. So it happened there and teacher didn't like that. He usually shout at them, but now they stop. But they don't do it in front of the teacher . . . (i)t's not so bad now, like the first time I saw it."

As Zukiswa, who traveled from the old African township of Langa, explained in describing her difficulties with Afrikaans, teachers were frequently oblivious, through the assumptions they made, to the differences of students, particularly their linguistic competencies and cultural backgrounds. The teachers unconsciously premised their work on the model of what they understood a colored child to be. Obviously, many thought, Southern Suburbs Secondary children had to be able to speak Afrikaans. Zukiswa said:

> Ja. My Afrikaans teacher doesn't explain anything. He just, I mean,
> I speak Xhosa, so I find it difficult to speak Afrikaans, because
> Afrikaans is a very difficult language for me. He just tells us to
> page in the textbook, and do this work, and then he sits there. He
> does nothing. Sometimes he falls asleep. He doesn't explain, and then
> one day he was checking our books and found that I didn't do much work.
> He asked me why, and then I told him that I didn't understand the work.
> Sometimes he doesn't even to come to class. Sometimes, you're scared of
> him. You just don't go to his classes.

This experience, of having to cope in an environment in which different assumptions about student competence were the rule, was one that many students had gone through. Not all of those experiences were as culturally veiled as Zukiswa's. Andile, whose English was even weaker than Zukiswa's, spoke of trying to ask a question in a class, "(a)nd teacher don't understand me. Now I start think. . . . I ask the teacher, ne (*you know*)? I ask the teacher . . . I don't, I ask the teacher . . . [he cannot find the word and then speaks in Xhosa] . . . [Long pause] . . . hey, this name. . . . And the teacher don't want to (word in Xhosa). And then shout [at me]. . . ."

In the domain of language use, students were to learn regularly that the Xhosa they spoke was not acceptable at all to some teachers. Predictably there were moments when teachers, because of their inability to understand Xhosa, were constantly suspicious of what children were saying, and were prone to misinterpret student behavior. Miriam, a young woman from the informal settlement of Westlake, explained: "(t)he colored teachers they get upset when you speak Xhosa, but some of the teachers of course are interested. I don't see why they should have a problem with Xhosa, because they speak Afrikaans with the Afrikaans students. While it's a[n] English class, they don't speak English all the time."

Zania, for example, told a story in which her friends' use of Xhosa was interpreted as rudeness, "(t)his teacher is a racist, because if we are speaking Xhosa in class, he used to throw us out. He don't want to hear anyone speaking Xhosa. . . ."

The classroom, predictably, featured regularly in the students' accounts of their encounters with colored students. Sometimes, the stories they had to tell related to situations that were ambiguous in their significance. On these occasions it was debatable whether color or simply personal dislike underlay colored students' treatment of African students. On other occasions, there was little ambiguity, particularly when the language resorted to by colored students was framed in explicit racial terms.

Among the more ambiguous racial experiences were the kind that Phyllis and George had gone through. Asked how she knew that some of the pupils in her class were racist, Phyllis, a young woman from Langa township, replied, "(b)ecause when you ask them for something, they won't give you,b ut they have. But if it's the colored girl, she will give that girl. . . ." George, who traveled from Khayelitsha, almost 25 kilometers away, spoke in similar vein of his colored peers brushing off his overtures. He said, "I think some are . . . some of them are nice. . . . But some of them, they just don't like us, I don't think. Like when you ask one of them something, to explain something to you, is just say, he don't know, she don't know. But she knows. It's just because maybe because of my skin, color of my skin."

Lindi, an older girl, and others were to repeat this refrain, "(p)eople . . . are not nice in my class. Ja, they don't like to talk to me, or it's not even to me, to us. . . . To us, like, my friends. And when we were talk to the class, they just laugh. They don't listen to you. And, ja, that's . . . their attitude is not right. . . . Zukiswa, who had come to tolerate the students in her class, and who described them as being "nice people," said that when she first came to Southern Suburbs Secondary, ". . . at first I hated them, all of them. Because I thought they were. . . . Because they didn't talk to us. They were just sitting in a different place, talking something else--talking about something else. . . . Maybe they thought we were different or something. . . ."

That *something*, explained Zania, also from Langa, was unmistakably the idea that Africans were inferior. The colored students, she felt, only related to their African counterparts when the racial hierarchy between them was clearly understood. She made the point that "they [the colored students] want us to call them madams, you see, to give them the kind of respect . . . of 'oh here's our colored (mistress)'. . . . If you want something from (them) you must always be. . . ." She did not conclude the sentence, but embedded in her train of thought was the idea that to get anything one had to display the correct sense of subservience.

In the midst of seeking to provide an overview of the quality of experience that African children went through at Southern Suburbs Secondary, it is important to emphasize, and repeatedly so, that these were not the sum or even the larger part of younger people's experiences at school. In the range of experiences African students went through at school, there were many moments of affirmation and genuine love that they would encounter. Lindi, for example, told the story of the kindness shown her by a teacher. "The other day," she began, "we were bunking his class, all of us, my friends. And then he came to fetch us, we were sitting on the law. Ja. . . . He didn't chase us back into the class. He talked to us, and we told him the problem, why we were bunking his class. He say that is you don't understand his work, you must come to him." And, indeed, there were also long periods of time where they would simply do the things of schooling, playing, laughing, fighting, arguing, studying for tests, learning, and so on. As I show later, many of the students said clearly that they were happy at Southern Suburbs Secondary. Students liked doing the things that went with schooling. Lindi, for example, told us, "I like studying for tests." Jonas concurred that he enjoyed the routine of learning, doing homework, and just of coming to school. Thabo explained that he liked schoolwork.

Inherent, however, in the day-to-day experience of schooling, appeared to always lurk the latent potential for racism. Minute cracks exposed a sedimented layer of negative racial consciousness beneath the patina of the normal order. It was this consciousness that was responsible for the undermining of African students' subjectivities. The formal activity of class was a place where this phenomenon—of being undermined—asserted itself. In their classes, while they were being taught, for example, the othering impulse of the formal curriculum was hard to suppress. Jonas saw this in the formal operation of the school,

Jonas:	Another thing I hate about this school. . . .
E. W.:	That you hate?
Jonas:	Ja. (laughter) The thing I hate about this school . . . is this, the school is very much a. . . . Like in terms of our history. We don't learn about our own history. We learn about the history of the other countries like Europe.

	So I'm not proud, I'm not. . . . I mean that makes us fail of course, because you learn about the history of somebody else from the other country, from the other continent in fact, it's boring. . . .
C.S.:	Is this a racist school?
Jonas:	I think the whole system . . . the system of the whole world in fact. . . .
C.S.:	Of the hole world?
Jonas:	Of the whole world in fact, because the system of education is being (indistinct) because the Black people are not learning about their own history. We must learn about Napoleon, the White man, the mighty Napoleon. I'm sick and tired of that. . . .

Despite the fact that many students, as was evident earlier in the chapter, spoke of being discriminated against at school, they liked their school. They enjoyed the company of their peers, the attitude of their teachers, and the discipline for which school stood. An important anticipatory point to make in listening to the students is that the quotient of *goods* that they took from or found in the school was sufficiently weighty for many to be able to tolerate the *bads* they encountered in it.

So much so was the case that of the 20 students, most had something positive to say about the school. Only two students were unambiguously negative. Much of what the students had to say related to their peers and the routine of school. Zukiswa had this to say, " . . . I like the . . . people there at the school. I enjoy them. . . . They are very nice people. They are not difficult to talk to. They are always nice. Some of them are naughty, but they are nice too." Priscilla spoke of the students in her class who, she felt, looked out for her needs. "I like that . . .," she explained, "if I don't understand, they can . . . they explain for me. Yes . . . and if I maybe I'm not at school, they phone for me. They ask for me, why I didn't come to school." The social aspect, making friends, was very important for many students.

Thabo was to agree and took the matter further, " . . . this school. Ja, it's a nice school. I like this school, because of the . . . in terms of the attitudes of the student and the teachers." Zania's assessment was similar. She said, "(b)eing here, it's very good for me. It's very interesting, terrific, and I enjoy it. And I'm proud of my school, teachers, and the students, because we used to help each other. Going out, like hiking, and going to the movies. I like this school, and I also like coming to school because some of my teachers are just good to me. . . . And we used to go out with out teachers."

Student testimony of the support they received from particular teachers constituted a strong factor in their affection for the school. Individual teachers stood out in their recollections in the ways in which they performed little acts

of kindnesses for them. Three accounts, set out below, are worth repeating. The
first comes from Miriam, who explained:

> Altogether, like our school there's a lot of nice teachers who
> understand the students. And always tries to . . . om humanity
> in hulle in te preach en so aan. Ek hou van skook because dit
> is lekker. . . . (*to instill in them a sense of humanity and
> so on. I like school because it is enjoyable.*) Most of the
> teachers I know. Really, I like them. I like die activities
> wat hulle somtyds het, al is dit so baie min. But dis fine,
> dis lekker. Hulle stel belang in 'n . . . like, me now. Hulle
> sal altyd vir my--like (*I like the activities they organize,
> even if they are rare. But it's fine, it's enjoyable. They
> take an interest in me. They'll always like--*) like I'm
> involved in drama and that--they'll always like encourage
> me, like in my schoolwork. I mean, it's nice that there's
> someone cracking on your shoulder now and again. It's nice
> when they keep on like that. Hulle's nice met 'n mens.
> *(They're nice to a person).* They're not racist to one.

Mathakhoza's story confirmed Miriam's:

> . . . they're always . . . and if maybe there's something
> that you don't understand, they can . . . they help you
> out. Ja. There's this teacher I actually like. Out of all
> of these teachers, my Afrikaans teacher. He can see if you
> don't understand, and he's . . . she's the one who makes
> a plan so that you . . . she can maybe provide extra
> classes for you so that . . . so he can help you out with
> your work. Even on Saturdays, she'll ask you to come to
> school, just to come and help you. And she'll take you
> back home.

Zukiswa, too, had found her teachers in general to be caring and
sensitive, and made school something to which she looked forward. She began
by explaining her relationship with a particular teacher, and then went on to talk
of some of her other teachers:

> He talks to us. He doesn't just tell us to page in our
> textbooks, and do this work. He just talks to us, and
> explains things, and sometimes he talks to us individually.
> Ja, I know, but there are a lot of us in the class, so he
> doesn't have much time to do that. But sometimes when he
> gets the chance. And he's a very easy person to talk to,
> because we're not afraid to ask him something. And my

other teachers, they are also nice. They're also not
difficult people, because they also are easy people to
talk to. I mean we're not scared to come up and ask them
if we don't understand something. . . . Ja, it makes
whatever subject easy. Ja, even in my Maths class, my
Maths teacher, he's approachable, ja. I can ask him to
explain something, and when I'm stuck, I don't feel scared.
I just go to him, and tell him that I'm stuck, I can't
continue with this. And then he shows me how to do it.

There were many other reasons for liking school. Among these were
the academic and personal. Many students liked school because, as Zania put it,
"It increase my knowledge." George's explanation was similar, "(N)o, I like it,
to get more knowledge. So that I can know what's happening with this and
this."

"I like education," said Andile, "and education is very important for
me. And I want to pass this year." For Mathakhoza it was a straightforward
issue. "Yes school is boring," she said, "but sometimes I enjoy to be here at
school. Because here at school, I've got many friends." What was important
about these friends, she said, was that they " . . . are the ones who usually show
me the right way, and who usually correct me when I speak wrong. I like
speaking languages."

Phyllis felt that coming to Southern Suburbs Secondary exposed her to
new information:

I like school because you get to know some things which you
didn't even know. Like in History. We saw the video, we didn't
know that years ago it was like that. The Whites were just taking
our lands from us . . . but they were not even belonging here in
South Africa. And their political . . . people were detained, and
they have to chase us away, . . . from Sophiatown [a landmark
township in Johannesburg and the only place in the city where
Africans were able to own property]. And so most of the people
were in exile, because of that. Ja, ja. Now we are just discovering,
and we are just knowing some things which we didn't even know.

ETHNICITY AT CITY CENTRAL

City Central was, for many years, *the* institution to attend if one lived in the
city. It provided social status for students that they could not get elsewhere.
Whether students came to it because their parents had made that decision for
them or because they wished it for themselves, the act of coming constituted a
first opportunity and a first step for students to formally identify with the

institution. And many students did, indeed, come to identify strongly with City Central. While some, like Shahiema, Rukeya, Liezl, and Sheila, who all lived in suburbs adjacent to the school, were extremely critical of it, most had very positive feelings toward City Central. Even Shahiema and her friends were proud of being students at City Central. For example, while the testimony of Andre, who had to travel by bus to come to school, was stronger than that of his peers, it was not unusual:

> There's something about City Central, the spirit around it, this
> whole atmosphere. It makes you hunger for education. I think that's
> what's lacking at other schools. There was this guy at our school,
> at City Central. He left last year, and he was interviewed recently.
> He went to a so-called White school. And he was interviewed. And in
> this interview . . . he made some very, I think, rude statements,
> very inflammatory statements about this school. . . . We've always
> had a proud tradition of discipline, of standing up for what we
> believe in. Like Mr. X. [a former principal], he was willing to
> sacrifice for what he believed. We were taught to stand up for
> what we believe in. Never to lie down or back down in the face
> of adversity, but to really strive for things. And that is
> something which helps all City Central students once again.
> They go out of their way to get what they want in life. It
> makes them strong.

What Andre was to say about *his* school and the way in which he chose to speak was, in many ways, a validation and fulfillment of the school's formal objectives. *Being strong* and *standing up for what one believed*, formed, as anyone familiar with the school would confirm, central planks of its mission. What, however, students were loyal to and what they would be prepared to stand up and be strong for was not always clear. To be sure, the politically informed ideals of nonracialism and individual excellence could be seen running through the school's everyday rhetoric, but the contextualization of those ideals in classroom and other school settings often, and inevitably, produced situations that revealed the heterogeneous facets of, and multivalent forces in, the school.

It was in their relationships with teachers that students were called upon to work with the variegated meanings that emanated from the school's formal structure. This work was manifest in the process of instruction, during moments when teachers assigned and evaluated tasks, and in their face-to-face encounters with teachers.

The experience of working with teachers in the process of instruction was a mixed one for many students. Most students, and this was hardly a surprise, found school tedious and boring. Liezl was perhaps more disaffected than most. She found that, "when the teacher's talking I don't really listen to what she's saying because it's like . . . boring. You know? It's like . . . it doesn't grab me. So when I study, then only I go over the work, and I learn the work. Then I know what's going on. But not during class. I can't listen and stuff." School did indeed *get to* many more students. Deirdre, regarded by some of her teachers as an exceptionally creative student, enjoyed the times when she was able to "write my own point of view and things specially in composition," but found school to be "right now . . . boring. It's boring, you have to sit in a class and the teacher just teaches, and he just talks and everybody's supposed to sit there and listen. You're not made part of the lesson." For Nadine school was "endlessly tiring. . . . Sometimes I just don't feel like doing it, then I just don't do it."

Others, such as Zaaid and Andre, were pragmatic about their experiences in classes. Zaaid explained that he "never stud(ies) and stuff like that. But I always, I don't know, like to do things on the last minute. . . . The night before I know I have to do it, and then I'm serious about it. But I'm not so serious about it [in class]." For Andre it was a matter of:

> having been silly [about schoolwork] all these years, thinking
> I'm not going to do that teacher's homework, because he's
> this and that. I've actually . . . matured . . . . I realize
> I've got to take responsibility for myself. And yes, homework
> is a drag . . . but then you've got to look where your
> priorities are. . . . This is my future I'm planning here now,
> and I'm not going to play around with my future.

Two distinct perspectives of their teachers' work were evident among the students. Some students construed much of what they went through with teachers in class as being politically irrelevant. Rukeya, for example, felt that the pedagogical style of teachers revealed how much teachers were part of the wider social (apartheid) context in which they were embedded. She implicitly, rather than directly perhaps, challenged the conformist and conventional approach of teachers, which "failed to let students . . . read and make their own assumptions." School, she felt, could be a time for "see(ing) the issues. Draw out, for instance, the novel. Let me just give some easy thing like Red Riding Hood. [Look at it] (f)rom a political aspect . . . try and apply your thinking to . . . how it will affect the way students think about politics, about issues like birth control. . . ."

Many students preferred to think of their teachers as being stimulating, a view that was very much more in keeping with the image of the school. Andre spoke of a long-standing argument that he was conducting with a teacher who resented this (Andre's) support for a rival political party. Irritated as he was by the argument, Andre felt, nonetheless, that it was a good thing that he could have his say. In general, he said, the teachers at City Central helped him to speak his mind:

> I can point to one person, Mr. A. my history teacher. He actually
> made me feel good about myself, because I always, I have a great
> knowledge of general [information]. . . . I read the newspapers
> a lot. And he told me that . . . that didn't actually make me a
> nerd, and I shouldn't be afraid of expressing those things.

Fouzah also recalled the time during the national elections when teachers regularly spoke of the issues involved in the process, and encouraged the students to debate the merits of different party positions. "Because although they [the teachers] had their personal opinions," she said, "they spoke to us from an open point of view, and left it up to us who we went to decide for without any pressure from their side." Ashraf was always conscious of how fastidious teachers were around the use of pejorative terms and how they sought to make their work politically relevant. He explained that:

> Most of our teachers are progressive. They . . . none of them
> . . . they'd never make racist jokes and things. They're very
> adamant about the struggle, and all those things. . . . The
> teacher that most imprinted this was Miss B. . . . She was
> . . . she taught me History in Standard Seven. That was the
> last year I did History but you know, I can still remember,
> and I like her for it . . . what she brought out and
> everything. . . .

The world in which colored students found themselves, as their African peers at Southern Suburbs had discovered, was complex. As students struggled at Southern Suburbs, so too, differently, did their colored counterparts at City Central. Issues of color were undoubtedly profoundly troubling for students at City Central. Brought up in the politically correct atmosphere of City Central, and conscious that their every step was being monitored ideologically, students had to work with the push and pull of different calls on their racial sensitivities. They struggled, however, to keep the apartheid order at bay. This struggle was apparent in their attempts to deal with the impact of the new South African reality in their lives. Try as the school did to help them deal with issues such as affirmative action, student opinion at City Central was almost uniformly against the practice. There were two components to the argument that students made against affirmative action. The first was informed by an existential anxiety, and the second by an apparent concern for affirmative action reversing White domination in favor of Black domination.

Articulating the first argument, Zaaid, an outspoken young man, said, " . . . jobs are already so little. And like with affirmative action, it's going to be hard to find a job . . . . People now . . . can see no jobs, how they must live, and I wouldn't want to live like that. . . . It worries me sometimes." Monique, who was a member of the trendy crowd at the school, added, "I

probably wouldn't be able to get a job very easily. . . . Because a friend of
mine can't get a job and she was denied a job because somebody who was a
Xhosa-speaking like applied as well and got the job. . . ."

It was the second argument that was deployed more often. "I don't
think [it's right]," said Nazia, a studious girl from the area close to the school,
"I don't think so at all because it is totally wrong. It's as if apartheid is starting
all over again." Nadine, her friend, agreed:

> I don't think that's . . . okay. . . . (I)n some ways, I
> think it's fair and in some ways I think it's not fair.
> I think it was very unfair in people what happened in the
> past. But it was the past and I think it's now like . . .
> it's like apartheid is starting all over again. . . .(T)he
> Blacks are going to be favored and they're going to get
> all the jobs. . . .

Outwardly, students claimed--consistent with their formal membership
of and allegiance to City Central--that race was not an important feature in the
making of their judgments and in their everyday relations. In reality, it was an
unspoken but articulate dynamo that inserted itself and conditioned their
everyday behavior. While racial names such as "kaffir" were taboo in the
school, the condition of race was something from which they could not escape.
Deirdre, a girl who was much admired for her style, upon being asked whether
racism still existed in South Africa, said:

> (d)efinitely. A lot. . . . (Take) myself for example. If
> I sit in the bus and a so-called colored, old woman or aged,
> comes into the bus then I automatically get up. But if it's
> a so-called Black woman then I don't. Sometimes, without me
> really wanting to do it, then I'd like hesitate to get up
> because it's as if, because it's been put to us so that
> Black people . . . aren't human.

Try as they might, students had difficulty in dismissing the label
colored that was placed on them. While many rejected the term, on occasion,
as in the case of Alan, from the colored township of Kensington, a commitment
to and acceptance of the term came because, as Alan saw it, coloreds were
acceptable to neither Whites nor Blacks:

> Yes, I would (describe myself as colored). The reason being
> that--me and (indistinct noise on tape) had endless arguments
> about this. And actually that girl Michelle . . . she'll tell
> me, "but you're black, man," and I say, "no, I'm colored."
> Michelle . . . she'll tell me "why?", and I'd say like,

because they're *[he means politicians--CS]* always telling
you that coloreds and Blacks fall under the same . . .
coloreds fall under Blacks, right. But here, too, you're
not Black, and you're not White. You're colored. You're
in the middle. . . . I don't think I'd want to be called
Black actually. And I don't think I'd ever be called
White, so colored is fine.

Andre was to make an even stronger intellectual argument for using the
term colored. Prefacing his comments in a politically correct way by describing
himself as South African, he then switched the line of his thought:

I look at myself as a South African, as a human being. I
don't look at myself as colored. Okay, I admit it, I've
grown up used to being called colored. I'm colored. And
my neighborhood (is a) colored neighborhood. I've grown
up with it. What can I do? It's going to be in me, no
matter. . . . It's no use I'm going to try and get it
out of me, like some people are trying. Also, there are
things that I am proud of as a colored person. Well
firstly my neighborhood. No matter what, the people
have always stuck together, the colored people. That's
one thing that colored people are renowned for--standing
together with each other, helping each other. And that's
what I am proud of.

At the same time, there were many in the school who were astute observers of
the different discourses at school. Ashraf, described by all as a "great guy,"
deplored the racism he saw around him, and inveighed against colored
chauvinism. He admired the formal ethos of the school and had support for this
stance among several of his peers. One of them, Sadia, was outraged when she
overheard a fellow student Mr. Mandela as "dom darkie" (*stupid darkie*).

CONCLUSION

The argument with which this chapter has sought to take issue is that the
apartheid school is simply a reproductive structure and has the function of
bringing children into *correspondence* with the apartheid order. The
counterargument it seeks to make, using the experience of the 50 young people
who were interviewed, is that reproduction by itself is neither a particularly
good nor a particularly useful hermeneutic for understanding the complexity of
the race-school link. In the first place, it homogenizes the character of school
and assumes that its project is single, uniform, and uncontested, and in the

second, it suggests that school is a battlefield upon which just *two* adversaries stand, the rulers and the ruled.

The point of departure in this work is, therefore, that school is not a totalizing metanarrative. It neither embodies nor stands for a particular meaning that is canonically superimposed upon the everyday transactions of school. Speaking of the citizen in a decolonized nation, Spivak (1993, p. 48) says that "a person can inhabit widely different epistemes, violently at odds with each other yet yoked together by way of the many everyday uses of the *pouvoir-savoir.*" School is a space where young people encounter and play with the different epistemic logics that surround them, and where, as Spivak (1993, p. 49) said, "the narrow and the general sense infiltrate each other, bring each other to crisis, although they are not inscribed into a continuum."

In bringing this work to a close, this section seeks to show how the discursive terrain of school impacts on the identities of young people. It makes the argument that the identities of young people develop are divided internally; that their subjectivities are unavoidably the products of a series of intersecting encounters that leave them, in Flax's (1993, p. 95) terms, in a number of different positions at different times and places. Their identities are, by definition, incoherent and discontinuous. They are of their apartheid pasts, but simultaneously against it. Identity formation in school is a process in which young people bring resources, find new ones, and always work to make sense of their positions relative to others. In the apartheid school, this work is conducted as a series of rhetorical maneuvers in which young people are constantly required to do work or to *own up*, to coin an expression, to an image of what it is that they are supposed to be. It is this which produces what Bhabha (1994) called *recognition and disavowal*. The very act of going to school is a form of *owning up*. At a particular level, children *own up* to being the coloreds or the Africans or the Whites or the Indians the apartheid order says they have to be to attend that particular school. The act of *owning up* is, however, never a straight admission. What it is, is a response to a series of social compulsions. One is forced to acknowledge the call of apartheid in one's life, much as, as Althusser (1971) explained, one was forced to acknowledge ideology. Some of the compulsions carry more authority than others, and so one ignores them at one's peril. One ceases to exist, for example, if one chooses to operate outside the Official Order. It is the strategic and rhetorical maneuver around these compulsions that are explored below.

OWNING UP TO THE OFFICIAL

Owning up to the Official Order is for young people, African and colored, a complex and continuing experience for ambiguity. For African children, the act of coming to Southern Suburbs is both a break with and an acknowledgement of their apartheid subjectivities. In leaving their township schools, they are signaling their rejection of the ensemble of meaning associated with their apartheid pasts. Leaving is behind *Bantu Education* for the forbidden vistas of the White or the *almost-White* colored world. The process of leaving is profoundly decisive. It has the impact, as Gaganakis (1991) said, of separating, culturally and spatially, the young people who have decided to move from their own township peers.

Some of the students at Southern Suburbs commented that they liked the school because "they were meeting new people." The point is relatively straightforward. Inherent in it is the idea of young people constructing new subcultures, informed by the very act of leaving the township, which set them apart from their township lifestyles. At the same time, in entering the colored environment of schools like Southern Suburbs, they enter acknowledging their difference. They *are* different. They come from a different place and a different history. Although coming to Southern Suburbs is thus tantamount to a statement about their township lives, it is simultaneously a recognition of their *otherness* within it. With respect to their pasts, their entry into Southern Suburbs is thus a complex statement of betrayal and recognition-betrayal of the township in leaving it and recognition of their affiliation with it in meeting their contrary colored peers. (At the same time, for a few students, and the significant division of opinion within their number must be emphasized, coming to Southern Suburbs is unequivocally the expression of a desire to relinquish the township altogether). In *owning up* township students thus stand before and in relation to the Official Discourse with considerable ambiguity. It seeks to have them acknowledge their African separateness, and in ways that remind them of their subordinate status; their response, however, is to wish it away by seeking to relocate themselves outside of it. Their identities are very much divided between the attractiveness of the outside world-the new school-and the familiarity of their inside worlds-the township. A *divided* self thus manifests itself in its participation at school.

The process of *owning up* for colored students is no less complex. They do so, however, within the racial constraints of the discourse of the Official Order, which has them acknowledging and conforming to its bureaucratic prescriptions. They are, in terms of these bureaucratic prescriptions, still colored people who have to present colored birth certificates and identity documents and who have come from colored primary schools. School tells them that they are human beings, not coloreds. Inherent in this process is thus an element of a *denied* self.

OWNING UP TO THE FORMAL AND THE INFORMAL

It is in the interplay between the formal and the informal discourses, however, that the process of speaking to their identities becomes most complex. For African children, the formal and informal discourses collude in seeking them to acknowledge their inferior and subordinate positions. For colored children the relationship between the formal and the informal discourses is a contradictory one. The formal addresses them in the oppositional tones of the universal human who stands above apartheid, and the informal grounds them in the separately lived reality of apartheid.

The formal and informal discourses constitute a medium, or media, in which young Africans are called upon to signal and affirm their relative position to the colored children they meet at school. They are constantly called on to accept the fact that their histories are signs of an inferiority that is irremediable. Their Blackness is testimony of it. Their responses to these invocations, however, reveal the full range of their rhetorical strategies. Sometimes they are submissive and acquiescent, at other times they are strident, defiant, and proud.

In having to *own up* to what school, in its formal and informal modes, asks of them, students *measure* what it is they should be doing and how they should be responding. Having decided to come to Southern Suburbs and having made the break with the township, they continue their involvement with the apartheid order, but seek to reposition themselves within it. When the formal and informal discourses of school thus serve to set on them, they are able to recognize to what they are being subjected. Their choice, however, in seeking to secure new positions within the order calls on them to respond to the attack of their colored peers and teachers in ways that are by turn defensive an acquiescent, and resistant and unyielding. Their desire for the better life, which Southern Suburbs stands for, means that they accept their subordination inside school.

At the same time students do take exception to the hidden curriculum of race. Teachers who say things like *"you people,"* leave them feeling deeply frustrated. Rebelling against school and teachers is, however, not an option that is able to gain them ground. Occasionally, of course, the agenda becomes unbearable and they either take stands by themselves, as Mathakhoza did, or they rally together as the boys did when they were about to be punished for an infraction they considered not to have been their responsibility. For the rest, however, frustrated as they were, their often-conscious assessment was that as long as they constituted a minority group inside the school, they would have to abide by its discursive dictates. Their subjectivities were thus presented in a state of self-repression.

Signally, however, self-repression gives way to self-expression outside of the formal arena. In their encounters with their colored peers, they were able to represent themselves more confidently. Where they retreated in the face of teacher abuse, they fought back when such abuse came from their peers. They refused to accept the positioning to which their peers subjected them. The estimation they made there was that terrain was safer, and less hazardous.

In making sense of the impact of school on African students' identities, what Spivak (1993, p. 49) referred to as the "narrow and the general sense infiltrat(ing) each other, bring(ing) each other to crisis, although they are not inscribed into a continuum," is useful in understanding the interpolated nature of students' lives. Visible in students' identities are the figures of their apartheid lives that constantly infiltrate, condition, and sometimes even bring to a crisis their school lives. School makes possible this infiltration, conditioning, and, one might add, counterconditioning. They are called on in their school lives in the mode of address of apartheid. Their apartheid pasts, however, provide them with the rhetorical means to deal with this invocation in ways that simultaneously affirm and contest that apartheid past. It is in this sense that subjectivities that are produced in the arena of the school are at once *divided, repressed,* and *displayed* and *resilient.* Subjected, put upon, and oppressed as they are, they are always active readers of their contexts and thus able to strategize how to deal with their various encounters.

For colored children the play between the formal and the informal is equally complex, but has different results. Where the formal and the informal discourses in their African peers' lives are congruent in the outcomes they seek to precipitate, in their lives those same discourses have an ambiguous relationship. The essence of this ambiguity is contained in the contradictory makeup of the two discourses. Discrete as these discourses are, and capable of determining their respective domains as they might be, in their difference they provide young people with significantly different interpretations of the world. It is in working with these different interpretations that students develop what Flax (1993) called "troubled identities."

At the heart of this *trouble* is the considerable weight of the formal discourse, which requires young people to *own up* to a universalism that the school constantly flourishes in front of them. Against this stands the informal discourse, which insistently calls on them to *cut loose* and concentrate on being themselves and even being colored.

What this at-homeness or familiarity with the informal discourse of coloredism set up was that City Central students were able to present themselves as subjects able to project two distinct sides to their subjectivities. They were unmistakably the products and the producers of both the formal and the informal discourses. Evident in their lives were the clear signs and markers of these discourses. It is this manifestation that provides substance for the application of the term "troubled identities." Students reveal themselves to be, like people with multiple subjectivities elsewhere, adept in several, often discontinuous, environments.

Important to recognize, however, is that as discontinuous as the formal and the informal discourses are in terms of the world views they project, they are not strictly standalone discourses. Interestingly, students call into use in their informal interactions the truths of the formal discourse. A central truth that some deployed in the informal world was that of their membership of the human race -"we're all the same." While individuals such as Sheila and Shahiema were able to penetrate the universalist miasma surrounding some of the highmindedness invoked by their peers, for virtually all of the other students, and even for Sheila and Shahiema themselves on occasion, the trope of universalism was a powerful took in their rhetorical arsenal.

Of course, the informal discourse was also present in their approach to the formal life of the school. It constantly undermined the singularity of the formal by poking fun at its self-importance. As the students indicated, they were "turned off" by school. In turning away from it, they looked for fulfillment in the tricks and ways of the informal. Having said that, it is important to recognize how much discourses influence each other and to see how difficult it was for students to avoid the encounter with the racial discourse of apartheid. Even when they thought they were standing above apartheid, it infiltrated their highmindedness. It lay there obscured and disguised.

Important in bringing this chapter to a close is recognizing how differently the discourse configuration serves African and colored students. I have tried to argue that school is an important site for symbolic work, and that it is not just a conduit for ruling-class aspirations. What I have shown is how complex the apartheid school is as an experience for young people. I have not only argued that school is a contested terrain, I have also tried to show up the nature of the discursive contestation as a dialectic in which collusion, contestation, agreement, and dissonance constantly operate in people's lives. Willis (1977, p. 146) spoke of the "unintended and contradictory importance of the institution of the school." He said that aspects of the dominant ideology are defeated there, but that the defeat is pyrrhic. This work seeks to argue that elements of the apartheid ideology are, to be sure, defeated on the school campus. African children find in school the material for their dreams of a better life. Colored children see themselves painted differently to the portraits embossed for them on their birth certificates. But, in equal measure, apartheid has more than held its own. Its ways and tastes remain evident in the behavior of children. The children emerge with identities that are end products of a form of social compromise. They are manifestly, therefore, the products of their oppositional worlds. But they are also the children of apartheid; their parentage is unmistakably imprinted with its characteristics.

What this conclusion points to is how difficult it is to read off from the school a meaning of the larger society. School and education are sites in which young people, as active subjects, measure what they can and cannot do. In making strategic choices, they explore dimensions of their subjectivities that the racial order seeks to close down. They emerge from their schooling experience with the ethnic badges of colored and Xhosa culture and, invariably, they are profoundly conscious of the racial hierarchies that surround them. They are, however, considerably more than the stereotypes that the hegemonic racial discourse prepares for them.

REFERENCES

Adam, H. (1971). *Modernizing racial domination: South Africa's political dynamics.* Berkeley, CA: University of California Press.

Althusser, L. (1971). *Lenin and philosophy and other essays.* New York: Monthly Review Press.

Behr, A. L., & MacMillan, R. G. (1971). *Education in South Africa.* Pretoria, South Africa: Van Schaik.

Bernstein, H. (1972). Schools for servitude. In A. LaGuma (Ed.), *Apartheid: A collection of writings on South African racism.* London: Lawrence and Wishart.

Bhabha, H. (1994). *The location of culture.* London: Routledge & Kegan Paul.

Bowles, S., & Gintis, H. (1976). *Schooling in capitalist America.* New York: Basic Books.

Brookes, E. H. (1968). *Native education in South Africa.* Pretoria, South Africa: Van Schaik.

Bundy, C. (1979). *The rise and fall of the South African peasantry.* Berkeley: University of California Press.

Callinicos, A. (1992). Race and class. *International Socialism, 55,* 3-40.

Chidester, D. (1996). Mutilating meaning: European interpretations of Khoisan languages of the body. In P. Skotnes (Ed.), *Miscast: Negotiating the presence of the Bushmen* (pp. 25-39). Cape Town, South Africa: University of Cape Town Press.

Chisholm, L. (1994). Making the pedagogical more political, and the political more pedagogical: Education traditions and legacies of the Non-European Unity Movement, 1943-1985. In W. Flanagan, C. Hemson, J. Muller, & N. Taylor (Compilers), *Vintage Kenton: A Kenton Education Association commemoration* (pp. 225-241). Cape Town, South Africa: Maskew Miller Longman.

Christie, P. (1990). *Open schools. Racially mixed Catholic schools in South Africa, 1976-1986.* Johannesburg, South Africa: Ravan.

Christie, P., & Collins, C. (1984). Bantu education: Apartheid and ideology. In P. Kallaway (Ed.), *Apartheid and education* (pp. 160-183). JohannesBurg, South Africa: Ravan.

Comaroff, J. (1985). *Body of power, spirit and resistance: The culture and history of a South African people.* Chicago: University of Chicago Press.

Cross, M. (1992). *Resistance and transformation: Education, culture and reconstruction in South Africa.* Johannesburg, South Africa: Skotaville.

DeKiewiet, C. W. (1941 & 1996). *A history of South Africa: Social and economic.* Oxford, England: Oxford University Press.

Dube, E. F. (1985). The relationship between racism and education in South Africa. *Harvard Education Review, 55*(1), 86-100.

Dubow, S. (1995). Ethnic euphemisms and racial echoes. *Journal of Southern African Studies, 20*(3), 355-370.

DuPreez, J. M. (1983). *Africana Afrikaner: Master symbols in South African school textbooks*. Alberton, South Africa: Librarius.

Flax, J. (1993). *Disputed subjects: Essays on psychoanalysis, philosophy and politics*. London: Routledge & Kegan Paul.

Foucault, M. (1989). *The archaeology of knowledge*. London: Routledge & Kegan Paul.

Gaganakis, M. (1991). Opening up the closed school. In D. Freer (Ed.), *Towards open schools. Possibilities and realities for non-racial education in South Africa* (pp. 78-96). Manzini, Swaziland: Macmillan Boleswa.

Grossberg, L. (1997). *Bringing it all back home: Essays on cultural studies*. Durham, NC: Duke University Press.

Hirson, B. (1979). *Year of fire, year of ash: The Soweto revolt, roots of a revolution*. London: Zed Press.

Horrell, M. (1964). *Bantu education to 1968*. Johannesburg, South Africa: South African Institute of Race Relations.

Jaffe, H. (1994). *European colonial depotism: A history of oppression and resistance in South Africa*. London: Karnak House.

Johnstone, F. (1976). *Race, class, and gold*. London: Routledge & Kegan Paul.

Kallaway, P. (Ed.). (1984). *Apartheid and education: The education of Black South Africans*. Johannesburg, South Africa: Ravan.

Kallaway, P. (1991, April). *Education and nation-building in South Africa in the 1990s: Reforming history education for the post-apartheid era*. Paper presented at the Comparative and International Education Conference, Pittsburgh, PA.

Kros, C. (1993, October). *Eiselen: Idealists and idealism revisited*. Paper Presented at the Meeting of the Southern African Comparative and History of Education Society, Scottsburgh, South Africa.

Legassick, M. (1974). British hegemony and the origins of segregation, 1901-1914. In Institute of Commonwealth Studies *Collected Seminar Papers*. London: University of London.

Loram, C. T. (1917). *The education of the South African native*. New York: Negro Universities Press.

Macmillan, W. M. (1927). *The Cape colour question*. London: Faber & Gwyer.

Macmillan, W. M. (1929). *Bantu, Boer and Briton*. London: Faber & Gwyer.

Magubane, B. (1979). *The political economy of race and class in South Africa*. New York: Monthly Review Press.

Majeke, N. (1952). *The role of the missionary in conquest*. Cape Town, South Africa: Genadendal.

Nolutshungu, S. C. (1982). *Changing South Africa*. Manchester, United Kingdom: Manchester University Press.

No Sizwe. (1979). *One Azania, one nation*. London: Zed Press.

O'Meara, D. (1988). *Volkskapitalisme: Class, capital, and ideology in the development of Afrikaner nationalism*. Cambridge, England: Cambridge University Press.

Omi, M., & Winant, H. (1986). *Racial formation in the United States*. London: Routledge & Kegan Paul.

Rhoodie, N. J. (Ed.). (1972). *South African dialogue*. Johannesburg, South Africa: McGraw-Hill.

Sharp, J. (1988a). Introduction: Constructing social reality. In E. Boonzaaier and J. Sharp (Eds.), *South African keywords: The uses and abuses of political concepts* (pp. 1-16). Cape Town, South Africa: David Philip.

Sharp, J. (1988b). Ethnic group and nation: The apartheid vision in South Africa. In E. Boonzaaier and J. Sharp (Eds.), *South African keywords: The uses and abuses of political concepts* (pp. 79-99). Cape Town, South Africa: David Philip.

Soudien, C. A. (1996). *Apartheid's children*. Unpublished doctoral dissertation, State University of New York at Buffalo.

Spivak, G. C. (1993). *Outside in the teaching machine*. New York: Routledge & Kegan Paul.

Tabata, I. B. (1960). *Education for barbartism in South Africa*. London: Pall Mall Press.

Theal, G. M. (1984). *South Africa*. London: Fisher Unwin.

Theal, G. M. (1902). *The beginning of South African history*. London: Fisher Unwin.

Thompson, E. P. (1968). *The making of the English working class*. Harmondsworth, England: Penguin.

Van Onselen, C. (1982). *Studies in the social and economic history of the witwatersrand, 1886-1914*. Harlow, Essex: Longman.

Willis, P. (1977). *Learning to labor: How working class kids get working class jobs*. Farnborough, England: Saxon House.

Wilson, M., & Thompson, L. (Eds.). (1969). *The Oxford history of South Africa* (Vols. 1-2). Oxford, England: Oxford University Press.

Wolpe, H. (1972). Capitalism and cheap labour-power in South Africa: From segregation to apartheid. *Economy and Society, 1*(4), 424-456.

III

Changing Ethnic and Racial Maps and Education

6

Teachers, the South African State, and the Desegregation of Schools in the 1990s

Volker R. Wedekind
University of Natal

The year 1999 marked the second democratic election in South Africa and the end of Nelson Mandela's Presidency. The African National Congress (ANC) was returned to power by a significant majority (just short of 66%) and President Thabo Mbeki set an aggressive agenda of transformation. It is also nearly 10 years since President F. W. de Klerk announced his intention to unban the resistance organizations and dismantle the apartheid legislation. This is an opportune moment to reflect on one of the key challenges in the dismantling of the apartheid system and the construction of an embryonic South African identity: the desegregation of schooling. However, unlike much of the literature on the process of desegregation that has concentrated solely on the experiences of desegregation, assimilation, and racism in the formerly White, Indian, and colored schools, this article will seek to assess the role that the state has played in managing the process and its implications for education more generally.[1]

The politics of identity have been central to the struggles in South Africa. Access to power and resources have been related directly to matters of race and ethnicity and continue to be hotly contested. Indeed, President Mbeki has fueled the debate with his vision of an African Renaissance, prompting much discussion on what it means to be African. The multicultural vision of a Rainbow Nation promoted by the politics of reconciliation during the Mandela presidency replaced a resistance vision of nonracialism that had been characteristic of opposition during the 1980s. The concept of nonracialism had

---

[1]See Chisholm, 1999, for a critique of previous research.

in turn supplanted the Black Consciousness ideology of the 1970s. Suffice to say that it was inevitable, given the logic of apartheid, that matters of identity would dominate political processes.

Schooling and the politics of identity have long been linked in South Africa. Apartheid, and indeed colonial and settler governments before the formal system of apartheid were introduced, attempted to separate not only the different race groups in South Africa, but also the ethnic or linguistic groupings within those races. Despite massive resistance, particularly from 1976 onward, and despite a few minor reforms, the new democratic government essentially inherited an educational system with separate education departments for each race and ethnic group-some 15 departments. An enormous task of both organizational and social integration faced the government. Yet, given this history, the lack of attention to issues of identity and schooling by government is at first somewhat surprising. In his first statement (some 7,000 words) as the new Minister of Education, Kader Asmal did not mention the words race, racism, antiracism, multiculturalism, or nationalism at all, and makes one reference to racial integration as one component of teacher stress (Asmal, 1999). Similarly, when confronted with a Human Rights Commission report that detailed extensive racism in schools around South Africa, an Education Ministry spokesperson responded that the ministry did not envision instituting a program for teachers in race relations because "racial discrimination is outlawed by the Constitution and the Schools Act" (*M & G*, 1998, January).

However, when one examines the educational landscape of South Africa more thoroughly, it quickly becomes apparent that there are myriad issues that appear more pressing. Problems associated with racial desegregation and integration, or lack thereof, affect a very small percentage of relatively privileged schools, whereas the remaining 90% of the schooling system buckles under the strain of too few classrooms; inadequately trained and qualified teachers; schools without water, toilets, telephones, and electricity; and a breakdown in what is described as a culture of teaching, learning, and managing.

However, although the issue of desegregation may only affect a small percentage of all the schools in South Africa, there are at least four reasons why it is important to examine the processes that have taken place there. First, the desegregated schools are symbolically significant beyond their numbers in that they are viewed widely as a test case for the future of an open society in South Africa. Second, as Chisholm suggested and I will show later, "the introduction of choice appears to have had an impact on all parts of the system" characterizing "the educational landscape . . . by movement and flux" (Chisholm, 1999, p. 97). Third, the issue of preparing young people for life in a post-apartheid South Africa should not be viewed narrowly in terms of only those children that are in contact with other races and cultures at school; it is an issue that needs attention in all South African schools. Fourth, the process of desegregation is a useful test case for analyzing the relationship between the various levels of state policy and the experience of those at the receiving end of those processes. By drawing on a number of case studies conducted in Pietermaritzburg and other parts of South Africa, this chapter will examine the process of desegregation thus far, and argue that the links between national identity and schooling have not been adequately examined by policymakers in South Africa, and that issues related to this, including racism, are not simply issues that need to be ironed out in a few multicultural schools (Van Wyk, 1997).

Because culturally unique terminology is complex, the reader is advised to review a note on terminology for an international audience, placed at the end of this chapter.

EDUCATION IN SOUTH AFRICA: A BRIEF BACKGROUND

To understand the process of desegregation as it unfolded in the 1990s, it is necessary to briefly rehearse the key historical developments leading up to the decade under discussion here. The history of South Africa and its educational system is well known and well documented (see Cross & Chisholm, 1990; Hartshorne, 1992; Kallaway, 1984; Levin, 1980; Nkomo, 1990). The philosophy behind the concept of apartheid was one of apartness, or separate development, where each defined population group would develop its own education system in accordance with its needs and cultural traditions. The benevolent face of apartheid education was supposedly a non Eurocentric approach. However, it was very quickly reduced to a simple formula of separate and unequal, primarily in terms of its resource allocation. Despite minor additions to the curriculum in some departments (e.g., Inkatha's introduction of the Ubuntu botho program in KwaZulu schools [Mdluli, 1994], the House of Delegates' inclusion of Indian languages in some of its schools, and the Veld School programs in white Transvaal schools), the formal curriculum in all South African schools remained surprisingly similar in content. Variations between departments were matters of form, in that pedagogical styles varied and that assessment varied to some extent. Thus, apartheid education failed to produce a system that schooled people for different and separate cultural worlds (largely because those worlds could not be kept separate economically). In this sense, it would be misleading to attribute too much power to the schooling system in propping up the separate identities that exist in South Africa to this day.[2]

Rather than acting as a pacifying mechanism of social control (Harley, 1992), the apartheid system of schooling provided a key site of mobilization against the state (one need only look at the events of 1976 in Soweto, the 1980s boycotts in the Western Cape, and the role of the teachers within resistance organizations more generally). The resistance to apartheid education, specifically from 1976 onward, was mobilized almost entirely around issues of resources and seldom contained an overt or developed critique of the education system more generally. Small groups of intellectuals developed the slogans of People's Education for People's Power into embryonic visions of an alternative system, but to a large extent this was not popularized in a way that made any sense to either the learners or parents in the schools. So, unlike Cuba or Mozambique, for example (Carnoy & Werthein, 1977; Cross, 1993), school struggles had seldom been sites of educational progressivism, despite a proliferation of nongovernmental organizations that promoted progressive educational ideas.

EDUCATIONAL POLICY: POST-1990

Once President de Klerk announced the unbanning of the resistance movements in February 1990 and the repeal of the key pillars of the apartheid system (crucially the race classification legislation), the debates about the shape and the character of a new South Africa gained momentum. In the educational realm, major policy initiatives were set in motion involving both the political parties (specifically the ANC), the bureaucracy (through new curriculum initiatives) [see CHED, 1991a; CHED, 1991b], and civil society (dominated by academics within the National Education Policy Investigation [NPEI, 1992]).

The new government, inaugurated after the elections in 1994, tackled the education system primarily from a legislative perspective.[3] This is not to

---

[2]It is important to stress that schooling was undoubtedly a key part of the spatial separation that was central to the apartheid system. The point, however, is that there is little evidence that schools were central in teaching people specific identities.

[3]Besides the Constitution (Act 108 of 1996), which defines the competences of the national and provincial governments with regard to education, the following legislation was passed that defined the new educational system: South African Qualifications Authority Act 58 of 1995; National Education Policy Act 27 of 1996; South African Schools Act 84 of 1996; Abolition of Corporal Punishment Act 33 of 1997; Education Laws Amendment Act 100 of 1997; and Further Education and Training Act 98 of 1998. In addition, the government published a series of white papers outlining policy, and legislation related to workplace training also impacted the design of the new education system.

deny the significance of policy statements on free and compulsory education for the first 10 years and practical steps such as the school feeding scheme that introduced meals into primary schools. However, this major commitment to the deepening of the schooling effect was immediately constrained by lack of resources. In effect free education was only offered to grade 1 learners. The legislative focus is not surprising in that any transformation of the education system needed to be preceded by a legislative framework that legitimated the interventions. This legislative framework consisted of both structural and curriculum dimensions. Besides reorganizing the 15 separate departments into 9 provincial departments with a national department to oversee policy, the key structural changes related to the establishment of a National Qualifications Framework in order to ensure an integrated education and training sector that addressed the economic imperatives. The curriculum dimension included the complete reorganization of subjects into learning areas and the adoption of an outcomes-based approach under the banner Curriculum 2005. Curriculum groups were then established to design the outcomes for each of the learning areas based on a common set of essential outcomes (Lubisi, Parker, & Wedekind, 1998; see also Kallaway, Kruss, Fataar, & Donn, 1997, for a general overview of transitional education policy processes).

Like so many other national curriculum initiatives of the past two decades, South Africa's recent curriculum framework is driven by a dual thrust of economic skills and national identity needs. However, unlike, for instance, the British National Curriculum, the South African curriculum is not drawing on the resources of a historic tradition of what it means to be South African (for a review of the national curriculum as a vehicle for the inculcation of a national identity, see Goodson, 1993). Indeed, South Africa's past provides only limited resources for a national identity, so the curriculum is attempting to construct a new identity for a new citizen for the new South Africa drawn largely from fairly abstract ideals of antiracism, nonsexism, and multiculturalism. Although these ideals are clearly stated within both the policy documents and the curriculum framework, Vally pointed out that there is little evidence that has been translated into effective antiracism programs in schools (Vally, 1999, March 19).

Despite calls to develop a curriculum based on the culture of South Africa, the new curriculum is remarkable similar to efforts in other parts of the world in its attempt to create citizens who are thoroughly modern and able to compete in a globalized, information-based network society (see Castells, 1996, for a useful analysis of what this might mean). In many aspects South Africa is now attempting what has been recognized by historians as the common feature uniting the wide range of initiatives by states to fun and manage schooling: the construction of a national polity to promote the participation of the state's subjects in national projects (Goodson, 1993). Policy documents and curriculum initiatives try to hold in tension the need for reconciliation and the creation of an African humanist subject, with the need for skilled lifelong learners, able to negotiate the complex technologies and systems of the new millennium.[4]

The policy framework put in place by the first democratic government reveals much of the intentions of the post-apartheid state are not different from those faced by most post-colonial states: heightened expectations, poverty, limited resources, and multiple identities that potentially threaten the very fabric of the state.[5] Like other African states, South Africa adopted a classic approach to dealing with this on an educational front: policy that promotes the expansion of schooling and the deepening of the effect of schooling through curricular reform in order to signal equal access to modernity (see Bradshaw & Fuller, 1996, for Kenya; Fuller, 1991, for Malawi). The issue of equality of access within this policy thrust was politically the most pressing matter to tackle and needed to be addressed in terms of improvement of existing resources as well as the opening up of those pockets of privilege that existed through the segregated history of schooling. It is to the process of desegregation that I now turn.

THE CASE OF DESEGREGATION

Methodology

This study draws on data that are part of ongoing research[6] into social relations in secondary schools around the city of Pietermaritzburg, in the province of KwaZulu Natal, as well as a case study of widely reported tensions at a school in the North West Province. The study began in the early 1990s.[7] Data for this

---

[4]Increasingly, business consultants attempt to marry notions of African philosophy such as *ubuntu* with modern business practices, and this is likely to filter into the curriculum in some form.

[5]This was illustrated by the very real threat of long-term instability when the Inkatha Freedom Party threatened to boycott the 1994 elections and the White right wing spoke of the possibility of race war.

[6]The research has been funded by the National Research Foundation's "Global Change and Social Transformation Programme" as well as grants from the University of Natal Research Fund.

[7]Aspects of this research have been published elsewhere (see Harley, 1994; Harley & Wedekind, 1999; Penny, Appel, Gultig, Harley, & Muir, 1993; Sader, 2000; Wedekind, Lubisi, Harley, & Gultig, 1996; Wedekind & Sader, 1998, July), including detailed descriptions of the methodology. My thanks to all the colleagues that have collaborated on this study.

chapter have been drawn primarily from 16 lengthy interviews with teachers and 22 interviews with principals conducted between 1991 and 1998, as well as data from a semistructured questionnaire completed by 1,480 learners. In addition, case study material has been drawn from newspaper reports and the published reports of a range of governmental nongovernmental organizations.

The State Attempts to Integrate Schools

For a variety of reasons related to earlier reforms of the apartheid system and levels of autonomy within the educational system, desegregation had begun in a limited form during the 1980s. However, once the key apartheid legislation was repealed in the early 1990s, the process of desegregation happened far more rapidly. With the first democratic government in place in mid-1994, it became a matter of some urgency that school that had been enormously privileged should be seen to be open to all South Africans. The new government wished to ensure a fairly rapid redistribution of resources, but was also very conscious to make allowances for the appeasement of the minorities. For this and other reasons, schools were often left to their own devices, with the state stepping in a sa mediating body.

The process of desegregation followed different courses depending on the department to which schools were attached. Independent schools had accepted Black Africa, Indian, and colored children in small numbers since the late 1970s, and catered largely to the Black middle classes. The Department of Education and Training (DET), which was responsible for Black African education outside of the homelands, simply issued a statement to the effect that it was open to all race groups, knowing there was little likelihood there would be much demand for its schools. The schools controlled by homeland governments did not have policy restricting access, but were seldom faced with applications from White, Indian, or colored learners. The House of Delegates and the House of Representatives (the legislative bodies controlling schooling for Indians and coloreds respectively) simply opened their schools by fiat, with provisos that local Indian and colored communities would receive preference and that the ethos of the schools would be maintained.

By far the most complex process was the opening up of schools administered by the four provincial departments for Whites. Politically these were controlled by the House of Assembly, and it was the Minister of Education responsible for these departments that introduced a number of models that schools could adopt. These included complete privatization, partial privatization, and continued state funding, with degrees of autonomy handed to the school's governing bodies to control matters such as admissions. Parents were asked to vote on these options, with principals and teachers often being forced to campaign for a special model. The degree of real choice was somewhat questionable. Complete privatization was not economically viable for even the most affluent communities, and retaining the status quo meant a significant drop in funding. Essentially schools were forced to adopt a model that opened admissions, but under the control of the governing body. Schools were also given greater powers to charge school fees. How then did the school principals and the teachers experience this process, and what was the role of the educational bureaucracy directly responsible for managing this process?

Attitudes of Educators and Managers

All the principals and all but one of the teachers in the Pietermaritzburg study applauded the desegregation of schools.[8] Most importantly, the emergence of "open" schools represented an important symbolic victory for anti*apartheid* sentiment and for the principle of social justice.

As a new orthodoxy, the open schools were regarded almost uncritically by the interviewees as a "good thing." Nevertheless, managers and educators in the open and township sectors of schooling emphasized somewhat different reasons for their enthusiasm for desegregated schools. In the early 1990s, teachers and principals in both sectors were markedly optimistic about the prospect of political change and the potential benefits this would have for the education system in South Africa. In a political era with strong messages of reconciliation emerging from the major political figures, principals placed strong emphasis on healing relationships between people divided by the racial classification system of *apartheid*. Specifically, for the Black African principals, the physical "mixing" of races was viewed unproblematically, and self-evidently, as a noble enterprise.

A common theme focused on the benefits to learners of different races being able to play together and learning to understand each other: "When a White child [looks] at a Black child, she would run away from him because he's the enemy . . . And a Black child who looks at a White child, she or he sees nothing but an oppressor. You see, it's that twisted idea, as far as I'm concerned." Justification for integration was frequently made with reference to

---

[8]This finding should not be seen as representative. Skuy and Vice's attitudinal survey found that only 59% of White teachers supported integrated schooling (Skuy & Vice, 1996). The home language of the teachers was a highly significant factor in differentiating between those who held positive attitudes and those who held negative attitudes toward integration. In our study only one of the interviewees was Afrikaans speaking, the group most likely to hold negative attitudes toward integration.

the past: "[Learners] . . . have grown up in a society where we are racially divided and perhaps put, ah, they were put in different schools, just for, for reasons of color and nothing else." There was a need to integrate schools to avoid "nasty incidents." It was thus necessary for schools to prepare young people for "the future dispensation," and it was maintained that this process should begin early in the primary school.

There seemed to be widespread support for the broader project of building a South African society that moved beyond the divisions of the past. The government message had clearly been accepted. There was, however, a layer of complexity to the open school principals' and teachers' support for opening their enrollments. Their sense of what was morally right was not untrammeled by pragmatism and economic expediency at different levels. Enrollments in several of these schools had been falling. This had implications for the schools' staff allocation and meant possible redundancies.

A mix of morality and other concerns is captured in the following interchange:

Interviewer:	Now, what would you say was the actual rationale behind the, you know, the opening of the school, or the decision to open the school?
Principal:	Well, I think if this country is going to provide skilled manpower to drive your economy . . . you can't just allow the White people to do that. The White people, when you look at demographics, are declining very fast in terms of their numbers, whereas the Black populations are increasing, so it stands to reason that if you want to maintain the high standard of living actually . . . you have to open up your system. Education, I think, is the most important place. It's got to start there. And I think it's clear common sense and it's also humanitarian—it's the right thing to do.

The pragmatism behind opening enrollment is put more starkly by a teacher at another school:

Interviewer:	Why did the school begin to admit pupils from other race groups?

Teacher: At that stage our school was in an area,
                                where we were losing the support of the
                                Indian parents . . . they preferred to take
                                their pupils elsewhere-our classroom were
                                becoming empty, so we had to fill up with the
                                African pupils.

While the general support for the desegregation of schooling in schools
around Pietermaritzburg was encouraging (and not entirely representative of the
South African picture as a whole), neither the somewhat idealistic notion that
mere mixing would in itself produce tolerant learners on the one hand, nor the
understandable utilitarian nature of the decision by many schools on the other
hand, meant that much planning was going into managing the process. Indeed,
while the principals may have wished to ponder their overall policy regarding
integration, learners were already sitting in their classes, and effective programs
had to be designed for them. Faced with this demand, institutions appeared to
rely on what had worked for them in the past.

THE EXPERIENCE OF DESEGREGATION

Maintenance of Standards

There can be little doubt of the strength of goodwill and the need to "do the
right thing" with respect to the victims of discrimination. Principals of White
schools had in many instances taken great pains, sometimes against the odds, to
secure the vote necessary to open their enrollments. Some principals in open
schools had campaigned for the opening of their schools despite opposition from
members of their own staff and parents.

Even among the strongest supporters of desegregation, there was an
overriding concern for academic standards and the ethos of the school. While
the open school principals were strongly supportive of desegregating their
schools, they wished to achieve this in ways that did not threaten their ethos or
the "standards" in their schools. To do this, it was necessary for them to seize
the opportunity to control the process of admission on their own terms. The less
affluent schools enjoyed a greater measure of freedom in making decisions, but
the economically more powerful state schools were best placed to manage
change in such a way that their ethos and standards were not assaulted.

Controlling Admissions

Open school principals-particularly those from the higher status schools-showed a keen awareness of the possible effects of an uncontrolled "critical mass" of children from different ethnic or racial groups entering their schools. Standards and ethos could be compromised by sheer weight of numbers: "Obviously, if you're going to have a massive influx of people who've come from a deprived background, yes, the style of teaching is going to change. . . ." Control measures took the form of admissions tests,[9] almost universally in English and mathematics. Here is an example of more liberal practice in a less affluent school:

> "Uh, basically, I asked my English teacher to set an English test for Standard 6, Standard 7, Standard 8, and we've tried to make it as elementary as possible, so that it's not an unfair test to the pupils. The same with mathematics, Standard 5 level and we, we even accepted pupils with 30%."

More powerful schools were more cautious:

Principal:	English and mathematics. Those are the two that we really look at. Afrikaans if they do Afrikaans at any sort of level, but English and Mathematics are the two that we. . . .
Interviewer:	Now obviously those tests you use as a screening device?
Principal:	Right.
Interviewer:	Do you go beyond that, as say, well, hang on now, within those somebody's quite good at math, but look his English is not so good, or vice versa. And then do you attempt to try to offer some support system when they arrive here?
Principal:	Yes, well, first of all, let's go back to selection. We also look at home background. Very important. We ask things like, "Do you have television at home, where do your parents work, what brothers and sisters do you have?" and we get some sort of feel of

---

[9]These are not unconstitutional.

the home background. Have they, have they
ever had a coloring-in book at home, do they
cut things out with scissors, etc., etc. So
that's how we do it. Then we do have a
backup system, we do have a lady coming to
help again with English comprehension, and
she'll help with mathematics. . . .

Despite some fairly complex admissions procedures and criteria, none
of the schools in the study had a formal policy on admissions and the streaming
of learners. This lack of transparent policy frameworks within which decisions
could be made (and challenged) is part of a broader issue that will be discussed
below.

While schools could not refuse admission after the 1994 elections,
teachers interviewed in 1998 still reported that admissions tests were being
administered, not as an exclusion mechanism but rather as a means of streaming
the learners into ability groupings. This academic selection process has the
consequences in many schools I have visited that the top stream has almost no
Black African learners and the lower streams comprise very few learners who
are not Black African. In effect a *de facto* internal segregation continues,
allowing schools to maintain standards at one end of the spectrum and offer
remedial classes at the other. In some Afrikaans medium schools, an English
stream was introduced, catering primarily to Black African learners. The
consequence again was an internally segregated school.

Social and Academic Assimilation

It was a social imperative that learners should "fit in." Admission policies were
built around the common-sense view that younger learners would fit in more
easily than the senior learners.[10] A typical comment: "I don't like taking boys
later than Standard. We've tried some aged about 15, 16. They don't . . . there
are problems, you've got social problems. They don't integrate."

The dominant cultural standards were most commonly described as
"western," as in the following statement:

Okay. One of the problems that you always have to face is which culture is the
culture that you should follow . . . . There's no doubt in my mind that we aim

---

[10]A distribution favoring junior learners was clear in enrollment figures
provided.

at the Western culture. We aim at what they are doing in Australia, the rest of the world. So the boys coming to my dining room, they are taught table manners that would be acceptable to any of the modernized Western countries, and all the social graces that go with that. But at the same time, the boys are taught to respect the cultural differences of other people, and to actually maybe assimilate some of them, because some of the boys here bring different types of habits which are actually better than we find elsewhere, and that becomes part of it. So we aim to take the best of each of the cultures, but predominantly it's the Western culture that dominates.

This was the typical pattern: dominant "Western" cultural standards, but with "respect" being accorded to other cultures. At no institution was a clear account provided of what was actually being done, as part of the school curriculum, to develop respect for other cultures. It appeared rather as if principals and teachers were of the view that an inherent part of Western culture was the bestowal of respect to other cultures. It was almost as if principals felt they could rely on Western "social graces" in this regard, and that the necessary cultural recipe was already embedded in the school ethos in a way that rendered explicit programs dealing with issues of culture and ethnicity unnecessary.

Similarly, the academic roots of assimilation lay in a confident belief that particular forms of knowledge were universal. Views on socially constructed knowledge were not evident here. Social and academic assimilation meant that beyond the level of cultural artifacts, differences were not viewed with much sympathy. If a cultural standard is universal, deviation from that standard constitutes "deprivation": " . . . if a child has come from a deprived background where they haven't had the things that we take for granted, electricity, and everything that goes with electricity, etc., yes, their perceptions are different." And if they're different they need remediation: "Standards are going to be a problem. One has to understand that, but I think a heavy, hard remedial program is needed, but all of us know the importance of praise and encouragement-boost them, well done, fantastic. . ."

In the majority of settings, assimilation and remediation was synonymous with "bringing learners up to standard" in the basics, as is evident in this explanation offered by the principal of a "colored" school:

 . . . at the beginning of this year, for the first 2 months in Standard 6, we only taught English and mathematics. We didn't have the other subjects, of course without the approval of my department. If they knew they might have hammered me for it, but I did it because I taught Zambia [in] 1967-74 and I knew the children coming from the primary schools in Zambia had the same problem when they only learned in the vernacular and when they came to high school, and we did that for a whole term and it was very successful in Zambia and I couldn't see why it wasn't going to be successful here.

Apart from concessionary gestures to the standards of other cultures, there was widespread agreement that all learners would be able to accommodate to the Eurocentric type of school provided they were keen and had the right attitude. If they were, they would adapt and do well. Some successful instances of this were cited:

Principal: . . . well here. And I use that as an example, where there was potential hidden and given the opportunity, and out it came . . . we've got a boy who came, and they said "ooh, brilliant mathematician!" Did well enough in our entrance exam, but had never put studded boots on. And had never held a rugger [rugby] ball. And he's now a star in our wing for our Under 15 side.

Interviewer: Yes.

Principal: And he just learn[ed] the skill--never caught a rugger ball, loved Kaiser Chiefs [local soccer club] or something like that, realized that he couldn't play soccer here, put his mind to his rugger, and has done fantastically.

All the schools in this study had adopted what Sader called a color-blind approach in that they emphasized the equality of learners, but at the same time ensured that the ethos of the school and community within which it was located was enforced (Sader, 2000). All the interviews rejected crude racism, but by their very actions of not acknowledging difference, they actually reinforced racial stereotypes such as "disadvantaged" when describing either social status or academic achievement.

Furthermore, principals and many teachers were clear that learners of other races wished to be inducted into the cultural and academic standards of the open schools:

First of all, just to say recently, and I didn't do this, the senior staff did it, they interviewed each child of color at the school. Now this is very interesting. That first of all the African children, they probably told us what we wanted, what they thought we would like to hear, but every one of them said that they were happy in the Eurocentric-type school. The parents sent them here specifically because they wanted our type of education and they didn't want to see African-type education, whatever that might be.

Although this view found its strongest expression in the independent and former White schools that were part of the study, it certainly was a widely held view that was not contradicted by colored and Indian teachers, nor by the Black African principals. Indeed, one of the most startling findings of the studies was the way in which open schools represented a notion of standards that needed to be aspired to by township schools. The interviews with Black African principals revealed that the open schools served as a powerful reference point with respect to both pedagogy and content. The dominant image of desirable curriculum change was, in the words of one principal, "syllabuses on the same lines as those in the Indian schools and colored schools and White schools." The implicitly articulated role of a township school in the face of existing disparities was to prepare learners for open schools:

> Our students have left (name of school) and gone to these Model B and C schools. What is encouraging is that we have received feedback from them and they are saying that they found nothing new in these schools. They have adjusted very well. Some of them are even leading in these schools, they are getting top positions, position one in other instances.

That a principal was able to derive encouragement from losing his best learners is a significant commentary on the process of affirmation taking place. If the open schools served as a benchmark, transformation was achieved to the extent that one's "products" were successful in those schools.

TEACHER PREPAREDNESS AND TEACHER INTEGRATION

Although the schools were willing to open their enrollment, or indeed had no choice but to open their enrollment, there was little preparation put in place to deal with this dramatic change. None of the school sin the Pietermaritzburg study operated with any policy that referred specifically to the promotion of interethnic, intercultural, or interracial relationships, or to the handling of racial incidents or racism in general.

Interviewer: Are there sections of the general school policy that would deal with similar issues about diversity—do you have general school policies?

Teacher: Not as far as education is concerned—like maybe with uniform and general discipline—but I have not heard of any policies as far as education is concerned.

Furthermore, there was little awareness among the teachers interviewed that there was any policy regarding desegregation. Fifteen of the 16 interviewees were generally unable to explain the education department's policy on the racial integration of schools.

The state thus legislated the desegregation of schools, but failed to make any policy unavailable and understood by the teachers concerned with dealing with the very pragmatic consequences of the legislation. Teachers were left largely to their own resources, and these were found to be somewhat limited. Teacher education had been divided along apartheid lines and had prepared teachers for teaching within ethnically defined education departments. With the exception of tow of the younger teachers who had been trained by universities in the early 1990s, all the teachers interviewed stated that their teacher training had not prepared them for desegregation, and that neither the department nor the school had provided adequate in-service education.

The consequence was that none of the 16 teachers interviewed has any indepth knowledge of the cultural and ethnic backgrounds of the learners enrolled in their classrooms. In part this was due to a well-intentioned desire to ignore the racial classification and systems of record keeping that were such a pernicious part of the apartheid system. In part this can be attributed to the "raceless" approach adopted by the schools. Interviews with teachers confirmed the findings of analyses of earlier interviews with principals who refused to talk about their learners in terms of race[11]: We have [name of school] boys here and we treat them equally. The raceless and all-learners-are-equal approach adopted by teachers and schools could be understood in terms of teachers attempting to adapt to an unfamiliar situation. This attempt by teachers to adapt is in itself a positive attribute that needs to be encouraged, especially in light of the situation teachers find themselves in, "where there are no clear guidelines, and much practice is developed in a trial and error way rather based in sound educational theory" (Akhurst, 1997).

However, Sader pointed out that this approach, which includes the failure to keep any records of the cultural backgrounds of learners, results in the dominant school ethos simply being taken as the norm (Sader, 2000). Without an acknowledgment of the differences within the class, it becomes very difficult

---

[11]Chisholm had a similar response from all her respondents at schools in Gauteng in which "acknowledgement of differences entailed racism" (Chisholm, 1999, p. 97).

to address those differences in any programmatic way. Teachers seemed totally unaware of the debates around multicultural and antiracist education (see McLaren, 1997), and seemed persuaded that the approach of treating all alike was fairest.

Sader concluded that teachers interviewed simply did not have the knowledge, experience, or in some cases the disposition to address matters of race and culture in their classroom. The support for teachers from the state were nonexistent, although there were a limited number of teachers that had been on courses organized by nongovernmental organizations that had addressed aspects of desegregation in schools. However, the teachers' assessment of these courses was not very positive.

Although teachers may not have had the knowledge, skills, or indeed disposition to effectively deal with the complexities of desegregated schooling, there was an additional problem facing schools. Learner populations are transient and change from year to year, resulting in fairly rapid changes in the racial composition of some of the schools,[12] yet teachers are much more permanent. The consequence of this was that the teaching staff at open schools remained largely racially homogeneous. Verma and colleagues identified the representative nature of the teaching staff as a key factor in reducing conflict in British schools, and thee was a general awareness that the situation in the Pietermaritzburg schools was not desirable (Verma, Zec, & Skinner, 1994). Teachers interviewed in 1998 spoke with some embarrassment about the lack of representativity among the teaching staff, with the no schools having more than 15% of teachers of other races.

In part the fact that so little had changed at this level can be explained in terms of teachers hanging onto jobs in an unsure employment climate and thus reducing the number of posts that became vacant. However, there is a further dimension. The South African Schools Act empowered schools to select their own staff, enabling schools to choose teachers that matched the culture and ethos of the school. With teacher education having been entirely segregated during the apartheid years, teachers were trained in distinct and separate traditions. Much suspicion about the quality of training at many Black colleges of education tended to prejudice Black teachers' chances when applying for posts in open schools.

The state's attempt to rationalize and redress some of the imbalances in staffing numbers by retrenching and/or redeploying teachers turned into an administrative and fiscal disaster. In an attempt to create flexibility in the

---

[12]One of the Indian schools changed from being roughly 70% Indian to being 80% African over a 2-year period.

system, the state offered teachers early retirement packages or opportunities for redeployment. The generous retirement packages were snapped up, thus draining the system of some of the most senior and experienced teachers and simultaneously draining the education budget to such an extent that many provinces were faced with huge deficits. However, the redeployment of teachers to other schools, and in some cases to other provinces, was bitterly opposed by the teachers, their unions, and some of the schools that were due to receive the redeployed teachers. The redeployment issue turned into a major embarrassment for the national Ministry of Education, which in turn laid the blame at the door of the provincial departments administering the process.

The policy had not been adequately thought through. The oversupply of teachers tended to be concentrated in urban areas, although the need was greatest in rural areas. However, it was always unlikely that teachers in the middle of their career, often settled with families, would be prepared to uproot and teach in rural areas without even the most basic infrastructure. Furthermore, in the Western Cape, the oversupply was such that surplus teachers were being asked to transfer out of the province.

When some schools were told that they were obliged to select teachers from the redeployment list, these former White schools' governing bodies took the Minister of Education to court on the grounds that they were "unlawfully limiting the statutory powers [of the school] to have appointed to the school, teachers recruited and freely chosen from the best candidates available" (Affidavit by Otta Helen Maree to the Cape High Court, cited in Jansen, 1998, p. 10). The schools won their case, forcing government to rethink their legislative framework. The state's devolution of school control to the community effectively meant that they were unable to bring about the rapid movement of teachers that the rationalization plan had partly intended.

THE ROLE OF LOCAL LEVELS OF BUREAUCRACY

The chaotic way in which the teacher rationalization plan had been implemented is part of a broader picture of different levels of bureaucracy seemingly working at loggerheads. Whether through inefficiency, lack of resources and skills, or deliberate efforts on the part of sections of the bureaucracy to undermine the desegregation process, there is extensive evidence from the Pietermaritzburg study to show that local bureaucracy has done little to assist schools in addressing issues of identity policies and its various consequences.

The township principals reported that the department had simply played no role whatsoever. Although the DET had officially declared itself to be an open department, two principals were in fact unaware of this development, and three others expressed reservations about their educational authority being open. One principal commented: "I do not think the DET is racially open because there is no institution where this can be supported or demonstrated, and the DET has not given us any guidance as to how we can prepare for an integrated school." Perhaps more sinisterly, during the transition period the actions of the White education authority had varied from a position of offering no support to an attitude of obstructionism. Certain officials reportedly even warned school principals "not to engage in politics."

But by far the most pervasive complaint from teachers and managers was the absence of guidance from the department. None of the teachers interviewed were familiar with departmental policies on integration, antiracism, or multiculturalism. At best they were able to guess that the department supported these notions: "I suppose they would support these ideas. . . . But I haven't seen it." More important than familiarity with department policy was the complete absence of in-service training for teachers and managers to deal with multicultural and multilingual classrooms. The consequences of this lack of any local support for teachers and managers in school was that none of the school sin the Pietermaritzburg study were equipped with knowledge, experience, training, or disposition to contribute toward coping with the stresses of desegregated schooling, let along contributing creatively toward the fostering of a new national identity.

COMMUNITY CONTROL

At the level of the school, there appeared another disjuncture between state policy and what happened in the local context. As has already been noted in relation to teacher employment and redeployment above, the South African Schools Act of 1996 legislated a model of community control over schools through substantially empowered governing bodies dominated by parents. However, one of the difficulties with this model was that it assumed that school had a definable community that they served. In the case of the Pietermaritzburg schools, learners commuted to school from all over the greater Pietermaritaburg-Msunduzi region and beyond, and in many cases the teachers and managers had little idea where their learners came from and had no contact with the parents. Parents living far from the school, often without communications resources such as telephones or vehicles, were simply not in a position to participate in parent meetings and governing body activities.

The consequences of this was that governing bodies remained dominated by the traditional community that schools used to serve. The state thus effectively strengthened the position of these powerful communities, which were in some instances able to use their position to resist change.[13] However, the following concern raised by a teacher from a former colored school highlights the complexity of the problem:

> The other thing that I am concerned about is also the different cultures-okay-we are more than 70% maybe about 80% Zulu peaking, so a large percentage of the children who are in our school do not come from our community-so as much as the government is saying that the community must have a say in the running of the school-the "the community must take ownership of the school"-which community? Can we honestly expect . . . kids who come from another community to be loyal to their school and the community in which that school is? Then, on the other hand, can we expect the community in which the school is based to be loyal and committed to a school that serves . . . primarily pupils coming from another community? Also they have come from another community with a totally different value system-which is different to the general tone and value system that is in place in this school. So constantly we are at loggerheads because before it used to be a gradual filtration. We in the community were a majority, so it was easy for us to create an influence on those coming in . . . . The tone and the policy is being undermined because it is being swamped--that is the problem that we are facing.

THE WORST SCENARIO: THE VRYBURG CASE

The picture that emerges from the discussion thus far is a process marked by localized *ad hoc* decisions taken by people that have had little or no training to deal with the complexity of desegregated schooling. Schools, often with deeply entrenched traditions, were faced with rapid changes in the learner populations. The teaching staff, largely divided along apartheid lines, were ill prepared for the changes, and appear to have received little support from their department.

The potential for the ad hoc nature of the desegregation process to have serious violent consequences was illustrated by a number of incidents of conflict at formerly White schools. The most well-documented case occurred at Vryburg in the Northwest Province. The Vryburg example is a useful case in illustrating how relatively manageable issues can escalate into violent confrontations.

---

[13]In 1996 Potgietersrus Primary school's governing body took the state to court to enforce an exclusionary admissions policy on the basis that the constitution protected cultural and language rights.

A Background

Vryburg is a small rural town in the Northwest Province of South Africa. It is a town that remained a part of South Africa while most of the surrounding area was incorporated into the "independent" homeland of Bophuthatswana. Vryburg Hoerskool was an Afrikaans medium secondary school that was faced with declining learner numbers in the early 1990s and decided to introduce an English stream. In the context of the local schools in the neighboring townships having few resources and being oversubscribed by 50%, Vryburg Hoerskool received a number of applications from Black children. In 1995 the school accepted 100 Black African learners, but in the following year fewer than half of those returned. In late april 1996, while the final constitution was being debated in the Constitutional Assembly, Vryburg Hoerskool became the center of a racial incident that ended with violent confrontations and burning in the wider community. The conflict was sparked by complaints about racism on the part of some of the teachers and White learners. But, as the Daily Mail and Guardian report of May 1, 1996, suggests, "the bitter conflict had as much to do with misunderstandings and bungled agreements as it did with the naked racism of a few individuals" (M&G, 1996, May 1).

The 1996 Crisis

Although the school had agreed to introduce an English medium stream, the department had failed to supply any additional English-speaking teachers. The existing teachers thus were faced with the choice of either teaching in an unfamiliar language medium themselves, or attempting to teach learners in a language with which the learners were not familiar or comfortable. Furthermore, lack of communication had led to misunderstandings about school feels-the government had made electoral commitments to the *principle* of free and compulsory education, yet it was not in a position to implement this beyond the first grade. However, student organizations in the Vryburg area reportedly informed learners that education at Vryburg was free (M&G, 1996, June 1). The school's legalistic approach to dealing with defaulting parents heightened the tensions, and when some parents complained to the Human Rights Commission (HRC) about racism, the matter boiled over into demands for the school's closure, sit-ins at the local education authorities' offices, and allegations of students holding senior provincial education officials hostage.

The intervention of the HRC and senior provincial politicians succeeded in bringing the situation under control. The provincial premier, Popu Molefe, set up a commission to investigate the incident and make recommendations to ensure that similar incidents did not occur. Given that the final constitution was still being negotiated at this point and that the provinces had only taken over responsibility for education 2 years earlier, the lack of policy and procedures to deal with such incidents can be understood. The case of Vryburg should have been a useful learning experience not only for the Northwest, but all of South Africa's education departments. However, 18 months later Vryburg Hoerskool was again the center of violent clashes that engulfed the whole town.

The 1998/1999 Crisis

In late February 1998, the governing body of the school decided to suspend four Black African learners for a week because they did not pay their fees. Protesting learners clashed with police in the town after allegedly taking the principal and two senior governing body members hostage. The local mayor and education officials claimed that it was a meeting to discuss the situation. Whatever the case, White parents barred Black African learners from entering the school the next morning and assaulted Black African learners and other Black African adults in the vicinity of the school. Black African learners were escorted away by the police to the nearby township, sparking off further violence from "angry youths" who "went on the rampage, burning cars, threatening Whites with violence and indiscriminately attacking passersby" (*M&G*, 1998, March 16). The "assault" had been witnessed by one of the few Black African teachers at the school, who reported that it had not been an assault, simply an altercation. The teacher reported this to the principal, who nevertheless encouraged the female learner to lay charges.

The day after the fighting on the playing fields, the school was cordoned off by the police with razor wire, and Black African and White learners were separated during the breaks. The following day Black African learners from the school staged a sit-in at the local education authority offices and demonstrated outside the school. Fifty were arrested by the police for holding an illegal gathering, but in a comedy of errors were able to walk out of the police station while Black and White police officers argued over who should charge them!

On Thursday, March 19, the Huhudi township, where many of the Black African learners lived, was reported to have descended into mayhem. Police were attacked after they attempted to stop a large group of residents from marching to Vryburg in support of the Black African learners. Their demands included the resignation of the school principal and the disbanding of the governing body. The following day the provincial government closed the school because "the safety of the learners and teachers can no longer be guaranteed. We want to give the task team the opportunity to finish its work and the community the opportunity to calm down. It is starting to get out of hand, and we do not want a situation where there is any loss of life" (David van Wyk, Spokesperson for Premier Molefe, quoted in the *M&G*, 1998, March 20).

On Sunday, March 22, 1998, ahead of the report of the investigating task team, the provincial Member of the Executive Council (MEC) for Education announced that Vryburg Hoerskool's governing body was to be disbanded and replaced by a government-appointed task team. The MEC was satisfied that the governing body had not performed properly. The move met with support from the South African Democratic Teachers Union and the Congress of South African Students. A new governing body was set up after a period of interim management and a new election.

The report of the task team revealed widespread segregation in classrooms and hostels and confirmed many of the allegations of racism. It made wide-ranging recommendations for changes, including the appointment of a Black deputy principal.

In September 1998 tensions flared up again when the Acting Deputy Director General for Education in the Northwest Province accused the parent community of racism. The issue that prompted the accusation was the fact that only 37% of the parents had paid their school fees and the school was in financial crisis. When approached for comment on the new crisis, the leader of the task team that had reported in March, Theresa Oakley-Smith, stated: "The situation is totally unacceptable. We spent 3 weeks there and made some strong recommendations about changes that needed to be made, both practically and regarding a change in attitudes. Very little has been done and the finger of blame for this should absolutely be pointed at the Department of Education" (The Star, 1998, September 21). The response from the Member of the Executive Committee for Education was that the task team had completed its work and should leave the school alone. He stated he was satisfied with the progress at the school.

In March 1999 the school was again in crisis after the suspension of a Black African pupil for allegedly stabbing a White pupil with scissors. Black pupils marched to the Department offices and demanded his reinstatement as well as the implementation of the recommendations of the task team from the previous year (*The Star*, 1999, March 3). The Department announced that it was about to begin interviewing for the post of a deputy principal for the school.

The Lessons of Vryburg

This case is illustrative of a number of problems facing the state and school sin coming to terms with the implications of forging a new South African identity. When the task team set up by the second provincial government finally delivered its report, it raised a number of alarming concerns. Chief amongst these was the despite the experience of 1996, there had been no transformation of the school, and the two streams essentially constituted two separate schools on the same premises. The school itself was clearly at fault, but the task team also condemned the failure of the provincial education department to be proactive and to play a supportive role in helping the school to transform. The task team found that a provincial strategy that had been drawn up to defuse the types of tensions reported above had been effectively ignored by local education officials. Furthermore, specific recommendations made by the first task team set up in 1996 had also not been implemented. Yet the very officials who had failed to implement the recommendations had been expecting a flareup for the past 6 months. The lessons of 1996 had been noted, and appropriate policy developed, but the state had bee unable to dive any of this policy through to the level of the school. This pattern repeated itself when the 1998 task team recommendations had not been implemented, with a further crisis flaring up in September, and had still not been implemented the following year in March 1999.

Vryburg was not an isolated incident. At the end of March 1998, another rural school in Schweitzer Reneke saw White leaders assault Black African learners with cricket bats. In early april 1998, an alleged incident of sexual harassment at one of the schools that was a participant in the Pietermaritzburg study led to fighting between Black African and White learners, although it did not result in the scale of conflict witnessed in Vryburg. The Human Rights Commission, in a report forewarning the events of Vryburg, claimed "racism in schools is a big problem" (*M&G*, 1998, July 1). The HRC report listed 29 incidents of racism in schools since 1995, but admitted that this was simply the tip of the iceberg.

Of course for every Vryburg there are also success stories. For instance, at the time that Vryburg had its first crisis in 2996, the *Daily Mail and Guardian* reported on a number of Afrikaans medium schools in the mining areas of the Witwatersrand that had integrated rapidly and successfully. In its first year as an open school, one of the schools had a learner population that was 60% Black African. Besides isolated cases of parents withdrawing their children from the schools, there had been no conflict over the transformation. The success of these schools was attributed to the positive attitude of the teachers, but crucially also to the role that Gauteng Provincial education department played in encouraging and supporting the teachers during the transition. "Parents, teachers, and governing bodies were primed of the anticipated changes way in advance," said Billy Motora, the district education officer (*M&G*, 1996, March 8). While no two schools face exactly the same circumstances, it is evident that the lack of departmental support and the policy vacuum evident in the schools in the Pietermaritzburg study make for an environment where the Vryburg scenario becomes more possible and more likely.

Although the discussion thus far has dealt primarily with issues of racial integration, the more general notion of a tolerant and open society as envisioned by the state remains somewhat distant in most of South Africa's schools. Children are still excluded from schools because they don't accept the religious ethos of the school or because of their sexual orientation, and although there are increasing cases where schools are being legally challenged, this happens primarily in communities where the parents are familiar with their legal rights and have the resources to employ legal counsel. While the most overt instances of racism tend to be restricted to those schools that have a racially heterogeneous population,[14] broader issues of prejudice are equally applicable to open and township schools. It is to an awareness of this more general notion of tolerance within the township sector that I now wish to turn.

"WE ARE NOT AFFECTED": LACK OF AWARENESS IN TOWNSHIP SCHOOLS

It has already been noted that principals and teachers at township schools supported the desegregation of schools and viewed it as a good thing. However, not one of the principals interviewed felt that township schools needed to address issues of culture and race within their curriculum. While they recognized a need for multicultural and antiracist programs within the open schools, the fact that they were unlikely to find students of other race groups attending their schools meant, for them, that such interventions were not necessary.

As victims of discriminatory resourcing and political turbulence, township schools were perceived to have little to offer. Geographically they were isolated from the metropolitan areas in which learners of other races

---

[14]This is not to discount the increasing instances in which Black children from different cultural backgrounds are forced to confront racism and prejudice in Black schools. There is an increasing tendency for children of diverse ethnic groups to be found in urban schools, and in the bigger metropoles, the influx of immigrants and refugees from other parts of Africa also increases the diversity in what appear to be homogeneous schools.

resided and poorly served by public transport. While no White, Indian, or colored learners had enrolled at township schools, there had been a movement of Black African learners to open schools. Principals could not be certain of exact numbers, but estimates in the various school ranged from 4 to 22 per annum since 1991, with one school reporting a figure of 50. It was speculated that migrations would have been prolific were it not for transport difficulties and costs of travel to the open schools. "Well to do" was an expression frequently used in describing the families who were moving into town and enrolling their children in the open schools. More significantly, 8 of the 10 principals specifically mentioned that it was teachers' children who were moving to the open schools.

Interviewer: In terms of teachers here at [name of school], are
                 there any that have sent their kids there [to open
                 schools]?
Principal: Yes, most of them!

Indeed, principals themselves were prominent among those who had moved their own children to open schools.

Integrated schooling, for the principals of DET schools, had a meaning circumscribed by the realities of the situation. It means that Black African children able to move to the open schools did move. There was no evidence of any concern among the township principals for preparing their own learners to integrate into the broader South African society and cope with the inevitability of confronting racism. For the principals, racism was only a problem when there is contact between races.

Interviewer: Do you have any policies or programs to deal with
                 issues of racism?
Principal: There is no racism here, because there are no other
                 races.

Clearly then, issues of integration in the broader South African society were not seen as central concerns of the school curriculum, irrespective of whether the schools were integrated or not. The vision of open schooling supported by the principals did not translate into direct changes within the curriculum, and remained a vision of a primarily demographic integration.

EDUCATION AND THE STATE

The discussion thus far has focused on the experience of desegregation. In many respects, from the perspective of the teachers, this process has been nothing but chaotic and extremely stressful for the practitioner in the field (Akhurst, 1997). However, it is necessary to try to understand how this relates to broader issues connected to the construction of a new South African identity, and crucially, what roles schools can play in this process.

The South African State

To understand the potential relationship between education, the state, and national identity and their relation to the various regional, cultural, and ethnic identities that occur within the state, we need to examine the nature of the South African state as we presently find it. In the case of South Africa, the world institution model articulated by John W. Meyer and colleagues is persuasively (Meyer, Boli, Thomas, & Ramirez, 1997). South Africa, like all other African states, had its geographic boundaries determined during the colonial era. The development of the colonial state into a settler state and then into the apartheid state is well documented. Of interest here is the recent shaping of the post-apartheid state. Meyer et al. argue that many features of the contemporary nation-state derive from worldwide models "constructed and propagated through global cultural and associational processes" (Meyer et al., 1997, p. 144). These models and the processes that propagate them help to explain the "many puzzling features of contemporary national societies, such as structural isomorphism in the face of enormous differences in resources and traditions, ritualized and rather loosely coupled organizational efforts, and elaborate structuration to serve purposes that are largely of exogenous origins (Meyer et al., 1997, p. 144). One need only examine both the constitutional process and the education policy process to recognize the ways in which the new South African state has been modeled, albeit eclectically, from examples of worldwide,[15] South Africa has a Bill of Rights, a constitutional court, and National Qualifications Framework, and outcomes-based education has been introduced. However, it does not have the history that spawned these structures in their original contexts and certainly does not have the resources to fully realize the purpose of these structures.

---

[15]Teams of experts were sent or were invited to study institutional arrangements in the United States, United Kingdom, Germany, Australia, and New Zealand.

The question then needs to be posted: Why has South Africa adopted these particular models for its political and educational dispensations? A generous explanation might be that the opportunity afforded by being able to start again was grasped, and the best of what was globally available was incorporated. Another explanation, however, might be that the political and educational models, like the economic dispensation, needed to fit within modern global patterns in order for the South African nation-state to be a recognized as a modern player. The constitutional state and the educational system signal to South Africa and the rest of the world that it is a modern society with modern institutions, regardless of the capacity to actually realize these institutions in practice. The national identity that is being promoted and propagated through these institutions is a profoundly modern one: democratic, rational, egalitarian, and productive. It is a national identity that is in many respects the alter ego of where South Africa has come from, with its history of sexism, racism, lack of democracy, and low levels of productivity. And, I would argue, it is an identity that does not have much purchase with the majority of the South African population in that it is based on abstract concepts that are not what Castells called "symbol mobilizers"[16] (Castells, 1997, p. 361). One of the dangers of relying on such symbolically weak identifiers is that they leave room for a range of competing identities to exist alongside or in opposition to the national identity.

The promotion and deepening of this new and modern identity is thus an extremely difficult task for the state and faces serious challenges form competing identity brokers that are able to draw on powerful symbol mobilizers. Among the key instruments that the new South African state has at its disposal is the schooling system, which has been central to efforts to do just this. Yet the role of the state in managing the sort of signals put out by the education system that could serve to strengthen this national identity have been rather limited. Indeed, the crucial process of preparing youth who are in schools at the moment for life in an open, tolerant, and modern society that has moved beyond the limited identities of the apartheid past has been left to teachers and school managers with very little guidance.

To understand why the South African state has failed to push through its national agenda, it is necessary to examine the nature of the state somewhat further.

---

[16]Ironically the persona of Nelson Mandela would provide an ideal symbolic personality or "prophet" (Castells, 1977) around which to mobilize an identity, but he has steadfastly refused to play this role and eschewed all moves toward a personality cult.

The "Fragile" State

The notion of the "fragile" state, as developed by Fuller in his penetrating analysis of education in Malawi and Kenya, is helpful in understanding South Africa (Bradshaw & Fuller, 1996; Fuller, 1991). Fuller argued that states in Africa (and the developing world generally) are different from relatively more stable states in the West in that their limited resources make it difficult for them to negotiate the tensions between the expectations of their popular support base and the competing interests and interdependence of sectors of the local and international community with which they are bound. The fragility of the state, and its need for alliances with a range of interest groups, results in weaknesses in the capacity to actually push through reforms.

Bradshaw and Fuller (1996) described generally some of the characteristics of the fragile state that apply in large measure to the South African situation:

> Economic elites often are stigmatized or remain unorganized; a small or static wage sector limits the strength of "working-class interests"; fledgling labor unions are often contained politically; rural communities and urban families on the periphery of the modern sector may be touched little by the central state's attempts to change their economic practices and social commitments. State actors in third-world regimes may act from self-interest and with relative autonomy as they symbolically mandate "reforms." But technical and organizational capacities of these seemingly centralized regimes to *effectively implement* policy and programs are infamously weak.

The state is thus caught between a number of competing forces and can only impact on society if it is able to mobilize a range of forces behind it. In South Africa these competing forces include, amongst others, the economically strong White minority, the massive public service, the trade union movement, the rural and urban poor who constitute the ruling party's major support base, and the organizations of the global economy such as the World Bank and IMF. South Africa's transition was not a revolution in the traditional sense: It was a negotiated transfer of power that generated a dispensation marked by the products of compromise and deals. These legacies already place severe limitations on what the state is able to do. For example, the tensions between the national education ministry, which provides policy frameworks, and the various provincial governments' capacity or desire to implement those policies is evident in the discussion on desegregation. As Fuller (1991) suggested, local levels of bureaucracy cannot simply be seen as mechanically carrying out the wishes of the state.

A further example of the consequences of a fragile state can be seen in the power that economically powerful minorities are able to retain in defining local institutions such as the school. The state cannot simply step in and transform education for fear of alienating this group, but at the same time it is constantly under pressure from its own political constituency to act decisively to improve their lot. The common result is rhetoric, but little action. The rhetoric serves a symbolic function, because in many instances the limited resources and influence of the state place major constraints on as ability to actually deliver the educational and economic promises.

The developments in education over the past decade in South Africa clearly illustrate some of the difficulties a developing country like South Africa faces in terms of trying to forge a new national identity. The schooling system as a vehicle for social change remains relatively weak due to the fragility of the state and its inability to push through the necessary social reforms that can begin the implementation of the vision.

CONCLUDING COMMENTS

By examining the consequences of the fragility of the South African state, it becomes clear that the process of desegregation cannot be simply understood as having been badly managed. Poor management is most certainly an aspect of the problem, but it is part of a major wider challenge facing the state.

What, then, are the prospects for schooling to help build a national identity based on some of the principles set out in the introduction? And what does the future hold for the teachers and learners discussed in this study? It is difficult to be too optimistic about the first matter: National identities are seldom forged out of abstract concepts. Schools may eventually incorporate notions of citizenship into the curriculum, but this will not bind the nation around a national project. The history of South Africa does provide an emotive unifying concept that South Africans can work against,[17] but this tends to undermine the project of reconciliation. Unfortunately, more often than not it is emotions like xenophobia that unite South Africans.

However, while the South African state may not be able to mobilize a South African identity through the schooling project, this does not mean that schools should be abandoned as sites of contestation over identity. At present South African youth are as divided as ever. The survey of learners' social

---

[17]In much the same way as modern German identity has been built around a reaction to the Nazi period.

interactions, attitudes, and values conducted in Pietermaritzburg revealed a picture of schools where may not have been much overt conflict, but where a large degree of suspicion and limited interaction remained.[18] It is clear that desegregation and contact in schools is not enough to facilitate better social relations in schools. And teachers have a crucial role to play.

One of the dangers of the fragile state that Fuller highlighted is that the need to demonstrate that reforms are having an impact can result in a bureaucratization of the systems that reduces the ability of local agents to act creatively. And this is certainly not desirable. If teachers are to play a positive role in facilitating better social relations among the learners, it is important that their good will and creative skills are harnessed. The role of the state must be one that supports, encourages, and assists in providing skills, but avoids imposing itself on teachers. If teachers are able to play this role, regardless of whether they teach in what I have described as open or township schools, then there is a possibility that the youth in the schools will be able to make some sense of the multilingual, multicultural, and racially and ethnically diverse place that is South Africa. And that sense may serve as an embryonic national identity for people who call themselves South Africans.

A Note on Terminology for an International Audience

Terminology is always a vexed question when writing about South Africa. Descriptors and labels seldom adequately capture the complexity of the "thing" they attempt to describe. So much of South Africa's history has been affected by attempts to define and control the ways in which people are labeled that very few labels are not contested. Furthermore, in some instances, terms used in South Africa may have other connotations in other places. I have chosen to be guided primarily by the terminology used by the people interviewed in this study, although this does at times mean using different times than the official policy documents.

There is a need for a shorthand that allows me to distinguish between different types of schools. The key distinction that I wish to make for purposes of this chapter is between those school that used to cater primarily to the White, Indian, and colored (people who are not categorized as Whites, Blacks, and Indians) communities and that have seen some level of desegregation and

---

[18]These findings are similar to those of a survey conducted for advertisers seeking to understand the South African youth market. Although youth were into fashion, music, and sport, there were clear racial dividers in terms of what fashion, what music, and what sport (*M&G*, 1997, December 23).

integration during the course of the past 15 years, and those schools that (due to their location and lack of resources) have remained homogeneously Black African. The former grouping of schools were administered variously by the Houses of Assembly (White), Delegates (Indian), and Representatives (colored), and the latter were administered by the Department of Education and Training (DET) or various homeland education departments. This classification holds to a large extent in the parts of South Africa I discuss here (although there are exceptions), but doesn't necessarily apply to parts of the Eastern, Northern, and Western Cape Provinces. For economy I refer to those schools that have experienced some degree of desegregation as *open schools*, whereas those schools that have a homogeneous Black African pupil population are referred to as township schools. Both these terms are problematic. The first belies the fact that many of the schools that are referred to as open are very far from being genuinely open. The second does not adequately capture the true geographic spread of the category because this type of school does not only occur in the urban townships. In fact, the vast majority of these schools are located in the rural areas of the former homelands and are significantly worse off in terms of resources than the township schools. By collapsing the two types of schools into one category, there is a danger of contributing to the continued marginalization of rural schools, to which I would like to alert the reader.

It is already evident from the above that racial classification remains a feature of South African life. The colonial and apartheid system classified and divided in order to discriminate, and the consequences remain acutely evident when discussing education. The primary apartheid classification separated South Africans into four categories: Africa, colored, Indian, and White. The term *Black* is used in two ways: first, as a collective term for the first three categories, and second, as a synonym for African. The term African has also been the subject of much debate recently, with White, Indian, and colored people wanting to lay claim to being African. For this reason I have chosen to use the following terms: *Black African*, *Colored*, *Indian*, and *White*. I use them reluctantly and with the full understanding that each category can be deconstructed and reconstructed in different ways.

It is important to note that in South Africa, ethnic identifications occur within racial ones. By ethnic I mean identification based primarily on language, culture, place of origin, and religion. In many instances these identifications are as significant or more significant than the categories mentioned above. However, they were not very significant in the ways in which the apartheid state allocated educational resources and thus they are not discussed at length in this paper.

REFERENCES

Akhurst, J. (1997). Challenges to teachers as schools in South Africa become more integrated: An anti-racist perspective. *Journal of Education, 22,* 3-16.

Asmal, K. (1999). *Call to action: Mobilising citizens to build a South African education and training system for the 21st century.* Pretoria, South Africa: Department of Education.

Bradshaw, Y. W., & Fuller, B. (1996). Policy action and school demand in Kenya: When a strong state grows fragile. *International Journal of Contemporary Sociology, 37*(1-2), 72-96.

Carnoy, M., & Werthein, J. (1977). Socialist ideology and the transformation of Cuban education. In J. Karabel & A. H. Halsey (Eds.), *Power and ideology in education* (pp. 573-588). New York: Oxford University Press.

Castells, M. (1996). *The rise of the network society* (vol. 1). Oxford, UK: Blackwell.

Castells, M. (1997). *The power of identity* (vol. 2). Oxford, UK: Blackwell.

CHED. (1991a). *Curriculum model for education in South Africa: Discussion document.* Pretoria, South Africa: Department of National Education.

CHED. (1991b). *Educational renewal strategy: Discussion document.* Pretoria, South Africa: Department of National Education.

Chisholm, L. (1999). Change and continuity in South African education: The impact of policy. *African Studies, 58*(1), 87-103.

Cross, M. (1993). Curriculum policies and processes in Mozambique, 1930--1989: The colonial legacy and the challenge of national reconstruction. In N. Taylor (Ed.), *Inventing knowledge: Contests in curriculum construction* (pp. 69-91). Cape Town, South Africa: Maskew Miller Longman.

Cross, M., & Chisholm, L. (1990). The roots of segregated schooling in twentieth century South Africa. In M. Nkomo (Ed.), *Pedagogy of domination.* Trenton, NJ: Africa World Press.

Fuller, B. (1991). *Growing up modern: The Western state builds third-world schools.* New York: Routledge.

Goodson, I. (1993). "Nations at risk" and "national curriculum": Ideology and identity. In N. Taylor (Ed.), *Inventing knowledge: Contests in curriculum construction* (pp. 260-277). Cape Town, South Africa: Maskew Miller Longman.

Harley, K. (1992). African education and social control in colonial Natal. *Perspectives in Education, 13*(2), 27-52.

Harley, K. (1994). Landmarks in the history of "open" schooling in Natal: The search for social control. *Journal of Education, 19*(1), 37-51.

Harley, K., & Wedekind, V. (1999). Vision and constraint in curriculum change: A case study of South African school principals. In B. Moon & P. Murphy (Eds.), *Curriculum in context* (pp. 179-195). London: Paul Chapman.

Hartshorne, K. (1992). *Crisis and challenge: Black education 1910-1990.* Cape Town, South Africa: Oxford University Press.

Jansen, J. (1998). Grove Primary: Power, privilege and the law in South African education. *Journal of Education, 23,* 5-30.

Kallaway, P. (Ed.). (1984). *Apartheid and education.* Johannesburg: South Africa: Ravan.

Kallaway, P., Kruss, G., Fataar, A., & Donn, G. (Eds.). (1997). *Education after apartheid: South African education in transition.* Cape Town, South Africa: University of Cape Town Press.

Levin, R. (1980). Black education, class struggle and the dynamics of change in South Africa. *Africa Perspective, 17,* 17-41.

Lubisi, C., Parker, B., & Wedekind, V. (1998). *Understanding outcomes-based education: Teaching and assessment in South Africa.* Cape Town, South Africa: Oxford University Press.

McLaren, P. (1997). Multi-culturalism and the postmodern critique: Toward a pedagogy of resistance and transformation. In A. H. Halsey, H. Lauder, P. Brown, & A. S. Wells (Eds.), *Education: Culture, economy, society* (pp. 520-540). New York: Oxford University Press.

Mdluli, P. (1994). Ubuntu-botho: Inkaha's "people's education." In W. Flanagan, C. Hemson, J. Muller, & N. Taylor (Eds.), *Vintage Kenton: A Ken Education Association Commemoration* (pp. 90-102). Cape Town, South Africa: Maskew Miller Longman.

Meyer, J. W., Boli, J., Thomas, G. M., & Ramirez, F. O. (1997). World society and the nation-state. *The American Journal of Sociology, 103*(1), 144-182.

N.E.P.I. (1992). *Curriculum: Report of the National Education Policy Investigation Curriculum Research Group.* Cape Town, South Africa: Oxford University Press.

Penny, A., Appel, S., Gultig, J., Harley, K., & Muir, R. (1993). "Just sort of fumbling in the dark": A case study of the advent of racial integration in South African schools. *Comparative Education Review, 37*(4), 412-433.

Reeves, J. (1998, September 21). More tension at Vryburg School. *The Star.* Retrieved from: www.iol.co.za.

Sader, M. (2000). *Teacher perceptions of the process of desegregation in selected Pietermaritzburg schools.* Unpublished Master's Thesis, University of Natal, Pietermaritzburg.

Skuy, M., & Vice, H. (1996). Attitudes of White teachers towards racial integration of schools in South Africa. *Educational Research, 38*(2), 135-146.

Tabane, R. (1999, March 3). Stabbing: School allows pupil back. *The Star.* Retrieved from: www.iol.co.2q.

Vally, S. (1999, March 19). School race survey shows shocking practices. *Sunday Independent.* Retrieved from: www.iol.co.za.

Van Wyk, J.-A. (1997). The intercultural culture of schools: Problems and challenges for a post-apartheid South Africa. *Journal of Negro Education, 66*(4), 539-545.

Verma, G., Zec, D., & Skinner, G. (1994). *The ethnic crucible: Harmony and discord in secondary schools.* London: Falmer Press.

Wedekind, V., Lubisi, C., Harley, K., & Gultig, J. (1996). Political change, social integration, and curriculum: A South African case study. *Journal of Curriculum Studies, 28*(4), 419-436.

Wedekind, V., & Sader, M. (1998, July). *"Bruin ous," "boers" and "blacks" vs popular, pretty and cool: Race, youth identity and schooling in South African secondary schools.* Paper presented to the WCCES Congress, Cape Town, South Africa.

For economy all references to newspaper articles appear in the text. *The Daily Mail and Guardian* has been abbreviated as *M&G. Retrieved from: www.mg.co.za.mg/archive*

Demographic Diversity and Higher Education Reorganization in South Africa: The Applicability of U.S. Models

James B. Stewart
Pennsylvania State University

Fatima Abrahams
University of Western Cape

The Republic of South Africa clearly faces monumental challenges in transforming its system of higher education to provide equitable opportunities for members of all groups. Aside from initiatives propagated by educational planners, previously marginalized groups are demanding a variety of changes in the configuration and modus operandi of historically White universities (HWUs). Many of the demands center on the problem of integrating the knowledge and experiences of diverse cultural, ethnic, and national groups into historically monocultural institutions. Areas targeted by change agents range from the composition of faculties and administrations to the structure and content of curricula. In some sense, there are parallels to pressures faced by higher education institutions in the United States over the past three decades associated with the modern civil rights movement and subsequent challenges to the status quo. The limited progress achieved in realizing the goal of equal educational opportunity in U.S. higher education constitutes a potentially useful object lesson for South Africa, where the issues are, arguably, more complex.

In both South Africa and the United States, historically Black universities (HBUs) had their origins as vehicles to support state-mandated racial segregation. Despite this fact, HBUs in both countries have successfully graduated many distinguished alumni who have contributed notably to community well-being and the social transformation of their respective societies. As efforts to desegregate HWUs proceed in both countries, the usefulness of HBUs has been questioned increasingly. Through a process that has manifested intense debate and tension, they have been relegated to marginal roles in plans to create educational systems that will meet societal needs in the next century.

This analysis examines selected challenges and responses associated with efforts to diversity higher education enrollments and transform institutional cultures in South Africa. The two major foci of the investigation are (1) the cultural conflicts associated with the alteration of the student body composition of HWUs and strategies to ameliorate these conflicts, and (2) the role of HBUs in the new configuration of higher education. The desegregation process in the United States provides the frame of reference for the analysis. Comparisons and contrasts between the two higher education environments are used to highlight critical issues.

A brief historical background describing the evolution of universities in South Africa is provided in the next section. Elements of the proposed reorganization of higher education in South Africa are then discussed, highlighting critical challenges facing both HWUs and HBUs. The significance of these challenges is underscored through a review of enrollment projections and recent enrollment trends. Potential strategies to address the issues facing HWUs and HBUs are then discussed. The discussion of HWUs focuses particular attention on affirmative action and multicultural education policies. The prospects for HBUs are examined in the context of the experiences of similar institutions in the United States. The analysis concludes with suggestions regarding how each country can learn from the other's experiences in attempts to cultivate cross-cultural literacy and collaboration skills required for meeting the challenges of globalization in the 21st century.

THE EVOLUTION OF SOUTH AFRICAN UNIVERSITIES

Three distinct higher education cultures have evolved within South Africa. The origin of the modern system of higher education dates back to the establishment of the University of the Cape of Good Hope in the early 1870s, which later became the University of South Africa (UNISA) (Dreijmanis, 1988; Ridge, 1996a). One cultural tradition, represented by the five major Afrikaans-medium universities (the University of the Orange Free state, Potchefstroom University for Christian Higher Education, the University of Pretoria, Rand Afrikaans University, and the University of Stellenbosch), sometimes referred to as "volkuninversiteite," has been linked traditionally to the ideology of Afrikaner nationalism. Although the Afrikaans-medium universities have all served as instruments of Afrikaner nationalism, differences in political ideology exist among them. As an example, the University of Pretoria is generally considered to be more conservative than the University of Stellenbosch (Dreijmanis, 1988).

The four major English-medium universities (the University of Cape Town, the University of Natal, Rhodes University, and the University of the

Witwatersrand) constitute the second major higher education cultural formation. These institutions have defined themselves as open universities committed to unrestricted inquiry as opposed to instruments of a particular political ideology (the University of Port Elizabeth is dual medium). Before 1959 the English-medium universities admitted Black students with limited government intervention. But between 1959 and 1983, Black students had to secure permission from the Department of Education to attend White universities. In 1983, the Universities Amendment Act was passed. It provided that colored, Indian, and White universities had the right to admit any student, subject to a numerical quota or ceiling, for the admission of students of population groups other than that for which the institution was designated. The quota provisions were not enacted (Dreijmanis, 1988).

Institutions of higher education designed to serve non-White South Africans constitute the third distinct cultural tradition in South Africa. The first higher education institution established for Africans was the South African Native College, founded as a private institution at Fort Hare in 1916 and renamed the University College of Fort Hare in 1952. Until 1961 Fort Hare also served as the major higher education provider for the colored and Indian populations. The university colleges of the North and Zululand were established in 1959, each designated to serve specific ethnic groups. Since 1979 African students can enroll at any African university irrespective of ethnicity. Vista University, a nonresidential institution for urban Africans, was established in 1981 at six locations. The Medical University of Southern Africa (Medunsa) was created in 1976. In addition to these institutions, several traditional colleges were established in several of the former homelands. The University of the Transkei was founded in 1976 as a branch of the University of Fort Hare, the University of Bophuthatswana (now the Northwest) was established in 1979, and the University of Venda in 1981 (Dreijmanis, 1988; Ridge, 1996a).

Higher education institutions were also established for other non-White population groups. The University College of the Western Cape was formed in 1959 to serve the needs of the colored population. The University College of Durban-Westville was established in 1959 to serve the Indian population (Dreijmanis, 1988).

With the end of apartheid, the new regime and higher education authorities face the monumental challenge of harmonizing these disparate higher education cultural traditions in the context of demands for wider access and expectations that higher education will contribute directly to critical societal development needs. The approach taken to attempt this harmonization is discussed in the following section.

A NEW HIGHER EDUCATION SYSTEM: VISION AND CHALLENGES

The outlines of a framework for the creation of a nationally coordinated system of higher education are presented in the Education White Paper (Department of Education, 1997). This reorganization of higher education is conceptualized as part of the broader political, social, and economic transformation of South Africa. Key objectives of the transformation include "political democratization, economic reconstruction and development, and redistributive social policies aimed at equity" (Department of Education, 1997, p. 4).

A vision of "a transformed, democratic, nonracial, and nonsexist system of higher education" is offered that entails:

1. Promot[ing] equity of access and fair chances of success to all who are seeking to realize their potential through higher education, while eradicating all forms of unfair discrimination and advancing redress for past inequalities

2. Meet[ing], through well-planned and coordinated teaching, learning, and research programs, national development needs, including the high-skilled employment needs presented by a growing economy operating in a global environment

3. Support[int] a democratic ethos and a culture of human rights by educational programs and practices conducive to critical discourse and creative thinking, cultural tolerance, and a common commitment to humane, nonracist, and nonsexist social order

4. Contribut[ing] to the advancement of all forms of knowledge and scholarship, and in particular address[ing] the diverse problems and demands of the local, national, southern African and African contexts, and uphold[ing] rigorous standards of academic quality

Increased access to higher education for Black women, disabled, and mature students is expected to be one outcome of the reorganization process as well as "new curricula and flexible models of learning and teaching, including modes of delivery, to accommodate a larger and more diverse student population" (Department of Education, 1997, p. 6). Partnerships are expected to be forged for the purpose of contributing to "an enabling institutional environment and culture that is sensitive to and affirms diversity, promotes reconciliation and respect for human life, protects the dignity of individuals from racial and sexual harassment, and rejects all other forms of violent behavior" (Department of Education, 1997, p. 6).

The vision set forth in the Education White Paper would seem to provide substantial space for both HWUs and HBUs to play important roles in the reorganized system. HWUs have had the advantage of more plentiful resources, which has enabled the establishment of a solid instructional and research infrastructure that can provide the foundation for skill development and innovative applied research initiatives. Conversely, it is reasonable to expect that HBUs have developed unique strategies for meeting the needs of students from historically disadvantaged groups. Moreover, given their geographical location and the fact that most were designated to serve specific subpopulations, in the aggregate HBUs clearly constitute a unique resource for addressing issues of linguistic and cultural diversity. However, their ability to contribute significantly in other ways to realization of the vision set forth in the Education White Paper is constrained by the legacy of neglect and discrimination under previous regimes.

The traditional approach to funding higher education in South Africa limits the ability of both HBUs and HWUs to respond to the new expectations. Most other African countries fund up to 100% of higher education. In contrast, South Africa is one of the five countries in the world that depends least on government for financial support (Motala, 1997). Direct funding comes from three sources: state subsidy, student fees, and endowment and gifts. There is a national state subsidy formula for post-secondary education that, for universities, is supposed to provide a subsidy equal to 80% of the standard unit cost per successful student in a discipline. However, it has never been funded in full (Ridge, 1996b). The government has made some efforts to increase its support. As an example, the 1996 Budget Review indicated plans to increase funding to higher education by 28% over the previous year. As a result, the overall level of subsidies to universities was anticipated to increase from 62.1% to 68.6% (Chisholm & Vally, 1996).

The new funding framework is designed with the goals of ensuring more student access, improving quality of teaching and research, increasing student progression and graduation rates, and providing greater responsiveness to social and economic needs. Whatever the goals of the changes in funding levels and allocation formula may have been, one unquestionable outcome has been serious dislocation problems for most higher education institutions. As an illustration, the University of Natal, an HWU, announced plans in 1997 to eliminate 660 jobs and close some departments in the face of a R60 million deficit (Motala, 1997).

HBUs have been decimated by the elimination of full state subsidies. Application of the same complex funding formula to HBUs as their counterparts, coupled with the combination of declining student numbers and massive amounts of outstanding student fees, has meant financial disaster. As an example, the University of Fort Hare was forced to fire over 900 workers in 1997 and declare bankruptcy. In 1999 the auditor general's office appointed three auditing companies to audit six cash-strapped universities, all of which are HBUs (*Tertiary education bodies look at merger benefits*, 1999; Ministry of Education, 1999, June).

The challenges to the realization of the vision set forth in the Education White Paper are not limited to issues of fiscal shortfalls and/or financial mismanagement and they are not limited to HBUs. During the second quarter of 1996, "at least 12 institutions of higher education experienced bitter and often violent clashes between students and university administrators and between White and Black students (Motala, 1996). The confrontations erupted over several issues, including academic and financial expulsions; charges of racism, incompetence, and corruption of lecturers and administrators; and discontent with the pace of transformation (Motola, 1996).

Conflicts over demands to create a more multicultural institutional culture have also emerged. As an illustration, at Potchefstroom University Black and White students clashed over the use of Afrikaans as the sole medium of instruction. Black students and supportive workers were attacked by police and White students while protesting against the existing language policy (Motala, 1996).

These conflicts underscore the reality that policies that focus principally on altering the demographic composition of student bodies and faculties will be inadequate to achieve the desired outcomes of the reorganization. This fact is recognized in the Education White Paper, which declares: "An enabling environment must be created throughout the system to uproot deep-seated racist and sexist ideologies and practices that inflame relationships, inflict emotional scars, and create barriers to successful participation in learning and campus life. Only a multifaceted approach can provide a sound foundation of knowledge, concepts, and academic, social, and personal skills, and create the culture of respect, support, and challenge on which self-confidence, real learning, and enquiry can thrive" (Department of Education, 1997, p. 14).

The problem is that the development of the type of strategies envisioned in the Education White Paper are lagging behind anticipated changes in the composition of student bodies at the various institutions, as can be seen by examining the headcount enrollment data presented in Table 7.1.

Although university enrollments are expected to increase by 12% between 1997 and 2001, enrollment in Technikons are expected to grow much faster (22%). The distribution of students between universities and Technikons will have shifted by nearly 10 percentage points between 1993 and 2001, reflecting a greater emphasis on technical training in support of labor force development. Within the university sector, the share of enrollments at HBUs has declined continually, and the total enrollment at HBUs is expected to remain virtually flat through 2001. Although enrollments at English-speaking HWUs are expected to increase by 13% between 1997 and 2001, the magnitude of the

TABLE 7.1

Total Head Count Enrollment by Sector 1993, 1997,
2001 (Projected) (000)

Sector	Actual 1993	Actual 1997	Planned 2001	Change 1997-2001
HBU--Number	102	104	105	1 (1%)
HBU--Percent	21%	18%	15%	
HWU (Afrik)--Number	72	93	133	40 (43%)
HWU (Afrik)--Percent	15%	16%	19%	
HWU (Eng)--Number	52	56	63	7 (13%)
HWU (Eng)--Percent	10%	9%	9%	
UNISA--Number	123	126	122	-4 (-3%)
UNISA--Percent	25%	21%	18%	
UNIV TOTAL--Number	349	379	423	44 (12%)
UNIV TOTAL--Percent	71%	64%	62%	
HBT--Number	26	53	56	3 (6%)
HBT-Percent	5%	9%	8%	
HWT--Number	59	80	114	34 (43%)
HWT--Percent	12%	13%	17%	
TECH SA--Number	62	82	92	10 (12%)
TECH SA--Percent	12%	14%	13%	
TECH TOTAL--Number	147	215	262	47 (22%)
TECH TOTAL--Percent	29%	36%	38%	
TOTAL	496	594	685	91 (15%)

Source: Bunting, I., & Bunting, L. (1997). "National enrollment trends in public higher education, overview of projected student enrollments between 1997 and 2001, *Higher Planning Statistics. Report 2 Planning statistics for the Western Cape*, 7-10. Pretoria: Department of Education (September).

increase is relatively small. The largest anticipated growth in university enrollments is anticipated to occur at the Afrikaans-speaking universities. Enrollment in this subsector is expected to grow by 40,000, or 43%. Finally, UNISA enrollment is expected to decline by 4,000, or 3%. Total enrollments at HBUs include enrollments at the University of the Western Cape, an institution originally founded to serve the population designated at "colored."

Table 7.2 presents comparable information for first-time enrollments. First-time enrollments at HBUs are expected to increase significantly between 1997 and 2001. However, comparing these figures to those in Table 7.1 indicates that increases in first-time enrollments are not expected to translate into significant growth in total enrollments. This reflects high attrition-rate projections for HBUs. First-time enrollments at Afrikaans-speaking universities are expected to increase, but at a significantly slower rate than that of total enrollment, reflecting expectations of relatively low attrition rates. First-time enrollments are expected to decline at the English-speaking universities, although total enrollment will rise.

Table 7.3 contains total enrollment data for White students. Several trends are noteworthy. First, a slight decrease in White university enrollments is expected. Consequently, the enrollment growth projected for universities is anticipated to be provided totally by Black (non-White) students. Second, only 1,000 White students attended HBUs in 1993 and 1997, and no change in this level is anticipated for 2001. This suggests that the principal burden of adjusting to significant demographic changes will be born by HWUs. First-time enrollment data for White students is presented in Table 7.4 confirm the trends reflected in Table 7.3.

Enrollment data for African students are presented in Table 7.5 As implied by the data contained in previous tables, the most significant change in African enrollments will occur at Afrikaans-speaking HWUs. In 2001, African students are expected to comprise 49% of enrollments at these institutions. In contrast, African students are expected to constitute only 32% of enrollments at English-speaking HWUs in 2001. Despite the expected growth in enrollments of African students in HWUs, the expected enrollment of African students in HBUs will still be larger than the combined enrollment of African students at English-speaking and Afrikaans-speaking HWUs in 2001. The first-time enrollment data in Table 7.6 underscore the trends discussed previously.

In summary, although university enrollment projections indicate a significant increase in African student enrollments in HWUs, the role of HUBs in providing higher education opportunities will persist. As a consequence, it is imperative that the requisite fiscal and other resources be provided. Enrollment projections indicate no expectation that HBUs are seen as a venue in which interracial collaboration skills will be fostered, as few White students are expected to enroll in this subsector. The major cultural adjustments are likely to be necessary at Afrikaans-speaking HWUs, where the largest enrollment

TABLE 7.2

Total First-Time Undergraduate Enrollment 1993,
1997, and 2001 (Projected) (000)

Sector	Actual 1993	Actual 1997	Planned 2001	Change 1997-2001
HBU--Number	23.4	18.2	21.3	3.1 (17%)
HBU--Percent	23%	14%	15%	
HWU (Afrik)--Number	14.9	15.2	16.3	1.1 (7%)
HWU (Afrik)--Percent	14%	12%	12%	
HWU (Eng)--Number	8.2	12.5	10.8	-1.7 (-14%)
HWU (Eng)--Percent	10%	9%	9%	
UNISA--Number	13.7	14.8	13.5	-1.3 (-9%)
UNISA--Percent	13%	12%	10%	
UNIV TOTAL--Number	60.2	60.7	61.9	1.2 (2%)
UNIV TOTAL--Percent	58%	48%	45%	
HBT--Number	10.6	19.0	19.2	.2 (1%)
HBT-Percent	10%	15%	14%	
HWT--Number	13.5	24.6	37.6	13.0 (53%)
HWT--Percent	13%	19%	26%	
TECH SA--Number	19.7	22.0	23.3	1.3 (6%)
TECH SA--Percent	19%	18%	16%	
TECH TOTAL--Number	43.8	65.6	80.1	14.5 (22%)
TECH TOTAL--Percent	42%	52%	56%	
TOTAL	104.0	126.3	142.0	15.7 (12%)

Source: Bunting, I., & Bunting, L. (1997). "National enrollment trends in public higher education, overview of projected student enrollments between 1997 and 2001, *Higher Planning Statistics. Report 2 Planning statistics for the Western Cape*. Pretoria: Department of Education (September).

TABLE 7.3

Head Count Enrollments by Sector
White Students
1993, 1997, 2001 (Projected) (000)

Sector	Actual 1993	Actual 1997	Planned 2001	Change 1997-2001
HBU--Number	1	1	1	0 (0%)
HBU--Percent	.4%	.5%	.5%	
HWU (Afrik)--Number	65	59	59	0 (0%)
HWU (Afrik)--Percent	14%	12%	12%	
HWU (Eng)--Number	33	28	27	-1 (-.4%)
HWU (Eng)--Percent	14%	15%	15%	
UNISA--Number	54	47	45	-2 (-2%)
UNISA--Percent	24%	25%	24%	
UNIV TOTAL--Number	153	135	132	-3 (-2%)
UNIV TOTAL--Percent	67%	72%	71%	
HBT--Number	0	1	0	-1 (-100%)
HBT-Percent	0%	.5%	0%	
HWT--Number	44	32	32	0 (0%)
HWT--Percent	19%	17%	17%	
TECH SA--Number	32	19	22	3 (16%)
TECH SA--Percent	14%	10%	12%	
TECH TOTAL--Number	76	52	54	2 (4%)
TECH TOTAL--Percent	33%	28%	29%	
TOTAL	229	187	186	-1 (-.5%)

Source: Bunting, I., & Bunting, L. (1997). "National enrollment trends in public higher education, overview of projected student enrollments between 1997 and 2001, *Higher Planning Statistics. Report 2 Planning statistics for the Western Cape*. Pretoria: Department of Education (September).

TABLE 7.4

First-Time Undergraduate Enrollment by Sector
White Students
1993, 1997, and 2001 (Projected) (000)

Sector	Actual 1993	Actual 1997	Planned 2001	Change 1997-2001
HBU--Number	0	.1	0	-.1 (-100%)
HBU--Percent	0%	.3%	.0%	
HWU (Afrik)--Number	14.1	10.6	10.1	-.5 (-5%)
HWU (Afrik)--Percent	35%	3.3%	30%	
HWU (Eng)--Number	4.8	5.3	4.4	-.9 (-17%)
HWU (Eng)--Percent	12%	16%	13%	
UNISA--Number	24.4	21.1	19.5	-1.6 (-8%)
UNISA--Percent	60%	65%	58%	
UNIV TOTAL--Number	0	.2	.1	-.1 (-50)
UNIV TOTAL--Percent	0%	.6%	.3%	
HBT--Number	9.0	8.0	10.2	2.2 (28%)
HBT-Percent	22%	25%	30%	
HWT--Number	7.2	3.0	3.7	.7 (23%)
HWT--Percent	18%	9%	11%	
TECH SA--Number	16.2	11.2	14.0	2.8 (25%)
TECH SA--Percent	40%	35%	42%	
TECH TOTAL--Number	40.6	32.3	33.5	1.2 (4%)
TECH TOTAL--Percent	33%	28%	29%	
TOTAL	229	187	186	-1 (-.5%)

Source: Bunting, I., & Bunting, L. (1997). "National enrollment trends in public higher education, overview of projected student enrollments between 1997 and 2001, *Higher Planning Statistics. Report 2 Planning statistics for the Western Cape*. Pretoria: Department of Education (September).

TABLE 7.5

Total Head Count Enrollment by Sector
African Students
1993, 1997, and 2001 (Projected) (000)

Sector	Actual 1993	Actual 1997	Planned 2001	Change 1997-2001
HBU--Number	86	93	91	-.2 (2%)
HBU--Percent	42%	28%	22%	
HWU (Afrik)--Number	5	28	65	37 (132%)
HWU (Afrik)--Percent	2%	8%	16%	
HWU (Eng)--Number	10	16	20	4 (25%)
HWU (Eng)--Percent	5%	5%	5%	
UNISA--Number	54	63	58	-5 (-8%)
UNISA--Percent	26%	19%	14%	
UNIV TOTAL--Number	155	200	234	34 (17%)
UNIV TOTAL--Percent	76%	60%	57%	
HBT--Number	17	43	44	1 (2%)
HBT-Pe	8%	13%	11%	
HWT--Number	11	38	71	33 (87%)
HWT--Percent	5%	11%	17%	
TECH SA--Number	22	55	62	7 (13%)
TECH SA--Percent	11%	16%	15%	
TECH TOTAL--Number	50	136	177	41 (30%)
TECH TOTAL--Percent	24%	40%	43%	
TOTAL	205	336	411	75 (22%)

Source: Bunting, I., & Bunting, L. (1997). "National enrollment trends in public higher education, overview of projected student enrollments between 1997 and 2001, *Higher Planning Statistics. Report 2 Planning statistics for the Western Cape.* Pretoria: Department of Education (September).

TABLE 7.6

First-Time Undergraduate Enrollment by Sector
African Students
1993, 1997, and 2001 (Projected) (000)

Sector	Actual 1993	Actual 1997	Planned 2001	Change 1997-2001
HBU--Number	19.6	16.6	18.4	1.8 (11%)
HBU--Percent	43%	22%	20%	
HWU (Afrik)--Number	.3	3.4	5.0	1.6 (47%)
HWU (Afrik)--Percent	.6%	4%	6%	
HWU (Eng)--Number	1.9	3.5	4.0	.5 (14%)
HWU (Eng)--Percent	2%	5%	4%	
UNISA--Number	6.6	7.3	6.9	3.5 (11%)
UNISA--Percent	14%	10%	8%	
UNIV TOTAL--Number	28.4	30.8	34.3	3.5 (11%)
UNIV TOTAL--Percent	59%	41%	38%	
HBT--Number	7.5	15.7	15.2	-.5 (3%)
HBT-Pe	15%	21%	17%	
HWT--Number	2.6	13.3	23.2	9.9 (74%)
HWT--Percent	5%	18%	26%	
TECH SA--Number	9.9	15.9	18.2	2.3 (14%)
TECH SA--Percent	20%	21%	20%	
TECH TOTAL--Number	20.0	44.9	56.6	11.7 (26%)
TECH TOTAL--Percent	41%	59%	62%	
TOTAL	48.4	75.7	90.9	15.2 (20%)

Source: Bunting, I., & Bunting, L. (1997). "National enrollment trends in public higher education, overview of projected student enrollments between 1997 and 2001, *Higher Planning Statistics. Report 2 Planning statistics for the Western Cape*. Pretoria: Department of Education (September).

increases for African students are expected to occur, although English-speaking HWUs will also be required to adapt to changing demographics.

The problem of shifting student demographics has been compounded by recent enrollment trends. South African universities and Technikons experienced a 7% drop in enrollments between June 1998 and June 1999. Continuation of this trend could lead to an additional loss of 2,000 students by the year 2000. White student enrollments fell by 16,000 and Black student enrollments fell by 20,000. The largest losses were at the HBUs, where African enrollments fell by 7,000, while enrollment in historically Black technikons increased by 22,000. Enrollments at Fort Hare fell by 82%, those at the University of the Transkei by 25%, at the Medical University of South Africa by 22%, and at the University of the Western Cape by 20% (Pretorius, 1999, October 17; Robbins, 1999, November, 19-25; Vergnam, 1999, October 25).

In contrast to the experience of HBUs, enrollments at Afrikaans-medium HWUs increased by 56,000 and those at English-medium HWUs by 10,000. These enrollment shifts underscore the need for HWUs to accelerate their transformation efforts. Critical issues relevant to the success of HWUs in serving the needs of new entrants are examined in the following section.

HWUs and the Management of Demographic Diversity

The Education White Paper enunciates eight principles that are to guide the transformation process: Equity and Redress, Democratization, Development, Quality, Effectiveness and Efficiency, Academic Freedom, Institutional Autonomy, and Public Accountability. Equity and Redress entails "not only abolishing all existing forms of unjust differentiation, but also measures of empowerment, including financial support to bring about equal opportunity for individuals and institutions" (Department of Education, 1997, p. 7). The report also sets the goal of providing a full spectrum of advanced educational opportunities for an expanding range of the population irrespective of race, gender, age, creed, or class or other forms of discrimination (Department of Education, 1997).

The Education White Paper mandates that the "major focus of any expansion and equity strategy must be on increasing the participation and success rates of Black students in general, and of African, colored, and women students in particular, especially in programs and levels in which they are underrepresented" (Department of Education, 1997, p. 13). It is further noted that government's "commitment to changing the composition of the student body will be affected through the targeted redistribution of the public subsidy to higher education. The relative proportion of public funding used to support academically able but disadvantaged students must be increased" (Department of Education, 1997, pp. 13-14).

Each individual institution is expected to develop its own plans to curtail discrimination and foster positive intergroup intercourse. These plans are expected to have as one objective the creation of a secure and safe campus environment that discouraged harassment or any other hostile behavior directed toward persons or groups on any grounds whatsoever, but particularly on grounds of age, color, creed, disability, gender, marital status, national origin, race, language, or sexual orientation (Department of Education, 1997). In addition, institutions are required to (1) set standards of expected behavior for the entire campus community, including but not limited to administrators, faculty, staff, students, security personnel, and contractors, (2) promote a campus environment that is sensitive to racial and cultural diversity, through extracurricular activities that expose students to cultures and traditions other than their own and scholarly activities that work toward this goal, and (3) assign competent personnel to monitor progress in the above-mentioned areas (Department of Education, 1997).

It is clear,then, that the government intends to employ forms of "affirmative action" and guarantees of nondiscrimination to facilitate the transformation process. While the idea of nondiscrimination is relatively noncontroversial, the concept of "affirmative action" is as controversial in South Africa as in the United States. Many of the basic ideas have been adapted from the U.S. model but, as in the case of multicultural education, there are important distinctions. Castle (1994, p. 265) argued that in Western countries, including the United States, affirmative action "is understood to mean government and institutional policies directed toward equalizing opportunities-particularly in the workplace and higher education-for minority groups and women." She also asserts that "the 'quota' and 'timetable' systems associated with affirmative action have become notorious for discriminating against White males, and have been seen to entrench negative attitudes towards the employability and educability of ethnic minorities and women" (Castle, 1994, p. 266).

Castle (1994, p. 267) suggested that "two concepts of affirmative action are evolving in South Africa which are distinct from Western concepts and practices." The "human resource development concept" treats affirmative action as a management initiative, giving preference to Black employees over Whites in recruitment, training, and other support. The rationale supporting this approach has three dimensions: responsiveness to a skills shortage, contribution to maintenance of social stability, and facilitation of the integration of Black workers into organizations (Castle, 1994). The "affirmative action as structural change concepts" treats affirmative action as a mechanism to achieve "large-scale redistribution of resources and opportunities to historically denied or dispossessed people" (Castle, 1994, p. 273). Under this conception, "state power will be used to transform inequitable, unjust social, economic, and educational systems" (Castle, 1994, pp. 278-279). Castle (1994) predicted that a compromise between the two conceptions will necessarily emerge, probably dominated, at least in the short run, by the human resource development concept.

There are important dimensions of the debate about affirmative action in the United States that Castle overlooked, the discussion of which may be useful in mediating conflicting conceptions of affirmative action in South Africa. First, Castle fell into the trap of accepting the claims of affirmative action opponents regarding discriminatory treatment of White males and the stigmatization of beneficiaries of affirmative action at face value. Counter-evidence of the presumable discriminatory impact of policies is provided by the fact that of the more than 50,000 cases currently in the backlog of the Equal Employment Opportunity Commission, only a handful constitute so-called "reverse discrimination" complaints. The claims regarding the stigmatization of affirmative action beneficiaries is disingenuous because minorities have consistently been portrayed as "inferior" well before the advent of the Civil Rights movement. Biological theories of racial difference have, in fact, been resurrected in the debate to "explain" continuing Black-White disparities in various social indicators (Herrnstein & Murray, 1994). Note that this strategy involves invocation of the penultimate assertion regarding the lack of qualification of affirmative action beneficiaries--they are genetically incapable of ever attaining qualifications!

One of the critical differences in the debate about affirmative action in the United States and South Africa is that opponents in South Africa cannot claim that a set of policies has been in effect that has eliminated differential treatment and that guarantees equal opportunity. This is, in fact, the line of argument used by many opponents of affirmative action in the United States. Stripped to its essentials, the argument is that systematic discrimination no longer constitutes a significant barrier to equal economic opportunity as a result of the effects of enforcement of Title VII. However, this assertion flies in the face of overwhelming evidence that radical discrimination remains a significant problem (for example see various analyses in Stewart, 1997) and that the enforcement of Title VII was not nearly as aggressive as opponents of affirmative action project and thus had only a very limited impact on inequality (see for example, Anderson, 1996; Donohue & Heckman, 1991; Leonard, 1996).

While it is certainly true that in the debate about affirmative action in the United States a case for affirmative action has not been made akin to the South African "affirmative action as structural change" conception, this should be seen principally as a reflection shortsightedness of U.S. commentators. In particular, the debate is constrained by conceptual and linguistic conventions that limit the ability to examine affirmative action in the context of broader issues such as social commitment to equitable distribution of social benefits of higher education.

There is clearly a need for a model that describes the characteristics of a "transformed" institution. Figure 7.1 adapted from Stewart (1991) provides a schematic representation that can facilitate understanding of the transformation process. The figure focuses on various approaches institutions can use in managing diversity: a monocultural approach, a non-discrimination approach, or a multicultural approach. The categories are, of course, not mutually exclusive as institutions may, for example, take a multicultural approach in some areas and a non-discrimination approach in others.

The previous discussion of the evolution of higher education in South Africa suggests that the transformation process begins from an environment characterized by monocultural institutions of three types: Afrikaans-medium HWUs, English-medium HWUs, and HBUs. The transformation process envisioned in the Education White Paper explicitly proposes a multicultural approach to mission relationships (Indicator 1), constituencies served (Indicator 3), and conflict resolution (Indicator 5). In most areas, however, HWUs are operating somewhere between monocultural approaches and nondiscrimination approaches. To illustrate, the resolution of the various clashes discussed previously between students at some HWUs does not suggest that a multicultural approach has been integrated into the institutional culture.

One of the key areas highlighted in Figure 7.1 is staffing patterns (Indicator 4). A diverse and culturally competent staff is an essential ingredient for successful transformation. Unfortunately, this is one of the most difficult issues that HWUs must address. Pretorius (1999, October 17) reports that African academics remain significantly underrepresented, constituting only between 7% and 12% of university faculty. These numbers have increased only slightly in recent years. Additional efforts to diversity the faculty and staffing in general now have legal underpinnings via the recently passed Employment Equity Act.

Another key area reflected in Figure 7.1 is the extent to which the curriculum incorporates information relevant to the experiences of all major population groups (Indicator 10). One implication of the Education White Paper is that some form of multicultural education would be introduced into the curricula of transforming institutions. However, the concept of multicultural education is even more contentious in South Africa than in the United States.

Moore (1994) provides a useful discussion of the range of perspectives regarding multicultural education in South Africa. He indicates that "some educationalists believe that policy needs to accept that culture is a powerful force in society, shaping people's sense of who they are" and "cultural difference needs to be respected and used . . . to construct a new cultural base for national unity" (Moore, 1994, p. 261). However, there are also educators who believe that "in the South African context the concept of culture is inextricably bound up with apartheid racism" and that "students need to be able to deconstruct the

Institutionalization Indicator	Monocultural	Nondiscrimination	Multicultural
1. Relationship to other missions	No recognition of other than traditional missions; denial of need to augment mission	Perceived tradeoff between "excellence" and diversity initiatives; diversity initiatives are optional	Diversity and excellence are complements; diversity initiatives required of all units
2. Planning process	One; denial of need to reflect presence of sub-populations in plans	Top-down; temporary structures (e.g. committees)	Multimodal; clearly delineated responsibilities for plan review
3. Constituencies served	Serving special constituencies perceived as "reverse" discrimination	Limited; remediation thrust; attempts to force different interest groups to merge into artificial umbrella groups	Old and new constituencies served equitably via an empowerment thrust
4. Staffing	Existing staff assumed to have the capabilities to serve all subpopulations	Representation of target groups in staff positions serving special populations only; one-shot human relations workshops for staff in selected areas	Involvement of members of various target groups throughout organization; coherent staff development program
5. Conflict resolution	Crisis determined	Reactive; process oriented	Proactive; outcome oriented
6. Evaluation procedures	None	Ad hoc	Systematic
7. Budgetary support	Ad hoc, no special funds available	Exclusive use of special funds; limited commitment of resources obtained through normal budget channels	Planned funding strategy involving combination of reallocation; special funds and external resources
8. Programming	Monocultural	Special events/public figure lectures, orientation, (e.g., Black History month, MLK celebration)	Comprehensive innovations reflecting a synergism of curricular and cocurricular activities
9. Management	None	Diffuse; lack of centralized authority	Central coordination; clearly defined communication and decision-making channels
10. Curriculum	Monocultural	Additive	Integrated, Transformational

Fig. 7.1. Characteristics of institutions in various stages of transformation.[1]

Source: [1]Adapted from Stewart, J. (1991). "Planning for Cultural Diversity: A Case Study," in H. Cheatham and Associates, *Cultural Pluralism on Campus*. Alexandria, VA: American College Personnel Association.

concept of culture . . . if they are going to find new ways of understanding who they are and they can become" (Moore, 1994, p. 261).

Some of the informants interviewed by Moore (1994) appropriately observe that many of the basic ideas informing South African conceptions of multicultural education have been imported from the United States. These ideas cannot be applied directly to South Africa, in part because of differing context. In the United States and some European countries, multicultural education has been advanced to protect minority groups against a process of cultural suppression and/or cultural assimilation. In contrast, in South Africa the demand arises from what is defined as a majority group out of a struggle against *de jure* segregation and apartheid education (Moore, 1994). At the same time, the oppressive nature of apartheid education and its grounding in an ideology that emphasized cultural difference is problematic, particularly in the context of the ANC's goal of creating a nonracial, united, democratic society. From this vantage point, "multicultural education sounds suspiciously like making difference a more fundamental principle than national unity" (Moore, 1994,p. 241). However, as noted by one interviewee, it is not possible to move toward a nonracist educational agenda without addressing the legacy of apartheid education, that is, the "politics of apartheid and the history of apartheid education . . . ensure that multicultural education has a core place in educational discourse rather than antiracist education per se" (Moore, 1994, p. 242). Moreover, it is not clear that multicultural education cannot overcome its link to the apartheid past and contribute to the transformation process it is conceived as "exploring the necessary and complex interplay between unity and diversity, between a national culture and cultural pluralism" (Moore, 1994, p. 257).

The wide range of opinions regarding the role of multicultural education in South Africa is symptomatic of the need for further dialogue, with the goal of generating greater consensus about viable models that can contribute to the achievement of positive outcomes from the reorganization of higher education. As one interviewee observed, "We need, in South Africa, a curriculum which values diversity, tolerance, and appreciation of cultural differences and which also helps students manage cultural differences without resorting to violence or self-protecting isolationism" (Moore, 1994, p. 254). And, as another proffered, explorations of the utility of alternative proposals should focus on the question "How will this actually help people in their struggle for justice?" (Moore, 1994, p. 252).

Curriculum transformation issues are further complicated by official language policy. The South African constitution confers the right of persons to receive education in the official language or languages of their choice in public educational institutions, where it is reasonably practicable to do so. The newly created Council of Higher Education has been charged with developing a language policy framework. This framework will address various issues, including the language or languages of learning and communication (medium or mediums of instruction) in higher education institutions; the role of higher education in language development and promotion and in elevating the status and advancing the use of indigenous languages; the role of higher education in preparing sufficient language teachers, interpreters, translators, and other language practitioners; and the role of higher education in preparing South Africans for effective linguistic communication with the rest of Africa and the world in the fields of culture, diplomacy, science, and business (Department of Education, 1997).

In summary, HWUs will need to devote significant resources to achieve the transformation objectives set forth in the Education White Paper. Efforts to meet the expectations of students from traditionally underrepresented groups will require modification of both the existing institutional culture and administrative practices. Overall, the transformation process can be facilitated if a systematic approach is employed, based on a model of a transformed institution, such as the one presented in Figure 7.1. One of the major problem areas facing HWUs is the lack of diversity in staffing.

The challenges facing HBUs have very different dimensions, as described in the following section.

ENHANCING HBUS IN SOUTH AFRICA: PARALLELS TO U.S. HBUS

HBUs in South Africa and the United States face similar problems. In both environments enrollments have declined as a result of shifts toward HWUs. Both sets of institutions face ambiguous public policies that reflect, in part, their continued treatment as vestiges of systems of racial segregation. As a consequence, the specter of closing some HBUs has been raised in both countries (see Robbins, 1998, November; Stewart, forthcoming). At the same time, there are important differences in the situations facing HBUs in the two societies. The most critical is the difference in the scale of instruction compared to overall university enrollments. To illustrate, as indicated in Table 7.7, HBUs in the United States enroll a significantly smaller proportion of Black students than is the case for HBUs in South Africa. The proportion of bachelor's degrees granted to African American students fell from 35.4% in 1976-77 to 28.0% in 1993-94. Similar to the enrollment patterns in South Africa, although shifts occurred, HBUs continue to account for a significant proportion of total Black enrollments in 4-year colleges and universities (over 25%). Also similar to the circumstances in South Africa, a very small proportion of White students attend HBUs.

TABLE 7.7

Enrollment in HBUs as a Percentage of Total Enrollment in 4-Year
Colleges and Universities by Race/Ethnicity: Selected Years 1976-1994

White students	.3	.3	.4	.4	.5	.5
Black students	29.8	28.6	27.8	27.9	27.4	26.2
All minority students	19.5	17.5	15.5	14.5	13.6	12.3
Total	2.9	2.9	2.8	2.7	2.8	3.0

Note. U.S. Department of Education, National Center for Education Statistics (1996).
Historically Black Colleges and Universities, 1976-1994, NCES 96-902, by C. Hoffman,
T. Snyder, & B. Sonnenberg. Washington, DC: National Center for Education Statistics,
Table 5-Fall enrollment in all institutions and historically Black colleges and universities,
by type and control of institution and race/ethnicity of student: 1976 to 1994, p. 23.

Resource reallocations have favored HWUs as in South Africa. The
U.S. Department of Education, National Center for Education Statistics (1996,
p. 15) indicates that "increases in expenditure[s] for students at both public and
private HBCUs lagged behind increases in expenditures for student at all public
and private institutions between 1976-77 and 1993-94." Educational and general
expenditures per student at HBUs rose 4% (after adjustment for inflation),
compared to 11% for all public colleges over the entire 1976-77 to 1993-94
period (U.S. Department of Education, National Center for Education Statistics,
1996). These patterns have been manifested despite federal initiatives unrelated
to desegregation enforcement.

Proponents of HBUs have argued vociferously that they continue to play
an important role in the higher education community (see for example,
Committee L on the Historically Black Institutions and the Status of Minorities
in the Profession, 1995). Several types of evidence have been presented to argue
the case, including information about: (1) the achievements of HBU graduates,
(2) successes of HBUs despite limitations in funding and resources, (3) recent
gains in enrollments, (4) special efforts in the sciences, and (5) research and
outreach activities in both domestic and international settings. One of the most

significant observations is that although HBUs serve a disproportionatley disadvantaged clientele while maintaining low tuition, they have higher retention and graduation rates of Black students than HWUs (Committee L on the Historically Black Institutions and the Status of Minorities in the Profession, 1995).

Various factors are identified as contributing to these successes, including: (1) expertise in providing remedial preparation for students who start out with weak high school backgrounds, (2) provision of a supportive social, cultural, and racial environment, (3) greater involvement of students in campus activities, and (4) a high level of interaction with faculty, particularly Black role models. Success in producing graduates trained in the sciences and engineering is given special emphasis, as is the involvement of 52 HBUs in community outreach and development efforts (Committee L on the Historically Black Institutions and the Status of Minorities in the Profession, 1995). Many of these same arguments have been voiced by supporters of HBUs in South Africa.

Unlike the situation in South Africa, the U.S. government has for some time recognized the need to preserve and strengthen HBUs and has provided some legislative and administrative support to achieve this objective. Examples include: (1) the Strengthening Historically Black Colleges and Universities Program and the Strengthening Historically Black Graduate Institutions Program (authorized in Title III of the Higher Education Act of 1965), (2) Executive Order 12232 (1980), which established a federal program to overcome the effects of discriminatory treatment and to strengthen the capacity of HBUs to provide quality education, (3) Executive Order 12320, signed by President Ronald Reagan; (4) Executive Order 12677, signed by President Gerald Ford (1989), mandating that federal agencies take positive steps to increase participation of HBUs, and (5) Executive Order 12876, issued by President William Clinton (1993), which, in part, directed federal agencies to increase contract and grant awards to HBUs as well as cooperative agreements.

Recent initiatives include several grants by the Department of Housing and Urban Development to help revitalize communities around HBU campuses. A few HBUs have also received grants from the Department of Energy to increase the numbers of minority science students and retrain workers for jobs in high-tech fields. The Department of Energy has also funded a consortium, made up of 12 HBUs and 6 institutions with substantial enrollments of other minorities, to perform environmental research and technological development. It is also charged with developing degree programs in these fields and increasing environmental literacy by working with community groups (Committee L on the Historically Black Institutions and the Status of Minorities in the Profession, 1995).

Several partnerships similar to the type envisioned for HBUs in South Africa have been initiated. A number of HBUs have also formed partnerships with urban elementary and secondary schools. Some HBUs are expanding curricula to pursue a distinctive urban educational and outreach mission. Approximately 50 HBUs are taking part in international projects, many working under a National Association for Equal Opportunity in Higher Education-U.S. Agency for International Development Cooperative Agreement (Committee L on the Historically Black Institutions and the Status of Minorities in the Profession, 1995).

At the same time, although significant support has been provided by federal agencies to strengthen HBUs, in many ways it reinforces existing patterns of segregation. In particular, federal support for enhancements is provided in a manner that isolates HBUs from the larger arena of government-institutional partnerships. In addition, there is a clear disconnection between the direction of federal policy and patterns of state support for HBUs. State initiatives are largely defensive or reactive, undertaken as responses to desegregation lawsuits, rather than as proactive efforts to involve HBUs in the broader network of development initiatives.

One of the differences between the policy environments in the United States and South Africa is the overarching role of the judicial system in defining the range of feasible developmental opportunities for U.S. HBUs through decisions in desegregation cases. The most recent judicial ruling defining the parameters of higher education desegregation is *United States v. Fordice* (1992). In fact, the developmental thrust reflected in governmental policy discussed previously is partially neutralized by the directives emerging from judicial decisions and the interpretation and implementation of those directives by administrative agencies.

There are several assumptions embedded in traditional desegregation policy that inherently limit the capacity of desegregation planners to conceive of HBUs as other than a legacy of separate-but-equal educational policies. Desegregation policy focuses almost entirely on the eradication of "racially identifiable" institutions. One dimension of this process involves scrutiny of the extent to which program duplication exists between HBUs and HWUs. One assumption associated with this scrutiny is that the organization and operation of HWUs constitute the paradigm for "educational soundness." As a consequence, programs located at HBUs that are deemed to be duplicative are in jeopardy of being eliminated. Consequently, for HBUs to have a legitimate role in the educational policy arena, they must look more like HWUs, both in a demographic sense and in an operational context. A second assumption is that programs are totally interchangeable among locations. This approach ignores the possibility that there are some unique characteristics of a given environment that generate distinguishing educational outcomes, and have the potential to erode educational diversity in ways that reduce the capabilities of public systems to respond to new challenges. In contrast, interventions at HWUs are of insufficient magnitude to significantly affect these institutions' cultures or standard operating procedures. Program duplication has been used as a principal indicator of "educational soundness" in desegregation oversight and it was found to be pervasive among Mississippi's public institutions of higher education. Enhancements at HBUs can only pass judicial muster if they are deemed to promote desegregation, that is, increased enrollment of White students at HBUs.

Although the potential effects of desegregation implementation can have decidedly adverse effects on HBUs, it provides the only framework, whereby a planned approach to defining and enhancing the role of HBUs can occur in the United States. There is no process in the United States equivalent to the wholesale reorganization of higher education in South Africa that is underway. Stewart (forthcoming) has proposed a framework for using desegregation policy to enhance HBUs and strengthen their overall contribution to overall societal development. Stewart argues that policymakers should undertake comprehensive assessments of the contributions of HBUs to the overall system of higher education and institute specific policies to enhance the role of HBUs. He suggests that the following criteria be employed in making such assessments:

1.   Uniqueness/overlap of institutional missions.
2.   Quantity/quality of human capital outputs (number of graduates, placement rates, earnings profiles).
3.   Efficiency of resource use/absorptive capacity vis-a-vis new resources (educational production function, i.e.g, enrollments, faculty resources, budgets).
4.   Current versus potential institutional contributions to local, regional, and state economic development initiatives (quantity, quality, and distribution of benefits flowing from research and outreach activities).
5.   Institution-specific characteristics that contribute uniquely to higher education outcomes (e.g., service to disadvantaged populations and/or communities, higher retention rates, empowering institutional climate).

A similar approach can be used to address the difficult issues facing HBUs in South Africa. A useful starting point for this exploration is the insightful set of proposals offered by Christiansen and Slammert (1999). These authors propose that "HBUs could develop a research, teaching, and service profile centered around the development of a new transdisciplinary discourse" that would be "significantly different from the one at institutions with a more traditional orientation" (Christiansen & Slammert, 1999, p. 12). The authors argue that developing such a position would build on existing strengths at HBUs because there are already such projects underway. As they envision the unfolding of this model, the entire curriculum of HBUs would be drastically altered. One result would be that graduates from HBUs would not compete in traditional fields with graduates of HWUs. The capacity of HBUs to deliver such an innovative curriculum to students is enhanced, according to Christiansen and Slammert (1999, p. 18), by the fact that "HBUs have been forced to make innovations in teaching through integration of support structures into the mainstream curricula made possible through extensive academic development." The curriculum would be organized around projects that would develop experiential problem-solving skills. The natural environment, global perspectives (South African perspectives), and gender, race, and class are the content areas for the projects proposed by Christiansen and Slammert (1999). The authors argue that "clear links to experiences or applications, especially in businesses or in the local community, can be used to make the research as well as the teaching-learning process more relevant, more involving, and more in resemblance with work in the job situation, including reflecting the inquiry element of academic work in general" (Christiansen & Slammert, 1999, p. 22). Christiansen and Slammert (1999, p. 22) offer the following vision to illustrate the potential benefits of their proposed reorientation of HBUs: "It is much more exciting to study authentic articles from recent issues of leading journals instead of textbooks, and perhaps even more exciting to try to combine numerous perspectives in solving even the smallest problem in a Black business or underdeveloped community!"

Clearly, the proposed reorientation of the research, teaching, and service activities of HBUs addresses many of the issues articulated in the Education White Paper. In particular, it presents a unique mission for HBUs that would reduce competition with HWUs for scarce resources. The proposed research and outreach orientation focuses directly on contributions to the overall transformation and development process. The innovative character of the proposal has the potential to facilitate cultivation of both community and business partnerships and the successful solicitation of funding from external donors.

There are elements of the experience of HBUs in the United States that can be incorporated to enhance the proposed model. As an example, such an orientation should be attractive to a significant number of non-Black students and could serve as means to both increase and diversity enrollments at HBUs. Such an outcome would seem to be consistent with the long-term vision of the ANC, although, as demonstrated previously, there is currently no expectation that this type of "integration" of HBUs would occur. One benefit would be that White students would be forced to function in a setting where they would have to adapt to the majority culture. Such an experience would prepare them to function as change agents in White communities, promoting the process of racial reconciliation.

Although the proposal embodies a transdisciplinary model, that is, one that transcends existing disciplinary boundaries, its vision is limited by the focus on individual HBUs rather than considering transinstitutional opportunities. In particular, as noted previously, some HBUs in the United States have developed consortia as a means of combining resources and expertise to take advantage of both economies of scale and to share specialized expertise with sister institutions. Such an approach would seem to have the potential to facilitate implementation of the proposed model. Specifically, informal networks of like-minded change agents in several institutions could begin to meet and develop plans to undertake pilot projects designed to explore the feasibility of a larger scale effort. Such an approach would avoid both bureaucratic barriers and existing fiscal and capacity limitations at individual HBUs.

Such a consortia approach can also be useful in mobilizing HBUs to respond effectively to other issues highlighted in the Education White Paper. As an example, a consortia of HBUs could play a vital role in developing the proposed language policy. It is highly unlikely that any other approach can address this complex issue.

Collaboration between South Africa and U.S. HBUs can also contribute to the realization of the international educational objectives contained in the Education White Paper. U.S. HBUs have the experience of being the beneficiaries of the dominant role that the United States plays in the contemporary global order, while simultaneously experiencing continuing discrimination and marginalization. HBUs in South Africa will need to develop the expertise to walk such a tightrope as South Africa becomes even more integrated into the global economy.

Finally, the proposal presents a vision of a form of multicultural education that would seem to provide a potential consensus between the competing perspectives discussed previously. To the extent that this model can be developed formally, it can be shared with HWUs, which, as discussed previously, will bear the brunt of anticipated changes in the demography of higher education enrollments.

LESSONS FOR THE FUTURE

HBUs in South Africa and the United States face significant challenges as the 21st century begins. The ability of HBUs in both countries to survive in the next century can be enhanced through collaboration. HBUs in the United States need to strengthen their commitment to outreach and global education and develop a unique vision that reduces competition with HWUs. HBUs in South Africa must develop improved administrative capabilities and the skills necessary to cultivate mutually advantageous partnerships. Students in both countries will be confronted with difficult questions of identity in the next century. The creation of opportunities for dialogue between student bodies can help students in both societies to define their place in an ever more complex world.

The foundations for greater collaboration between HBUs in the United States and South Africa has been formalized through the award of the USAID Tertiary Linkages Project to the United Negro College Fund in the United States. In many respects, the future vitality of HBUs in both countries may depend on a visionary and focused approach to managing this project. To paraphrase the words of DuBois (1903), it may be the key to ensuring that the problem of the 21st century will not, like the 20th century, be the problem of the color line.

REFERENCES

Bunting, I., & Bunting, L. (1999). National enrollment trends in public higher education, overview of projected student enrollments between 1997 and 2001. *Higher Education Planning Statistics. Report 2 Planning Statistics for the Western Cape.* Pretoria: Department of Education (September).

Castle, J. (1994). Competing conceptions of affirmative action in South Africa. *Perspectives in Education, 15*(2), 265-284.

Chisholm, L., & Vally, S. (1996). Finance and governance in recent conflicts over policy. *Quarterly Review of Education and Training in South Africa, 3*(4). Retrieved May 28, 1999, from www.sn.apc.org/sangonet/education/epu/epu34-2.htm.

Christiansen, I., & Slammert, L. (1999). *Historically Black universities at the crossroads.* Belleville, South Africa: Centre for Educational Development in University Science, University of the Western Cape.

Committee L on the Historically Black Institutions and the Status of Minorities in the Profession. (1995, January/February). The historically black colleges and universities: A future in the balance. *Academe, 80*(1).

Department of Education. (1997). *A programme for the transformation of higher education* (Education White Paper). Pretoria, South Africa: Department of Education. Retrieved April 13, 1999 from www.polity.org.za/govdocs/white_papers/highed.html.

Dreijmanis, J. (1988). *The role of the South African government in tertiary education.* Johannesburg, South Africa: South African Institute of Race Relations.

DuBois, W. E. B. (1903). *The souls of Black folk.* Bedford Series Edition. Boston: Bedford Books (1997).

Herrnstein, R., & Murray, C. (1994). *The bell curve, intelligence and class structure in American life.* New York: The free Press.

Ministry of Education. (1999, June). *Status report for the minister of education.* Pretoria, South Africa. Retrieved October 1, 1999, from www.polity.org.za/govdocs/reports/education/statusreport.html.

Moore, B. (1994). Multicultural education in South Africa: Some theoretical and political issues. *Perspectives in Education, 15*(2), 237-263.

Motala, S. (1996). Contested visions: Between policy and practice. *Quarterly Review of Education and Training in South Africa, 4*(1). Retrieved May 28, 1999, from www.sn.spc.org/sangonet/education/epu/epu41-4.htm.

Motala, S. (1997). New policies and the challenges of budgetary constraints--Introduction. *Quarterly Review of Education and Training in South Africa, 5*(1). Retrieved May 28, 1999, from www.sn.apc.orgsangonet/education/epu/epu51-2.htm.

Pretorius, C. (1999). Dramatic rise in number of Black students. *Sunday Times* (October 17). http://www.suntimes.co.zu/1999/10/17/news/news18.htm, visited November 9, 1999.

Ridge, S. (1996a). *Historical perspective on tertiary education in South Africa*. Belleville, South Africa: University of the Western Cape. Retrieved May 15, 1999, from www.uwc.ac.za/.

Ridge, S. (1996b). *Funding of tertiary education*. Bellville, South Africa: University of the Western Cape. Retrieved May 15, 1999, from www.uwc.ac.za/.

Robbins, D. (1999). Tertiary education: The size and shape of things to come. *Mail and Guardian* (November 24). Retrieved December 15, 1999, from www.mg.co.za/mg/news/99nov2/24nov.education-html.

Stewart, J. (1991). Planning for cultural diversity: A case study. In H. Cheatham and Associates, *Cultural pluralism on campus* (pp. 161--181). Alexandria, VA: American College Personnel Association.

Stewart, J. (Ed.). (1997). *African-Americans and post-industrial labor markets*. New Brunswick, NJ: Transaction Consortium.

Stewart, J. (forthcoming). The effects of public policy conflicts and resource allocation decisions on higher education desegregation outcomes in Pennsylvania. In B. Lindsay & M. Justiz (Eds.), *The quest for equity in higher education: Towards new paradigms in an evolving affirmative action era*. Binghamton: State University of New York Press.

Tertiary education bodies look at merger benefits. (1999, August 10). *Business Day*. Retrieved August 12, 1999, from www.africanews.orga/southafrica/stories/19990810_feat6.html.

United States v. Fordice, 505 U.S. 717, 112 S.Ct. 2727 (1992).

U.S. Department of Education, National Center for Education Statistics. (1996). *Historically Black colleges and universities, 1976-1994 (NCES 96-902)*. In C. Hoffman, T. Snyder, & B. Sonnenberg, Washington, DC: National Center for Education Statistics. Monograph.

Vergnam, L. (1999, October 25). Dramatic drop in student numbers hits universities. *Cape Argus*, p. 5.

8

Education and Identity Within a Psychological and Sociocultural Context

Saundra Tomlinson-Clarke
Rutgers, The State University of New Jersey

Approaching the 21st century gives pause to reflect on the many social and economic changes as well as technological advances that have influenced American lives. Globalization and technology have reduced the distance between people and cultures, affecting lifestyles both locally and internationally, as we now have access to immediate information and knowledge. These events have changed the context of education and the nature of learning. From an international perspective, " . . . nations and people are confronting increased cultural diversity in their economic, political, and social spheres. Many changes occurring within the borders of most nations force people of different backgrounds to interact in ways never imagined a generation ago" (Cushner, 1998, p. 1). Not only are Americans finding commonalities with people living in other regions of our nation, but mutual interests exist between people living in different parts of the world. As we learn to accept, respect, and appreciate cultural differences in the world, common goals among people include understanding the role of culture and socialization in the development of identity and understanding how identity affects our relationships with others.

Within the United States, the impact of changing racial-ethnic demographics on national and ethnic identity has been a focus of attention. An increased culturally diverse population has changed perceptions of the United States as a homogeneous, stable nation, created on a common identity of one people. Rather, the United States has become dynamic and increasingly heterogeneous, representing diversity in customs, languages, lifestyles, values, and worldviews. The increased diversity among America's people has resulted in a lack of agreement on a model of behavior that is representative of Americans and American culture. No longer are people willing to accept **one** model or an ideal that is representative of American culture or lifestyles. Wolfe

(1991a) refers to this phenomenon as the decentering of American society. Decentering of a society may not be unique to the United States, as many nations struggle with issues of cultural and linguistic diversity among their people. However, the sociocultural and sociohistorical roots that have influenced the development of American society are unique to this country.

The changing demographics of the United States and the globalization of world cultures also have influenced U.S. educational systems. Social issues in society and in the world are mirrored in our schools. Therefore, to effectively understand the influences of these societal changes on schooling and the identity development of children, it becomes important to examine education within the sociocultural context in which we live. In effectively conceptualizing the social and psychological effects of societal change on students, teachers, families, and communities, interdisciplinary approaches have been advocated.

This chapter briefly examines social and demographic changes in the United States that have had a major impact on society. An examination of struggles that the United States has experienced in its attempts to resolve discrepancies in access and equity among people is useful in understanding contemporary educational issues. Brown v. Board of Education, 1954 attempted to resolve educational equity by ending racial segregation in schools. Presently, multicultural education is promoted as a way to address differential educational outcomes for minority and majority students. Drawing on sociological and psychological perspectives, I discuss education within the sociocultural context of the 20th and 21st centuries, highlighting social issues currently affecting our educational systems. Also, I identify social and psychological factors associated with academic achievement, educational attainment, and identity development among elementary and secondary students. Finally, I argue that current conceptualizations of multicultural education, with a focus on the culturally different student, are ineffective in addressing social and educational inequities.

AMERICAN CULTURE AND IDENTITY

A common purpose formed the basis of a core American culture and identity. A notion of centrality was key in developing "shared beliefs, symbols, and interpretations" (Banks, 1997a, p. 8) by which the national culture was defined. The national culture reflected the "central and dominant culture of society" (Campbell, 1996, p. 26), derived from mainstream value orientations, ideologies, and worldview. The U.S. political institutions, influenced by the British (Banks, 1997a), reinforced the core values of the nation. For many, these beliefs in a U.S. common culture served to influence both mental and literal images of the American ideal. These images served to shape beliefs, attitudes, and behaviors of U.S. citizens as well as their relationships with people in other parts of the world.

These cultural assumptions based on the beliefs, customs, and traditions that defined the American culture were influenced by five interacting components. Stewart (1982) identified these components as follows:

1. The way in which people approached activities, the importance of goals, the nature of decision making and problem solving.
2. Social relations, definitions of roles, and status relations among people differing in role and status.
3. Motivation and achievement orientation.
4. Predominant worldview, and perceptions of the world.
5. Self-perceptions, self-definition, self-identity, and perceptions of place in the world.

Based on these five interacting components, differential judgments were made and value was attributed to people, and their social roles and their activities in society, defining their relationships with others. American culture continues to be influenced by these cultural beliefs, and is characterized by: (a) a future orientation, (2) mastery over the environment, (3) emphasis on the individual, (4) doing as the preferred mode of activity, and (5) good-bad dimensions of humanity (Kluckhohn & Strodtbeck, 1961; Sue & Sue, 1990). As an individualistic or self-focused culture (Helms & Cook, 1999), American culture is defined as synonymous with traditional Western thinking and is associated with the White middle class.

Diversity in the United States, however, is not a new experience. Immigrants arriving voluntarily and involuntarily to an inhabited land marked the beginnings of America's heterogeneity and the ongoing conflicts resulting from cultural differences. Although diverse groups of people were instrumental in building the United States, these racial, ethnic, and cultural differences were not appreciated or accepted by the majority (Gollnick & Chinn, 1998). The different circumstances that brought people to this country and the different status levels associated with their backgrounds greatly affected the ability and willingness of different groups to integrate into U.S. society.

For many, the United States was perceived as a country with opportunity and prosperity. Immigrants arriving voluntarily often perceived this country as the Promised Land, filled with opportunities for a free and equitable life. Many immigrant groups experienced acceptance and upward mobility within society. Some immigrants relinquished their ethnic and cultural identities, assimilating into the mainstream society. In contrast, however, people arriving to this country by means of forced and coerced migration were met with rejection and a system of forced separation. Salient differences prevented visible racial-ethnic group members from assimilating into society. Eighteenth-century beliefs that all people were not born of equal rights was the basis for creating a system of inequitable practices, maintained by laws (Banks, 1997a). The distinctions made between racial groups residing within the United States created a country separated by differences. Thus, the fundamental ideals that were basic to the development of the nation were incongruent with the discriminatory beliefs and inequitable societal practices that were enforced by laws. All people were not treated with equal rights.

As people opposed the way in which society constructed human rights and assigned roles according to race, ethnicity, gender, and social class, many challenged the system. Early struggles for civil rights began with men and women involved in the antislavery movements of the 19th century. Many of the challenges to national identity, however, were rooted in the civil rights and human rights movements of the 1950s and 1960s, respectively. Furthermore, the U.S. involvement in the Vietnam War changed people's perceptions of the country, causing many to question U.S. policies and practices. Decades later, with the end of the Cold War, international relationships have been changed dramatically. These sociohistorical perspectives provide a context for exploring contemporary issues in a dynamic society, and the impact of these changes on education and educational policies and practices.

EDUCATIONAL EQUITY

A historical look at the social issues affecting U.S. educational systems exemplifies the country's struggles with racial differences and inequality. *Plessy v. Ferguson* (1896) legally enforced a segregated society by asserting that distinctions made by race were not in violation of the 13th and 14th Amendments, if separate facilities are substantially equal. "Separate but equal" disguised and supported an agenda of discrimination and segregation, preventing equitable treatment under the law for all citizens of this country. This, one of the best known segregation cases, has had pervasive effects on the economic, social, and educational systems in the United States. Fifty-four years after *Plessy v. Ferguson*, acknowledging that students in a segregated system did not have equal opportunities and educational access, "separate but equal" was considered to be unconstitutional (*Brown v. Board of Education*, 1954).

Twenty-five years after *Brown v. Board of Education*, as we begin the new millennium, we find our society increasing in racial and ethnic diversity, and we face similar, yet more complex educational challenges with regard to differences. The goals of desegregating society and integrating our communities and educational systems have not been realized. Today, the educational experiences of children are likely to differ as a function of income, social class, and family background characteristics, "[A] nation often defined by its growing cultural diversity remains relatively homogeneous, with schools tending to reflect the ethnicity and social class of the neighborhoods in which they are located" (Hodges Persell, 1991, p. 285). Instead of an integrated society, we are observing a system of resegregation in communities and schools across the country (Gollnick & Chinn, 1998). This lack of uniformity in education has resulted in a system in which racial-ethnic minority students are denied equality and access to knowledge and opportunities associated with life success (Beckman, 1995). This is particularly evident in the inner-city communities and school where racial-ethnic minority students do not have access to the same educational opportunities as White students (Drew, 1995). As Drew noted, this is of particular concern in the areas of mathematics and science, where racial-ethnic minority groups and women have been traditionally underrepresented. To this end, the increasing cultural diversity of society will continue to have a major impact on our educational systems and the challenges of providing equitable access and opportunities to our nation's youth.

DEMOGRAPHIC PROFILE OF THE UNITED STATES

The United States, a nation built on a notion of centrality (Wolfe, 1991a), or common goals and purpose, has experienced dramatic changes in culture and identity over the past 50 years. As predicted, the American population has become increasingly culturally heterogeneous and complex (Blake, 1996).

Presently the U.S. population is estimated to be more than 273 million (U.S. Bureau of the Census, 1999). Of the U.S. population, 71.7% are identified as White, 12.2% are identified as Black, 11.6% are identified as Hispanic (of any race), 3.8% are identified as Asian and Pacific Islanders, and 0.7% are identified as Native American, Eskimo, and Aleut. The 1999 census data represent slight changes in the 1996 and 1990 census data, showing increases among American racial-ethnic minority groups. In the year 2000, one-third of the nation will be a member of a racial-ethnic minority group, with Blacks comprising the largest racial-ethnic minority group. It is reported that Blacks, Hispanics, Asians, Pacific Islanders, Native Americans, Eskimos, and Aleuts will comprise 40% of the U.S. population by the year 2020, and 50% of the U.S. population by the year 2050 (Gollnick & Chinn, 1998; U.S. Bureau of the Census, 1996). Presently Hispanics are the youngest ethnic group, with median age of 26.5 years (U.S. Bureau of the Census, 1999). However, by the year 2015, population projections predict that Hispanics will become the largest as well as youngest ethnic group, representing 15.1% of the total U.S. population. As the population of American racial-ethnic minority groups continues to increase in the 21st century, the population of non-Hispanic Whites will decline.

The ethnic population growth in the United States primarily has been a result of immigration. A dynamic world with "changing immigration laws, policies, unstable economic and political conditions, interethnic marriages, and wars" (Aponte & Crouch, 2000, p. 3) has accounted for the increased immigration to the United States. Recent immigration data spanning a 3-year period, from 1991 to 1993, indicated that the majority of immigrants to the United States were from North America (51.2%) and Asia (30%). Fewer immigrants to this country were from Europe (11.8%), South American (5.1%), or Africa (2.5%). Based on these immigration statistics, the majority of people immigrating to the United States from North America were from Mexico (34.7%), the Caribbean (9.1%), and Central America (6.1%). Asian immigrants to the United States were primarily from Vietnam (5.2%), the Philippines (5.1%), China (3.7%), and India (3.3%). These immigration patterns are reflected in the foreign-born and native-born U.S. populations, with Hispanic and Asian populations representing a higher percentage of the foreign-born U.S. population (Martin & Midgley, 1994).

Varying circumstances have brought a "new" immigrant to the United States. These immigrants may be looking for freedom and increased opportunities; however, they bring their own cultures and ethnic identities to what many perceive as a pluralistic society. Many seek to preserve their cultural heritage, customs, language, and worldview. Assimilation into the mainstream culture of the dominant society, the expectation may be one of cultural coexistence. Acculturation may also result when both new and old cultures are valued and integrated in developing a new culture. Cultural coexistence is the valuing and maintaining of one's cultures within society-the notion of pluralism. For many immigrant and native-born populations, education is viewed as the primary vehicle for their children's success.

Changes in the demographic profile of the country also have resulted in interrelationships between people. The racial-ethnic categories used by the U.S. Census Bureau have been called into question as the interracial, interethnic, multiracial, and multiethnic U.S. populations increase. Race became a factor in the census data due to the need to count slaves and free Blacks in fulfilling constitutional duties (Glazer, 1996). Although a multiracial category and questions of ancestry are now used, forced-choice categories may continue to serve political or hidden agendas. Maintaining the existing discrete racial and ethnic categories may no longer be relevant or accurately represent the demographic profile of an increasingly diverse society.

THE IMPACT OF SOCIETAL CHANGES ON AMERICAN LIFESTYLES

The fabric of American life has changed as a result of increasing cultural diversity in society. Based on sociological perspectives, Wolfe (1991b) identified 17 significant changes in American life that have had a major impact on U.S. society. These changes occurring in the 20th century, from the 1940s to the late

1990s, will continue to impact life in the 21st century. These changes are summarized and include:

1.   Changes in the demographic profile and image of the United States.
2.   Changes in the politics and values of American culture.
3.   Changes in work and working conditions.
4.   Increases in upward and downward mobility.
5.   Changes in the family, with the reality of dual-career families--causing some to link these changes to the decline of the family, still others to associate these changes with empowerment of women in society.
6.   Children as contested terrain, raising issues about healthy child development practices.
7.   Changes in housing.
8.   Changes in the U.S. economy and the relationship to the world.
9.   Uncertainty in foreign policy.
10.   Issues of race relations and harmony and equity in a country in which minority group and majority group experiences continue to differ.
11.   Effects of technological and social change.
12.   Development of subcommunities within society.
13.   Increases in information with decreases in understanding, resulting from a lack of context and history.
14.   Changes in relationships with one another.
15.   New social issues, and societal rules that may no longer be relevant or applicable.

These 20th century changes have challenged the thinking of Americans, forcing many to question beliefs about culture in a dynamic world. These issues define the social context in which we are living. In addition to affecting the individuals psychologically, these changes have influenced the social structure of families and communities. As we approach the new millennium, understanding these societal changes helps in understanding individuals, families, and communities and interrelationships within an increasingly competitive world economy.

These societal changes also have presented challenges and consequences for U.S. educational systems, affecting our schools and our learners (RAND, 1999). These challenges include:

1.   Educating an increasingly larger and more diverse
       society that is experiencing gaps in educational
       attainment among racial-ethnic groups.
2.   A need for increased education, particularly at the
       college level, to compete in the labor market.
3.   Increased demand, with declining public budgetary
       support.

DIVERSITY AND EDUCATIONAL OUTCOMES

With one in four Americans enrolled in the U.S. educational systems, U.S. schools reflect the diversity of population. In 1997, 78% of elementary and high school students were White, 17% were Black, 14% were Hispanic, and 4% were Asian (Sleeter & Grant, 1999). In addition to racial and ethnic diversity, the diversity of the student population is represented in religion and language differences, as well as differences resulting from social class, gender, and ability. To this end, the increasing racial-ethnic diversity of the population has had dramatic effects on the U.S. educational system and the schools that are educating our students.

As we begin the year 2000, population projections have estimated an increasing diversity in the school-age population, ages 6 to 17. Projections from RAND in the report *Closing the Education Gap* (1999) estimated that the school-age population among Asian Americans is expected to increase from 3% in 1990 to 6% in 2015. The school-age population among Blacks will show an increase, yet will remain constant from 15% in 1990 to 15% in 2015. Among Hispanics, with half of this population being of Mexican descent, the school-age population, which was 12% in 1990, will nearly double to 21% in 2015. In contrast to other groups, the school-age population among non-Hispanic Whites will decrease from 70% in 1990 to 58% in 2015, with a decrease by 3 million in absolute number.

Schools are closely connected to the society that they serve, and mirror the social issues in society. We can no longer assume that there is a common and agreed on culture or style of learning that should be used to educate students representing diversity in experiences. Neither can we assume that schooling results in positive outcomes for all students. These issues continue to be reflected in the differential outcomes that students experience as a result of an educational system that is not uniform and a society that is stratified by class, race/ethnicity, and gender.

Ethnicity and social class are characteristics associated with differential status in society, and are directly related to differential educational outcomes (Hodges Persell, 1991). Although social class has been used with different meanings (Helms & Cook, 1999), "social class more than either race or ethnicity tends to be a better predictor of school success, regardless of criterion descriptor" (Lutz & Iannaccone, 1995, p. 13). Socioeconomic status has been identified as the most powerful predictor of school performance, as related to academic achievement, school retention, and aspirations (Boocock, 1980). For example, children from families with higher levels of education and higher income are more likely to begin school earlier, attending nursery school or prekindergarten and attending private rather than public schools, than are children from families with lower levels of education and lower income (Martinez & Day, 1997). Martinez and Day also reported that dropping out of high school was more likely in low-income families (families earning less than $20,000) and less likely in higher income families (families earning $40,000 and over). Consistent with the disproportionate numbers of Blacks and Hispanics in the lower socioeconomic class, Blacks were reported to have higher high school dropout rates as compared to Whites; however, the dropout rates were not statistically different. Hispanics were reported to have the highest high school dropout rates.

On a positive note, educational attainment projections have predicted increases in high school and college completion rates for both the native-born and immigrant U.S. populations by the year 2015 (RAND, 1999). The RAND report also indicated that differences in high school completion rates among racial-ethnic groups in the United States are narrowing. Projections to the year 2015 have suggested increases in high school and college completion rates among native-born and immigrant Blacks. However, the educational attainment gap in higher education between racial-ethnic minorities and Whites is predicted to increase. Hispanics showed decreases in high school and college completion rates for both native-born and immigrant populations. This pattern of decreased educational attainment will be most pronounced in California, where there is a growing population of Hispanic and immigrant groups. Based on conservative rate assumptions, Ruark (1999) emphasized the magnitude of the RAND report's projections and the effect on educational attainment among racial-ethnic minorities. By the year 2015, Hispanics and African Americans will comprise 40% of the population of California, and will account for 75% of the high school dropouts, while Whites and Asians will account for 89% of California's college graduates.

In a society that is becoming more technologically advanced, and where increased educational attainment is necessary to compete in the labor market, dropping out or being excluded from education results in exclusion from the economic and cultural core of a diverse society, resulting in increased social inequities (Hodges Persell, 1991). To this end, Sleeter and Grant (1999) asserted, "African Americans, Hispanics, and Native Americans remain subordinate economically and politically . . ." (p. 4). Consequently, "[e]quality of opportunity has become a major objective for educational policy . . ." (Husen, 1990, p. 1). Acknowledging the importance of educational equity and equal opportunity for an increasingly diverse society, Hodges Persell posed an educational challenge: "How can education mitigate inequality based on class or ethnicity when, in practice, education reinforces inequality by virtue of vast differences . . ." (p. 285).

IDENTITY DEVELOPMENT

For children, learning about the world begins at an early age. A child's understanding of self and others develops as a result of interactions in the home, with family and friends, and in their communities. These early experiences and interactions influence the development of self-concept and worldview. Negative messages that racial-ethnic minority children receive affects the successful negotiation of normal developmental tasks, complicating the already complex tasks of childrearing (Diller, 1999). Parents must prepare their racial-ethnic minority children for the negative realities of a country and a world that have internalized racist stereotypes and prejudice. Consequently, the process of enculturation or "ethnic socialization" is fundamental in developing a child's self-concept and worldview (Bernal & Knight, 1993) and a child's feelings of self-worth.

Enculturation, therefore, is the process of transmitting cultural teachings of family and community, thereby developing ethnic socialization (Bernal & Knight, 1993). Ethnic identity, a shared-group identity that provides individuals with a sense of belonging and peoplehood (Smith, 1991) and sharing of a common historic origin and tradition (Banks, 1997b), is important in developing individual and family identity (Pedersen, 1994). In addition to a shared-group identity consisting of symbols and values, the outward signs of ethnic identity may be race, religion, and national origin (Smith, 1989). Three levels of identity-individual, group, and panhuman-influence the meaning that is attributed to any event, and to the development of identity (Smith, 1989). the individual or idiosyncratic level of identity is defined as that part of the person that makes him or her unique. The group level of identity consists of the shared aspects of one's identity. The panhuman level focuses on universally shared aspects of one's identity. Using this framework, ethnic socialization or enculturation influences an individual's beliefs about his or her uniqueness and self-worth, feelings of psychological membership, and sense of belonging in a group, or community, as well as a sense of belonging to the general universal culture of humankind. In addition to the development of self-identity and group identification, ethnic socialization directly affects intergroup relationships (Sleeter & Grant, 1999) and the development of in-group and out-group attitudes (Banks, 1997b).

SELF-IDENTITY AND UNDERSTANDING DIFFERENCES

The classic doll studies by Clark and Clark (1947) were used to determine the child's understanding of racial attitudes. Findings were based on a child's ability to perform three sequential learning tasks. These learning processes are:

1. *Racial classification ability*-applying racial-ethnic labels accurately to members of different groups.
2. *Racial identification*-applying a correctracial-ethnic category to one's self, involving an understanding of one's skin color and racial-ethnic categories.
3. *Racial evaluation*-evaluating his/her race/ethnicity based on the internalized messages from family, the community, and society (Aboud & Doyle, 1993; Diller, 1999; Proshansky & Newton, 1968).

Findings of these studies suggested that Black children have difficulty completing the last two learning processes, and often exhibited negative self-images (Diller, 1999).

Researchers (Baldwin, 1989; Branch, 1999) have criticized the methodology and findings in these early doll studies. Furthermore, replication and extension of the Clark Doll Tests in which children were given multiple-choice options rather than forced choices, produced different results. Assessing a child's understanding of racial-ethnic self-identity as well as a child's understanding of the significance of race and ethnicity in society based solely on the Doll Studies may be an overinterpretation of the findings. Considering the racial climate and social context during which these original studies were conducted is important in understanding the interpretation of the findings. The 1940s and 1950s were times of racial turbulence in this country, and Blacks suffered from discrimination and inequitable societal practices. Also, Proshansky and Newton (1968) acknowledged the limitations of their research, which was based on the available knowledge about racial identity at the time in which the research was conducted. Proshansky and Newton also stated that much of what was known about racial identity was based on sporadic rather than systematic research studies. Baldwin (1979) has suggested the need for extensive interviews, and I assert the need for extensive ethnographic studies, before assuming that these earlier studies reflect an understanding of children's self-identity or children's understanding of racial and ethnic differences in society.

The importance of a positive identity, however, cannot be underestimated. Negative covert and subtle messages that devalue a child's racial, ethnic, and cultural background are associated with a devalued self-image and unhealthy personal identity development. These unresolved inner conflicts result in disturbances in relationships with others, and decreased self-fulfillment.

Contrary to some beliefs, children develop an awareness of racial differences at an early age, between the ages of four and seven (Diller, 1999). Also, children begin to associate race with ability at an early age. The video *Children and Race* (1998) shows young Black and White children differentiating friends based on race, and associating ability with race. For example, Whites are associated with "being good at business," "being smart," and "good with most things," while Blacks are associated with "being good at sports." Racial-ethnic awareness and prejudice in children represents an understanding of self and self-identity as well as the awareness of differences (Aboud, 1988). The recognition of differences in self and others and prejudice increases with age. Although prejudice may decrease with age, self-identity and awareness remain high. A child's understanding and awareness of self and others, however, may have developed based on inaccurate and negative beliefs. This emphasizes the importance of early, positive experience and interactions in a child's life in developing a healthy identity and self-image.

Although there are numerous theories explaining prejudice in children, one proposed theory is extremely pertinent to this discussion. The **social reflection theory** suggests that prejudice seen in children is a reflection of society's values (Gollnick & Chinn, 1998). High-status groups in society are valued (in-group) and low-status groups are devalued (out-groups). Based on a stratified society, Whites represent the in-group and minorities represent the out-group (Aboud, 1988; Gollnick & Chinn, 1998). The social reflection theory also can be used for explaining prejudice toward women and homosexuals in a society where men and heterosexuals are valued and represent the in-groups.

EDUCATION AND IDENTITY

Research has suggested a strong relationship between identity development and health for minority groups. Research also has linked increased educational achievement for minorities to positive social outcomes. Sheets (1999) discussed the negative psychological outcomes in learning and development resulting from societal and school cultures and related practices that neglect and compromise ethnic identity development. "The achievement of a clarified or actualized ethnic identity does not immune individuals to the challenges of living in a society that is often hostile to ethnic and cultural diversity" (Gay, 1999, p. 200). However, Gay further asserted, "Genuine acceptance of one's ethnicity is positively related to psychological well-being, interpersonal relations, social consciousness, and personal efficacy" (p. 195). Positive development of one's ethnic identity enhances overall learning and self-development in an increasingly diverse society, experiencing increased educational and labor market demands.

Although it has been theorized that racial and ethnic identity development are associated with positive educational outcomes, a paucity of research has studied this relationship. A noted exception is a study by Brown and Simmons (1999). The model predicted a relationship between ethnic identity and current-year grades; however, a significant relationship between ethnic identity and educational aspirations was not supported by the findings. Understanding the complex relationship between identity development and educational outcomes warrants further investigation.

THE CHALLENGE OF UNDERSTANDING INDIVIDUAL AND CULTURAL DIFFERENCE

As previously discussed, the ways in which we understand others and the ways in which we understand our racial and cultural characteristics influences the social context in which we interact with others and ourselves. These are important aspects in understanding cultural socialization in today's increasingly diverse society. In striving toward a sense of cultural pluralism, it is important to understand and challenge existing beliefs that we hold and the assumptions that we make about cultural differences. Too often assumptions that we make are based on inaccurate beliefs about those in society perceived as culturally different, resulting in stereotyped attitudes and biased behaviors. In challenging these attitudes and behaviors, earlier research placed less attention on the individual and the need to understand oneself and the impact of race, ethnicity, and cultural characteristics in society. Neither were these factors linked to understanding how racial-cultural socialization influences attitudes, beliefs, and behaviors. Rather, the culturally different person became the focus for understanding difference.

These differences are often used as the primary basis for understanding culture. Distinctions, however, are still made about the cultural value preferences and value orientations among White middle-class Americans and American racial-ethnic minority groups, that is, Asian Americans, Native Americans, Black Americans, and Hispanic Americans (Kluckhohn & Strodtbeck, 1961; Sue & Sue, 1990). These racial and ethnic differences in cultural values and worldview are associated with personal identity and psychological development, and influence educational and career aspirations and goals. In addition to influencing self-identity and healthy psychological development, culturally based assumptions, attitudes, and beliefs about self and others affect relations with those in society perceived as similar in culture and experience, and those perceived as dissimilar in culture and experience.

At best, these identified cultural differences are viewed as characteristics that distinguish the cultural group. At worst, these differences are viewed as deficiencies that are in need of remediation. Earlier psychological and educational literature equated cultural differences with *culturally disadvantaged, culturally deprived, culturally deficient and socially deprived* (see Mio, Trimble, Arredondo, Cheatham, & Sue, 1999). These labels elicit images of individuals and groups that lack the intellectual skills and abilities and social behaviors to become successful within American society.

In today's dynamic world, these cultural distinctions do help in providing sociocultural and sociohistorical perspectives. To this end, such distinctions are useful as guidelines to understanding differences among people and groups. However, I have found, in my experiences of teaching multicultural course materials to both undergraduate and graduate students in education, counseling, and psychology, that those cultural distinctions are often viewed as "rules" to understanding differences. When applied as rules, these distinctions become static, rigid, and inflexible, often reinforcing stereotyped depictions of cultural groups. The cultural difference is the primary focus. This perspective lacks an understanding of both individual and cultural influences. Discussions of cultural differences should be viewed as fluid and changing, much like society, with the recognition that heterogeneity exists within cultures.

Consequently, educators have focused on student individual and cultural differences, as well as the nuances of the heterogeneous classroom. However, individual and cultural differences are not always salient (Sleeter & Grant, 1999) to the observer. Racial, ethnic, and gender differences are characteristics that are often apparent to the observer, and have received a great deal of attention in the multicultural literature. We, as educators, have become sensitive to and aware of the potential effects of these differences on the educational outcomes of students. However, other experiences that distinguish students are sometimes overlooked and neglected in understanding the social and psychological development of the student and educational outcomes. Among these experiences are the differential effects of socialization.

Gender socialization and the differential experiences of boys and girls in school (Sleeter & Grant, 1999) have received much attention in the multicultural literature. Likewise, racial and cultural (ethnicity and social class) socialization results in differential experiences for racial-ethnic and cultural groups in society and in school. Focusing on psychological development, Helms and Cook (1999) discussed the importance of an individual's "internalized experiences in response to racial and cultural socialization" (p. 9) as important forces in learning and development. Also, a person's perceptions and responses to racial and cultural socialization are important in understanding the psychological consequences of racial and cultural differences in the United States.

Less attention has been placed on the lack of change in the educational systems, policies and practices that occur outside of the classroom. The overall culture of the school-as reflected in the hierarchical relationships, the curriculum, the verbal relationships, attitudes toward diversity, and institutional norms-may be incongruent with the culture of the student's home. Also, as student demographics in the schools have changed, the demographics of the typical school board have lacked change (Lutz & Iannaccone, 1995). Likewise, teachers vary in their understanding of and involvement in the students, school, and community in which they teach. Understanding the interrelationships between the student, the family, and the community provide a basis for fostering positive identity development in students, enhancing overall learning and development. Duesterberg (1998) challenged educators to expand on their conceptualizations of culture in learning about their students and the communities in which their students live. Duesterberg stated that differences " . . . must be informed by understandings of culture that do not divorce culture from history, politics and socioeconomic conditions which shape cultural knowledge, cultural [and ethnic] identity, and cultural formation" (p. 508).

To this end, Tomlinson-Clarke and Ota Wang (1999) stressed the importance of understanding oneself and others as racial-cultural beings in society. To better understand our relations with others, it is first important to understand ourselves in relation to the racial and cultural characteristics by which we define ourselves and by which society defines us. Tomlinson-Clarke and Ota Wang discussed the importance of ecological models (such as Bronfenbrenner, 1986) in understanding complex, dynamic interlocking systems in which we live. These systems include:

1. *Microsystems*, which focus on the individual psychological understandings of self and interactions between other individuals (e.g., family members).
2. *Mesosystems*, which focus on the institutions that reside within communities in which individuals are directly influenced.
3. *Exosystems*, which consist of social, cultural, and political institutional structures that influence policies where the mesosystem resides.
4. *Chronosystems*, which temporarily account for the time in which the system is influenced.

SUMMARY

Parity in education is not the only answer to societal discrepancies in equity among different groups. Although many have suggested that multicultural education is an answer, it is far from the solution. Furthermore, education that is multicultural extends beyond an understanding and tolerance of cultural differences; rather, it enables students to think complexly and creatively and to act responsibly (Futrell, 1990, cited in Montgomery & Rossi, 1994). Parity in society is not a minority problem; it is society's problem that will continue to affect our lives in a variety of ways during the 21st century. We all must continue to challenge our thinking and actions.

Many of the social issues and inequitable practices to which U.S. society continues to struggle have been highlighted in this chapter. To this end, a major focus of the 1990s, which will extend into the 21st century, is developing strategies for providing educational access and equity to children and youth in a society that has maintained a fairly segregated educational system with respect to differences.

In sum, education that is multicultural and viewed as a process, with goals of changing the structure of educational institutions, increasing the relevancy of educational systems to an increasingly culturally diverse society, and providing educational equity to all students (Sleeter & Grant, 1999), is promising in addressing persistent U.S. educational concerns. From this perspective, these assumptions of multicultural education are fundamental in providing a meaningful education to all learners. Through multicultural education we might better understand individuals, education, and society within a sociocultural context. Understanding education within a sociocultural context becomes increasingly important as we attempt to develop and to implement equitable educational policies and practices designed to meet the challenges of the 21st century and beyond.

REFERENCES

Aboud, F. (1988). *Children and prejudice*. Oxford, England: Blackwell.

Aboud, F. E., & Doyle, A. (1993). The early development of ethnic identity and attitudes. In M. E. Bernall & G. P. Knight (Eds.), *Ethnic identity: Formation and transmission among Hispanics and other minorities* (pp. 47-59). Albany: State University of New York Press.

Aponte, J. F., & Crouch, R. T. (2000). The changing ethnic profile of the United States in the twenty-first century. In J. F. Aponte & J. Wohl (Eds.), *Psychological intervention and cultural diversity* (2nd ed., pp. 1-17). Needham Heights, MA: Allyn & Bacon.

Baldwin, J. A. (1979). Theory and research concerning the notion of Black self-hatred: A review and reinterpretation. *Journal of Black Psychology, 5,* 51-77.

Banks, J. A. (1997a). Multicultural education: Characteristics and goals. In J. A. Banks & C. A. McGee Banks (Eds.), *Multicultural education: Issues and perspectives* (3rd ed., pp. 3-31). Needham Heights, MA: Allyn & Bacon.

Banks, J. A. (1997b). *Teaching strategies for ethnic studies* (6th ed.). Needham Heights, MA: Allyn & Bacon.

Beckman, W. F. (1995). Race relations and segregation in the United States. In S. W. Rothstein (Ed.), *Class, culture, and race in American schools: A handbook* (pp. 125-128). Westport, CT: Greenwood.

Bernal, M. A., & Knight, G. P. (1993). Introduction. In M. E. Bernal & G. P. Knight (Eds.), *Ethnic identity: Formation and transmission among Hispanics and other minorities* (pp. 1-7). Albany: State University of New York Press.

Blake, J. (1996). *Comes the millennium*. New York: St. Martin's Press.

Boocock, S. S. (1980). *Sociology of education: An introduction* (2nd ed.). Boston: Houghton Mifflin.

Branch, C. W. (1999). Race and human development. In R. Hernandez Sheets & R. Hollins (Eds.), *Racial and ethnic identity in school practices: Aspects of human development* (pp. 287-309). Heidelberg, Germany & New York: Springer-Verlag.

Bronfenbenner, U. (1986). Recent advances in research on the ecology of human development. In R. K. Silbereisen, K. Eyferth, & G. Rudinger (Eds.), *Development as action in context: Problem behavior and normal youth development* (pp. 287-309). Heidelberg and New York: Springer-Verlag.

Brown, W. T., & Simmons, R. F. (1999). *Sources of variation in the educational achievement of African-American high school students.* Retrieved December 10, 1999 from *www.udel.edu/psych/rsimons/brwnabst.htm.*

Campbell, D. E. (1996). *Choosing democracy: A practical guide to multicultural education.* Englewood Cliffs, NJ: Prentice-Hall.

Children and race. (1998). *ABC News/Prentice Hall video library: Critical issues in multicultural education.* Upper Saddle River, NJ: Prentice-Hall.

Clark, K., & Clark, M. (1947). Racial identification and preference in Negro children. In T. H. Newcomb & E. L. Hartley (Eds.), *Readings in social psychology* (pp. 169-178). NY: Holt, Rinehart & Winston.

Cushner, K. (1998). Intercultural education from an international perspective: An introduction. In K. Cushner (Ed.), *International perspectives on intercultural education* (pp. 1-13). Mahwah, NJ: Lawrence Erlbaum Associates.

Diller, J. V. (1999). *Cultural diversity: A primer for the human services.* Belmont, CA: Wadsworth.

Drew, D. E. (1995). Class, race, and science education. In S. W. Rothstein (Ed.), *Class, culture, and race in American schools: A handbooks* (pp. 5-72). Westport, CT: Greenwood.

Duesterberg, L. M. (1998). Rethinking culture in the pedagogy and practices of preservice teachers. *Teaching and Teacher Education, 14,* 497-512.

Gay, G. (1999). Ethnic identity development and multicultural education. In R. Hernandez Sheets & E. R. Hollins (Eds.), *Racial and ethnic identity in school practices: Aspects of human development* (pp. 195-211). Mahwah, NJ: Lawrence Erlbaum Associates.

Glazer, N. (1996). Hard questions: Race for the cure. In L. Orozco (Ed.), *Perspectives: Educating diverse populations* (pp. 125-126). (Reprinted from *New Republic, 215*).

Gollnick, D. M., & Chinn, P. C. (1998). *Multicultural education in a pluralistic society* (5th ed.). Upper Saddle River, NJ: Prentice-Hall.

Helms, J. E., & Cook, D. A. (1999). *Using race and culture in counseling and psychotherapy: Theory and process.* Boston: Allyn & Bacon.

Hernandez Sheets, R. (1999). Relating competence in an urban classroom to ethnic identity development. In R. Hernandez Sheets & E. R. Hollins (Eds.), *Racial and ethnic identity in school practices: Aspects of human development* (pp. 157-178). Mahway, NJ: Lawrence Erlbaum Associates.

Hodges Persell, C. (1991). Schools under pressure. In A. Wolfe (Ed.), *America at century's end* (pp. 283-297). Berkeley: University of California Press.

Husen, T. (1990). *Education and the global concern.* Oxford, England: Pergamon.

Kluckhohn, F. R., & Strodtbeck, F. L. (1961). *Variations in value orientations.* Evanston, IL: Row, Patterson, & Co.

Lutz, F. W., & Iannaccone, L. (1995). The governance of local schools as influenced by social class, race, and ethnicity. In S. W. Rothstein (Ed.), *Class, culture, and race in American schools: A handbook* (pp. 13-33). Westport, CT: Greenwood.

Martin, P., & Midgley, E. (1994). Immigrants to the United States: Journey to an uncertain destination. *Population Bulletin, 49,* 1-47.

Martinez, B. M., & Day, J. C. (1997). *School enrollment--social and economic characteristics of students*. Washington, DC: U.S. Bureau of the Census.

Mio, J. S., Trimble, J. E., Arredondo, P., Cheatham, H. E., & Sue, D. (Eds.). (1999). *Key words in multicultural interventions: A dictionary*. Westport, CT: Greenwood.

Montgomery, A., & Rossi, R. (1994). *Education reforms and students at-risk: A review of the current state of the art. Section I: A nation at risk*. Retrieved October 3, 1999 from *www.ed.gov/pubs/EdReformsStudies/EdReforms/chap1dtml*.

Pedersen, P. (1994). *A handbook for developing multicultural awareness* (2nd ed.). Alexandria, VA: American Counseling Association.

Proshansky, H., & Newton, P. (1968). The meaning and nature of Negro self-identity. In M. Deutsh, I. Katz, & A. Jensen (Eds.), *Social class, race and psychological development* (pp. 178-218). New York: Holt, Rinehart & Winston.

RAND. (1999). *Closing the education gap: Benefits and costs*. Retrieved September 13, 1999 from *www.rand.org/publications/MR/MR1036/index.html*.

Ruark, J. K. (1999). Racial gap in college-graduation rates is likely to widen, RAND report says. *Chronicle of Higher Education*, 1-2. Retrieved September 13, 1999 from *chronicle.com/daily/99/09/9909102n.html*.

Sleeter, C. E., & Grant, C. A. (1999). *Making choices for multicultural education* (3rd ed.). Upper Saddle River, NJ: Prentice-Hall.

Smith, E. J. (1991). Ethnic identity development: Toward the development of a theory within the context of majority/minority status. *Journal of Counseling and Development, 70*, 181-188.

Smith, E. M. J. (1989). Black racial identity development: Issues and concerns. *The Counseling Psychologist, 17*, 277-288.

Stewart, E. C. (1972). *American cultural patterns*. LaGrange Park, IL: Intercultural Network.

Sue, D. W., & Sue, D. (1990). *Counseling the culturally different: Theory and practice* (2nd ed.). New York: John Wiley & Sons.

Tomlinson-Clarke, S., & Ota Wang, V. (1999). A paradigm for racial-cultural training in the development of counselor cultural competencies. In M. S. Kiselica (Ed.), *Confronting prejudice and racism during multicultural training* (pp. 155-167). Alexandria, VA: American Counseling Association.

U.S. Bureau of the Census. (1996). *Current population reports: Population projections of the United States by age, race, and Hispanic origin: 1995-2050*. Washington, DC: U.S. Government Printing Office.

U.S. Bureau of the Census. (1999). *Resident population estimates of the United States by sex, race, and Hispanic origin: April 1, 1990 to November 1, 1990*. Washington, DC: U.S. Bureau of the Census. Retrieved September 23, 1999 from www.census.gov/population/estimates/nation/intfile3-1.txt.

Wolfe, A. (1991a). Out of the frying pan, into . . . what? In A. Wolfe (Ed.), *America at century's end* (pp. 461-471). Berkeley: University of California Press.

Wolfe, A. (1991b). Introduction: Change from the bottom up. In A. Wolfe (Ed.), *America at century's end* (pp. 1-13). Berkeley: University of California Press.

IV

Language and National Identity

9

Educational Reform and Language Issue in Ukraine

Petro P. Kononenko
Taras Shevchenko University, Kyiv

Ivan Z. Holowinsky
Rutgers, The State University of New Jersey

THE PROBLEM

The breakup of the Soviet Union in 1991 was a critical turning point in the development of a national identity for Ukraine. Events of that year offered the opportunity for the reemergence of Ukrainian national identity, for the development of economic, political, and educational policies supportive of the contemporary Ukraine. A key element in the emergence of "new" Ukraine is the revitalization of the Ukrainian language. However, due to a centuries-long policy of suppression of the Ukrainian language, progress in the implementation of a new language policy has been slow.

The new constitution of Ukraine that has been adopted by the Parliament (Verkhovna Rada) declares that Ukrainian should be the official language of Ukraine. That decision by Ukraine's higher legislative body culminated centuries of struggle for the full recognition of the Ukrainian language. Owing to complex historical reasons, the struggle for Ukrainian became synonymous with the struggle for national self-recognition. In a unique way, the language became the most important symbol of statehood.

This chapter will analyze complex issues of the language within the context of Ukraine's cultural, demographic, and sociopolitical realities, past and present. The chapter will also discuss the sociopolitical importance of language in general and more specifically in the case of the Ukrainian language.

Two distinct historical periods can be identified. The first period, starting in approximately 1700 and lasting until the Bolshevik revolution in 1917, was characterized by the direct, forced Russification of the Ukrainian language under Tsars. The second period began with the emergence of the Soviet Union and ended with its breakup in 1991. During the period of the existence of the Soviet Union (1923-1991), equally strong but more subtle and dialectical methods of Russification were employed. The Russian language was declared as the language of "social interaction" within the Soviet Union and as a language of "great Lenin."

Upon her declaration of independence in 1991, Ukraine inherited the whole set of sociopolitical, cultural, and demographic problems. The current status of Ukrainian in education will be discussed within the context of historical realities. We will conclude this chapter with discussion on anticipated future trends in the usage of Ukrainian in education.

SOCIOPOLITICAL IMPORTANCE OF LANGUAGE

Every word is both a sign and a symbol. It represents concrete material reality and abstract symbolic relationships. A particular language united individuals with their clan, tribe, nature, history, religion, philosophy, etc. The language became indicative of the development of individuals and nations. It can be said that a national language has been an integral part of the nation building. From a historical perspective, theoretical foundations of nationalism in Europe were associated with the emergence of national literacy languages. A famous medieval Italian poet and writer, A Dante, advocated development of the Italian language at the time when Latin was still used widely. Dante maintained that a people's language is the natural language acquired by children since infancy. At the beginning of the 20th century, leading Ukrainian educator K. Ushynsky insisted that a nation should fight for its language. He believed that a language is synonymous with a nation. A nation can create a homeland, but not a language. Should a language perish, a nation will perish.

As *The New York Times* (1998) reported, roughly 6,500 languages would become extinct over the next century. About 60% of existing languages have 10,000 speakers or fewer. Many languages become extinct because they have not been used or because imperial policy favored the dominant language. For example, after Russia displaced approximately 60,000 Ubykh speakers from their ancestral place on the Black Sea into Turkey in the 1860s, the refugees eventually accepted the dominant Turkish language. It is reported that the last Ubykh speaker died in Turkey at the age of 88 in 1992. In the former Soviet Union, according to official data, prior to 1930 existed 194 languages. However, in 1959 there were 108 languages listed as in use. Eighty-six languages became extinct in the period of 29 years. It is clear that in Ukraine the fight for language became the fight for the national survival. In the 19th century, Ukrainian writers and poets led the fight for the Ukrainian language. Most noted among them was Taras Shevchenko, who more than anyone else understood Ukrainian mentality and shaped Ukrainian national consciousness.

A rich source of material for psychological interpretation of human behavior is contained in the writings of Taras Shevchenko. It should be noted that Shevchenko's poems were written 20 to 30 years before Dostoyevsky's major work, such as *Crime and Punishment* (1866), *The Idiot* (1868), or *The Brothers Karamazov* (1879-80).

However, while Dostoyevsky's works are widely read and interpreted, Shevchenko's writings have not yet been adequately researched as to their psychological content. To understand Shevchenko's ideas about human nature, we should consider him briefly as a person and consider his philosophy of life in the context of political and social realities of his time. Like Dante in Italy, Shevchenko in Ukraine is considered a national prophet responsible for bringing to the Ukrainian language international recognition.

Within the historical context of sociocultural evolution, verbal communication played a crucial integral part. We can accept as a priori the notion that the development of human societies would have been impossible in the absence of abstract verbal communication. It is an indisputable fact that language enables us not only to communicate in the temporal sense, but also to preserve information and cultural values for future generations.

Contemporary psychologists and psycholinguists emphasized the importance of language. Cassirer (1953), in his paper on the philosophy of symbolic form, informed us that the analysis of language shows that all linguistic expressions possess a definite independent character. Rieben and Carton (1987) also pointed out that speech gives us the power to free ourselves from the force of immediate impressions and to go beyond their limits. It is possible to do so because out intellect transcends the limits of space and time.

Throughout history it has been recognized that language controls behavior through indoctrination, education, and propaganda, as well as political pressure. Since the 19th century, modern empire states have been using language policy directed toward enhancement of their power and hegemony. At different times in the history of civilization, different languages achieved positions of preeminence. In medieval times Latin was the language of scholars and intellectuals. During the 18th and 19th centuries, French and English were recognized as languages of diplomacy, and German has been widely used by researchers and scholars in empirical sciences. However, a direct policy of linguistic suppression was not utilized either in Great Britain or France. Since the empires were almost by definition multilingual societies, the use of a particular language was dependent on legal, political, historical, anthropological, and other factors. As has been emphasized by George Shevelov, "The language question necessarily became not only an immediately linguistic question, but also, and often primarily, a political, sociological, and cultural question" (Shevelov, 1986).

HISTORICAL BACKGROUND

During the 18th and 19th centuries, there had been a sustained campaign of suppression of the Ukrainian language by the Russian authorities. The attitude of the Russian empire toward the Ukrainian language differed in a number of respects from linguistic policy either in France or Great Britain. The characteristics of Russian policy toward the Ukrainian language were the following: (1) government-controlled suppression, (b) centuries-long discrimination, and (3) the same policy basically as in Tsarist Russia and in the Soviet Union.

At the beginning of this century, governmental language regulations in Ukraine were based on the Ems decree signed by Tsar Alexander II in 1876. This decree was implemented by imperial censors to the extreme degree of absurdity. For example, even such classics as works of Shakespeare, Homer, Dante, and Shiller were not permitted to be translated into Ukrainian (Mynkiv, 1989). However, even more than a century earlier, since 1720, the Ukrainian language was banned from use in church. Even Ukrainian pronunciation of church Slavonic was outlawed. The draconic decree of Tsar Alexander also forbade any theatrical performances or public speaking in Ukrainian, the import of Ukrainian books published abroad, the teaching of any subjects in Ukrainian, as well as the use of any Ukrainian books in school libraries. As a result of such repressive policy, prior to 1914 the Ukrainian language was essentially absent within the Russian Empire from scholarship and science. It was entirely absent from education at all levels, from elementary school through university. The so-called "Fundamental Law of the Empire" stated: "The Russian language is the official language and obligatory in the army, the navy and all governmental and public institutions." Russian nationalists maintained that " . . . Russia can be great, united, and indivisible only if she is well bound by one cement, that of the one and only Russian official language" (Shevelov, 1986, p. 100).

During the 18th and 19th centuries five important decrees were issued limiting the use of Ukrainian language.

The Ems decree that proscribed printing of any texts, either original or translated, in Ukrainian also forbade any theatrical performances and public recitation in Ukrainian, the import of any Ukrainian books published abroad, and the teaching of any discipline in the Ukrainian language, as well as the preservation or circulation of any Ukrainian books in school libraries (Shevelov, 1986).

With the collapse of the Tsarist Empire in 1917, the War of Ukrainian National Republic with Russia (1917-1921), and the establishment of the Soviet Union, the problem of Russification of the Ukrainian language acquired new dimensions. It is not the purpose of this chapter to review the national policy of

TABLE 9.1

Tsarist Decrees Limiting the Use of Ukrainian Language

1720	Tsar Peter I issued an order prohibiting printing of books in Ukrainian language by Kyiv-Pechersk and Chernihiv printing houses.
1729	Tsar Peter II ordered that all official decrees in Ukraine printed in Ukrainian language should be reprinted in Russian.
1763	Tsarina Ketherin II prohibited lecturing in Ukrainian language at the Kyiv Mohyla Academy.
1769	Decree of the Moscow "Holy Synod" prohibiting printing of Ecclesiastical books in Ukrainian.
1876	Ems decree (Emsky Ukaz) of Tsar Alexander II.

Source: Shevelov, G. (1986)

the former Soviet Union. We will mention in the context of this paper only one important historical aspect. When an attempt by the Bolsheviks to foster revolution in Poland, Germany, and Hungary failed in the early 1920s, the leadership of the Communist party in Moscow began to focus upon strengthening the communist rule in the USSR. The Russian language was elevated to a dominant position, and to enhance its status there was a constant reminder that it was "the language of great Lenin."

The official and nonofficial policy of Russification over more than a half century resulted in an almost total elimination of Ukrainian language from scholarship and education. By the 1930s, intense total Russification in all aspects of life had been implemented throughout the Soviet Union. We will highlight only those aspects of Russification that relate to education.

The extent of how vehement the implementation of Russification was in the 1930s can be understood by reviewing such publications as *Mathematical Terminological Bulletin* or *Physical Terminological Bulletin*. Recently, Kochenka (1994) explained that difficulties with Ukrainian scientific terminology have their origin in the 1930s, when communist authorities disbanded the Institute of Ukrainian Scientific Terminology. Prior to its liquidation, the Institute had published over 40 terminological dictionaries in various branches of sciences. The campaign against Ukrainian terminology in sciences was based on such arguments as "against nationalism in mathematical terminology," or "uprooting nationalism in Soviet physical terminology." It is clear that Russification was a real goal, when we consider how "nationalism" was defined. It was defined as "avoidance of Russian terminology." This attitude was typical of the long-prevailing trend in the former Soviet Union.

In the dialectical vocabulary of the Communist Party of the USSR, the patriotic strivings of Ukrainians and other nationalities were viewed as bourgeois, nationalistic, separatist, and counterrevolutionary. To be accused of "nationalistic tendencies" was equivalent to the accusation of a crime against "the Soviet Motherland" (Dziuba, 1968). However, the expression of patriotism on the part of Russians was encouraged, and even the historical contributions of Tsars were glorified. The process of Russification of professional school personnel was reinforced by ideological indoctrination and pressure.

Russification in the USSR had been associated with an attempt to create "the new Soviet person," as documented by Dziuba (1968), Kolaska (1970), and Ovcharenko (1987). Fortunately, with the dissolution of the Soviet Union the anachronistic concept of "the Soviet Person" has been relegated to being a simple historical footnote (Lutovinov, 1998).

Ovcharenko (1987) reported that Russification started in nursery schools and kindergartens. As a rule, teachers communicated with each other and their students in Russian and compelled students to use Russian even during their leisure time. In this context it should be mentioned that even a preschool journal, *Doshkilne Vykhovannia* (Preschool Education), which was published in Ukrainian, contained children's songs in Russian. That policy was followed despite the fact that there was an almost identical publication of *Doshkolnoye Vospytaniye* (Preschool Education) published in Russian. Many books published for Ukrainian children were written in Russian rather than in the Ukrainian language. Tykhlovod (1974), surveying the literature on the Second World War published in Ukraine in the early 1970s for children, listed 10 books in Russian and 6 in Ukrainian. The contents of the books for Ukrainian children consistently deemphasized national identity. Instead, they attempted to create Soviet identity for non-Russian nationalities, a trend that was not emphasized for Russian children within the Russian-Soviet Socialist Federated Republic.

By the 1970s many schools in Kyiv did not teach the Ukrainian language even as a subject (Solchanyk, 1980). It has been reported that school boards of education had been frequently assigning to Ukrainian schools teachers of mathematics, physics, chemistry, or biology who did not speak or lecture in Ukrainian and who did not make a serious effort to learn Ukrainian. In addition, there was evidence of deliberate educational policy on Russification. For example, in 1978 the Cabinet of Ministers of the USSR issued a decree directed at further improvement in the study and mastery of the Russian language in non-Russian Union republics. The Deputy Minister of Education, Khomenko, wrote at that time: "It is important to install love for the Russian language, the language which codes experience of humanity for its happiness, of historical struggle for happiness, the language that was used to create priceless achievements in the sciences and arts" (Solchanyk, 1980).

In 1959, a new law was passed by the Ukraine's Supreme Soviet giving parents a right to choose between Russian and Ukrainian schools of instruction. However, because instruction at universities was given all in the Russian language, this seemingly egalitarian law enhanced the process of Russification. In 1975 the so-called Tashkent Conference was devoted to ways of improving teaching Russian to non-Russian children. During the 10-year period from 1970 to 1980, higher education textbooks in Ukrainian declined from 168 titles to 38, while those in Russian at the same time increased from 263 to 422. All doctoral dissertations were written in Russian.

As recently as the 1980s, the Higher Attestation Commission (VAK) in Moscow refused to take for examination candidates whose doctoral dissertations were written in Ukrainian. The situation often was absurd when even dissertations about the Ukrainian language and literature had to be written and defended in Russian (Pohribny, 1994). Even as late as 1990, a year before the dissolution of the Soviet Union, the Supreme Council of the USSR adopted in 1990 a law under the title: "On the languages of the peoples of the USSR." In that law Russian was declared the official language of the Union of the Soviet Socialist Republic.

One of the first actions that the new government of Ukraine took on itself after the declaration of independence was to restore the Ukrainian language to its rightful place as the national language. In an interview reported in Literaturna Ukraina (Literary Ukraine), Minister of Education Talanchuk (1992) suggested that destruction of the Ukrainian language and culture of the past 70 years was tantamount to the Chernobyl nuclear catastrophe. Associate Minister of Education Pohribny identified as a major national goal the introduction of the Ukrainian language into the teacher education program of pedagogical institutes and at the university levels (Pohribny, 1992). However, this effort has been hampered by decades of Russification. Furthermore, in some regions old-party functionaries, who were still in power, simply ignored directions of the Department of Education.

In comparison with public elementary schools, the language situation was even worse at the institutions of higher learning. For example, in 1990, 90% of instruction was conducted in Russian and 70% of scientific literature was published in Russian. One may understand the extent of this problem by simply reviewing a list of former "Soviet" periodicals that were available for subscription in the United States through the Four Continents Book Corporation. Among the 14 scientific journals available or published in Ukraine, 11 were in Russian, 2 in both Russian and Ukrainian, and only 1 in Ukrainian. It is peculiar that even journals referred to as Ukrainian were published in the Russian language, for example, *Ukrainian Biochemical Journal* and *Ukrainian Chemical Journal*.

Kononenko and Kononenko (1999) analyzed the extent of continuous discrimination of the Ukrainian language in Ukraine, even after 9 years of independence. The writers are pointing out that not only in Donetsk and Crimea, but also in other regions, the Ukrainian language is discriminated against, not allowed to function within the system of public education, scholarship, science, culture, manmade state administration. This discrimination is not only subtle, but open confrontation with laws of Ukraine. It should be clearly recognized that on many levels of state administration, there is a direct revision of the language law of Ukraine as adopted in the Ukraine's Constitution. This revisionist effort is promoted by former nomenclature and "aparatchiks" (Communist party functionaries).

THE IDEOLOGICAL, SOCIOPOLITICAL, AND DEMOGRAPHIC LEGACY

The collapse of the Soviet Union in 1991 provided an opportunity for educators and social and political scientists to study in depth education in transition from totalitarian Marxist-Leninist ideology to democracy and pluralism. The transition has not been completed in 8 years. As a matter of fact, the struggle still continues between the forces of progress and pluralism on one side and old bureaucratic *nomenclatura* on the other.

Among the former Soviet Republics, Ukraine is the most appropriate place to study this process for important reasons. Next to the Russian Federation, Ukraine is the largest in size and most prominent in importance among former Soviet Republics. Even though both countries had been dictated by totalitarian Marxist-Leninist ideology, political, linguistic, and religious factors complicated the relationship between Russia and Ukraine. For the above reasons, Ukraine, a country that for more than 70 years had a rigid totalitarian educational system, is a fertile ground to study complex issues and problems arising out of transition to pluralism, market economy, and educational reform.

Ukraine's current sociopolitical reality has its roots in its geopolitical past as a buffer between Europe and Asia. Since the beginning of the 18th century, Russia extended its hegemony over Ukraine. Gradually, through the process of political terror and economic exploitation together with cultural and linguistic Russification, Russia asserted its dominance and turned Ukraine into one of its colonies. In this process education became an instrument of colonization.

MARXIST-LENINIST IDEOLOGY

The educational system in the former Soviet Union was characterized by uniform requirements and centralized planning and administration. To begin with, there were no private schools in the former Soviet Union. All schools were establishments run and operated by the state. The Ministry of Education of the USSR developed policies for educational practices and determined the content of the curricula. The Ministries of Education of the Union Republics were directly responsible to the Ministry of Education of the USSR. Regardless of areas of specialization, all students were required to study several courses, such as Marxist-Leninist philosophy, the history of the Communist Party and of the Soviet Union, scientific communism, political economy, scientific atheism, Marxist-Leninist ethics and esthetics, and a foreign language (Pambookian & Holowinsky, 1987).

The main dogmas of former Soviet education can be briefly stated as follows: the a priori unquestionable acceptance of the primacy of the Communist ideology and leadership; the main goal of education as the upbringing of a "new person," a builder of a communist society; the importance of a collective in education; and the emergence of "new socialist personality." In the former USSR, the main purpose of education was indoctrination in the communist philosophy and way of life.

The concept of the collective was introduced into the Soviet educational literature and elaborated on by Antin Makarenko, who was considered to be a leading Soviet educator. Makarenko maintained that education should be an important but not exclusive activity in the life of students. As a convinced Marxist, he believed that physical education and labor played an important role in overall education and upbringing. He argued that abilities and traits are not fixed entities. He accepted the dialectical notion that society, as a historically evolving milieu, influences individuals, while maintaining that individuals create the social system and can change it. This belief-that education can create a new social order-became his central doctrine. Makarenko stressed that in order to reeducate a child, one must ignore the child's heritage. This philosophy placed him on a collision course with the child-study movement of pedology then prevailing in Europe (Holowinsky, 1988).

Basic to Makarenko's educational theory is a notion of the collective (Feldstein, 1977). Makarenko understood the collective as a link within society, and a child's collective as an integral part of a society in which the collective had evolved as a sociohistorical phenomenon. Therefore, he maintained that an individual should be educated as a integral part of society. In his view, the formation of a collective is a basic task of the socialist society.

Soviet educators and psychologists considered a school collective an integral part of Soviet society, bound organically to other collectives. They suggested that only through a collective can an individual become a member of society. Makarenko asserted that the individual's interests should always be secondary to the interests of the collective and the state. In this formulation, we see clearly the most succinct interpretation of the differences between democracy and the totalitarian system based on the dictatorship of the proletariat. In a democracy, the state serves the individual, and, in the former Soviet Union, the individual served the state. Negating the primacy of the individual, Makarenko maintained that an individual undergoes personality change under the influence of the collective. Employing dialectical logic, he stressed a notion of "paradoxical humanism." He believed that cruelty is the highest form of humanism because it forces an individual to change in spite of his own will. Paradoxical humanism reminds us of the notion expressed in the 19th century by Sechenov, who claimed that it should be possible to condition the development of a "new person." He maintained that it would be possible to "construct" people with "non-free will" in the sense that they would be conditioned to serve people, create good, and offer themselves for humanity (Yaroshevsky, 1974).

For more than 70 years, teachers in the former Soviet Ukraine have been indoctrinated in the single totalitarian ideology of Marxism-Leninism. This ideology and the strict Communist party control has been extended after WWII on the territory of Western Ukraine that, prior to 1939, was part of Poland. As reposted by Svorak (1997), in the 1944-45 school year all district superintendents of schools as well as their deputies were members of the Communist Party. It is interesting that all of them were sent to Western Ukraine from Eastern Ukraine. This legacy has to be underscored in order to appreciate the current efforts to bring Ukraine within the mainstream of European education.

CURRENT STATUS

The school system in Ukraine is composed of more than 26,000 units serving approximately 10.8 million students. The system contains 22,279 schools of various types. There are also 1,176 professional institutes (Drobnokhot, 1995). In 1995 there were also 754 higher education establishments of the first- and second-level accreditation, including 14 classical and 45 technical universities, 30 academies, and 72 institutes. The faculties of these institutions included 6,250 doctors of science, professors and 36,650 assistant professors and candidates of science (Yablonsky, 1995, June 21).

Due to decades of neglect by the former Soviet authorities, schools in Ukraine are in abysmal physical condition. As reported by Martyniv (1996), most of the schools cannot even provide for a basic sanitary environment for children without even mentioning the need for capital improvement. Conditions are even worse in the rural schools. Forty percent of these schools are operating in inadequate buildings. Classrooms are two or three times smaller than required, without central heating. The lighting is completely inadequate. Approximately 50% of the students are lacking one or two textbooks each. Moreover, up to 35 youngsters are crowded into one room. Normative tests have been introduced without preparing teachers how to use them. School psychological services and education of the gifted are virtually nonexistent.

At the same time it should be stressed that responsible educators recognize how crucial and indispensable quality education is in Ukraine at this time of nation building. However, before education will be able to fulfill its role, it must win a struggle against vestiges of old thinking embedded in Marxist-Leninist ideology. This is especially noticeable in scholarly areas such as history and social studies. Reforms in Ukrainian education during the transitional period have been characterized by the struggle between forces of progress and forces of reactionary past. Three brief examples will be mentioned to illustrate this problem.

Not only have most teachers and teacher trainers educated prior to the 1980s been indoctrinated in Marxist-Leninist ideology, but they have also been exposed to antireligious propaganda. As explained by Pashchenko (1994), atheistic indoctrination and antireligious propaganda in schools were mandated by decrees of the Central Committee of the Communist Party in 1932 and 1934. These decrees did not allow religious believers to hold teaching positions. Believers were also not permitted to be teachers in teacher training institutes. It was stipulated that children of ministers and priests were not allowed to become teachers unless they disassociated themselves from their parents. Against the background of long-standing indoctrination, it is easy to understand how some vestiges of Marxism-Leninism still can be found in the areas of special studies and humanities.

Lubar and Fedorenko (1994) point out the paradox of Ukrainian scholarship in contemporary Ukraine. For example, teacher training institutes still use old curriculum guides of the state that no longer exists. The disciplines of humanities are still thought in the spirit of communist ideology. As an example, Lubar and Fedorenko (1994) report that some disciplines, such as Marxist-Leninist ethics, atheism, history of the communist party, and scientific communism, have been renamed, but the content remains the same and the same instructors are teaching the "new disciplines." The new labels simply are: history of religion and agnosticism, political history, and politology.

Strangely enough, the popular trends of "deideolization" and "depolitization" of schools are preventing the development of national education because any strong criticism of Marxist-Leninist ideology is viewed by old nomenclatura as politization of schools. For example, Anatoly Pohribny, the former Deputy Minister of Education, has been removed from his position after being accused of fostering teachings of "scientific nationalism" (Pohribny,

1994). He has also been accused of discrimination against Russian-language schools. However, a look at simple statistics refutes this accusation. Although Ukrainians comprise 75% of the population of Ukraine, only 66% of elementary schools use the Ukrainian language in instruction. The situation is worse at the secondary and higher education levels, where only 37% of instruction is in Ukrainian.

In spite of existing difficulties, the restructuring of education in Ukraine made significant progress in the past couple of years. Yablonsky (1995, June 21) suggested that Ukrainian policymakers should consider the American model of higher education composed of junior colleges, colleges, institutes, and universities. Yablonsky suggested that before reforms are instituted, a detailed analysis of needs has to be made anticipating developments in the next 20 years. It is also important that needs assessment should be made by independent observers.

In the interview published in the newspaper *Chas* (Times) (1995, April 28), the Minister of Education of Ukraine, Zhurovsky, stressed the need to integrate education at all levels--elementary, secondary, and higher. In 1994 the Ministry of Education and The National Academy of Sciences of Ukraine signed an agreement of cooperation in the area of sciences and education. The goal is to create a single science education environment. One such concrete example is to create a physicotechnical department at the Kyiv Pedagogical University.

Ukraine as a sovereign nation has been recognized by approximately 200 nations, and the Ukrainian language after centuries of discrimination has been declared in the Constitution (Svoboda, 1996) as the official state language. However, the struggle for full acceptance of the Ukrainian language continues in many regions of Ukraine. The situation is critical in areas such as Donetsk Crimea and Odessa. It should be stated emphatically that in some regions and larger cities, there are reactionary attempts to change state laws and especially the language law. As stated by Kononenko (1995), there are attempts by some members of the Parliament to change existing laws. The danger is that if they succeed in changing the language law, there will be an attempt to change national symbols and the Declaration of Independence itself.

The 1999 conference that took place in Kyiv and was devoted primarily to the topic of the Ukrainian language concluded that the language is clearly discriminated against, especially in Eastern and Southern regions. For example, in Krimea where 625,000 Ukrainians live, only two high schools use the Ukrainian language in instruction. In Donbas there is a strong resistance against the introduction of Ukrainian in schools. Resistance to Ukrainian is evident in fields such as commerce, transportation, and business. Ukrainian language has not been yet introduced into the diplomatic corps, internal security services, or the armed forced. At the same time, one can observe increased numbers of publications in Russian with anti-Ukrainian orientation. Further, there is a shortage of Ukrainian textbooks in schools. This situation is especially critical in higher education. For example, the Accreditation Commission does not even require writing of dissertations in Ukrainian.

Osvita Ukrainy (Education in Ukraine) (1997) reported that in 1997, the school-age population in Ukraine numbered 1.3 million preschoolers, approximately 7 million elementary school student, and 1.6 million secondary school students. They are educated in 31,402 schools. The majority (15,898) are instructed in Ukrainian; 2,973 are instructed in Russian and 2,341 in both languages (Svorak, 1997).

In the spring of 1999, Ukraine's Parliament passed a broad-based education law that provides specific guidelines for general public education. The law provides for a legal basis for new types of schools that have been introduced in Ukraine since the declaration of independence, such as classical high schools (gymnasiums), lyceums, and junior colleges. A major change in general education is the introduction of 12 grades beginning with the school year 2001. The school system will be divided into: elementary-4 years; basic-5 years; high school-3 years. The children will enter the first grade at 6 years of age and graduate from high school at 18. This will approximate the structure of general education in most European countries. The law also will regulate the size of a class, which will be no more than 30 students, and the length of a lesson at 45 minutes.

In Ukraine there also exist numerous schools with non-Ukrainian languages of instruction. As reported by *Svoboda* (1997, June 4), schools with the Russian language of instruction are attended by approximately 3 million students. There are also 2,351 schools that offer bilingual instruction in Ukrainian and Russian (Svorak, 1997). Teachers of the Russian language are trained at 11 universities and 20 pedagogical institutes. In some regions of Ukraine, instruction in Russian at the elementary and secondary levels was rather high. For example, rates of instruction given in Russian in Donetzk, Luhansk, Zaporizhzha, Odessa, and Kharkiv are 93%, 90%, 67%, 65%, and 60%, respectively.

Although the population of Ukraine is 75% ethnic Ukrainians, only 50% of schools in Ukraine employed Ukrainian as the primary language of instruction. The status of the Ukrainian language as the medium of instruction in higher education is even worse than in elementary and secondary education. According to information provided by the Ministry of Education, the following percentages of students are educated in the Ukrainian language at the university level. Almost completely neglected are the efforts to print technical textbooks and instructional material in Ukrainian. This status quo stems from the legacy of long-lasting Russification imposed by the Russian and Soviet authorities since the early 18th century.

TABLE 9.2

Number of Schools for National Minorities in Ukraine

Minority	Number of Schools
Russian	3,470
Romanian	115
Hungarian	64
Moldavian	11
Polish	3
Jewish	3
TOTAL	3,586

Source: Ministry of Education of Ukraine, 9-25-1997, Personal Communication.

The overall status of the Ukrainian language in education in the 1990s did not improve much in comparison with the 1960s, as evident from the data provided in Chornovil. The publishing houses of the Universities of Kyiv, Lyiv, and Kharkiv published 2,297 titles of scientific and educationa literature during 1960--64, of which 795 titles were in Ukrainian, that is, 36%. Textbooks and handbooks in the technical sciences, highly specialized sciences, natural sciences, and educational literature for general and technical departments are published in Russian only (Chornovil, 1997).

Some interesting trends concerning the usage of Ukrainian language can be noticed in a survey conducted in 1998 at the University of Kyiv-Mohyla Academy (Brukhovetsky, 1999, May 21). Two hundred and eighty-five students participated in the survey conducted by Halyna Andreyko. The sample consisted of 88% Ukrainians, 8% Russians, and 4% of other nationalities. Results of the survey were reported in the percentages, and only limited statistical inferences can be drawn. However, it can be assumed that students at the University Kyiv-Mohyla Academy are representative in general of the Ukrainian student population. This will allow us to recognize some general trends. Eighty percent

TABLE 9.3

Percentage of Students Educated in Ukrainian Language by Instructors at
the Universities

District	Percentage of Students
Kherson	41
Odessa	40
Dnipropetrovsk	37
Mykoloiv	33
Kharkiv	22
Zaporizhzha	18
Donetzk	11
Luhansk	6

Source: Ministry of Education of Ukraine, 4-14-1998, Personal Communication.

of students reported that they use Ukrainian in their studies. Sixty-three percent indicated that they are fluent in Ukrainian. The extent to which Russian is dominant in Ukraine can be illustrated by the next two responses. Seventy-five percent of students in the sample indicated that they respond in Ukrainian when a stranger on the street talks to them in Ukrainian. However, only 20% talk to a stranger   spontaneously in Ukrainian. Their reluctance to use Ukrainian spontaneously in conversation may be a reflection of long-standing Russification practice in Ukraine. While 88% of students consider themselves to be Ukrainian, only 50% are interested in Ukrainian culture and history, and only 13% indicate that they are very familiar with Ukrainian traditions.

Since 1991, attempts to introduce the Ukrainian language as the language of instruction met with strong resistance from the Russian minority and former partocrats. The argument has been made that the state attempts to deprive Russian children of the opportunity to learn their native language.

ANTICIPATED FUTURE TRENDS

To restructure higher education, the Ministry of Education of Ukraine established an institute to upgrade qualifications of future leadership in education in 1993. On graduation from the institute, graduates receive a master's degree. The fields of study include sociology, psychology, and school management as well as business management (Drobnokhot, 1995). The institute attempts to establish cooperation with international educational establishments.

Derkach (1997), who is a university professor and a chairperson of Lviv UNESCO club, proposed recently that Ukraine should reorganize its general public education based on the European model of 12 years of general education prior to the university-level education. Precollege education would be subdivided according to what he referred to as a $4+4+2+2$ model.

The first 4 years of elementary education should focus on foundations in basic education as well as appreciation of personality development and sound upbringing. The goals should be to awaken in a child the need for civilized behavior, to stimulate appreciation for ethical values and cultivate respect and love for the country, its traditions and culture, as well as to develop interest in the environment and the desire to learn.

During the next 4 years of schooling, appreciation for objective reality should be developed. Children should acquire basic knowledge about living and nonliving matter. They should know the most essential facts about functioning of human organism from organic to psychological points of view. Children should also be made familiar with the most basic rules of society and government.

The last 4 years, or 9th, 10th, 11th, and 12th grades, are subdivided into 2 years of specialized education and 2 years of advanced education, which basically is university or college preparatory.

Further, looking into the next century, Lubar and Fedorenko (1994) made a proposal for higher pedagogical preparation in teacher training for the 21st century. They proposed that professional preparation of teachers be based on proven pedagogical principles and traditions of Ukrainian culture, customs, and ethnopsychology. It is expected that it will be possible to demonstrate that the new system of teacher training in Ukraine will be superior to the system in place during the Soviet times. The proposal recommends a four-stage preparation of future teachers: Preparation of 3-year duration for junior specialists, preschool teachers, and teachers of elementary schools; 4 years of preparation for teachers of secondary schools to obtain a B.A.; 5-year study for teachers of senior high schools; and 6-year study for teachers of classical academic secondary schools and junior colleges to receive an M.A. degree.

During the period of transition, where in some areas of education the views of old pedagogical nomenclatura still prevail, it may be of interest to observe that some reformers are beginning to question the ideological foundations of old Soviet pedagogy. Two examples will be cited from Krasovetsky (1995) and Skyba (1993, 1994).

Krasovetsky provided a critical overview of Makarenko's theory of education in a collective. He pointed out that the concept of collective as a "tool" or "instrument" of education should be rejected, but that the idea of a collective as a condition should be retained. Krasovetsky further emphasized that a collective could have a positive role if education will be accomplished through children's group activities guided by educators.

More specifically Krasovetsky (1995) focused on six principles of reconstructed pedagogy:

1. Ideological and political attempts to control school life as well as attempts to create a single model of child personality should be abandoned.

2. Every statement or recommendation suggested by Makarenko should not be accepted as absolute.

3. It is not true that collective is the only instrument of upbringing and education. What was frequently underestimated was the strength of intrinsic motivation.

4. The concept of collective responsibility for individual actions should be rejected. This clearly inhumane practice is open to serious abuses.

5. Humanistic pedagogy cannot accept a principle of unconditional surrender of individual interests to the interests of a collective. This principle led to tragedies because leaders frequently declared their own interests as those of the collective.

6. We should reject the notion that the decision of a collective must always supersede that of an individual.

Further, Skyba (1993, 1994) expressed strong criticism of Leninism, which has been the crucial foundation of all aspects of former Soviet society, including education.

As a departure from "Soviet education," Kobzar (1999, June 9-16) emphasized humanistic pedagogy within the historical context of the pioneering ideas of Comenius and others. As the key element of humanistic education, Kobzar considers a freedom of choice. The freedom of choice does require gradual learning of responsibility within a cultural and social context. An important part of humanistic education is the development of mutual trust and respect between learners and teachers. Cultivating self-respect among children is a very important task for an educator. Kobzar stressed that teachers should be tolerant when children make mistakes and should know how to build success and achievement by learning from past mistakes.

During this period of reconstruction of education in Ukraine, a recently formed educational association named in honor of Professor Hryhri Vashchenko has performed an important function. The association has over 30,000 members in Ukraine. Its goal is to promote humanistic and democratic ideas of education embedded in Ukrainian cultural values and tradition. The Vashchenko Educational Association organize in 1997 a scholarly conference in Kyiv in cooperation with the Institute of Ukrainian Studies of the Shevchenko National University. The main topic of the conference was democratization of education in Ukraine. Since the declaration of independence of Ukraine, many projects have also been initiated by universities in the United States and Canada to help in the process of restructuring of education.

Addressing the complex issues of language policy in contemporary Ukraine, President Leonid Kuchma, while on an official visit to predominantly Russian-speaking Kharkiv, stated that he does not "support forcible introduction of the Ukrainian language." Addressing Education Ministry officials, the president stressed, however, that Ukraine cannot neglect the nation's language and emphasized the need to create a favorable environment for learning Ukrainian. The president dismissed charges of oppression against Ukraine's Russian-speaking population as provocative allegations aimed at, on the one hand, stirring up interethnic controversies and, on the other hand, undermining Ukraine's international image as an emerging democracy. Ukraine's Constitution, President Kuchma said, guarantees free development, use, and protection of Russian and other minority languages, and this democratic principle must be upheld.

CONCLUSION

The current status of the Ukrainian language in Ukraine reflects the legacy of geopolitical and psychological realities. Since the middle of the 18th century until 1917, Ukraine was a part of Tsarist Imperial Russian subjected to intense linguistic Russification. From 1923 until the declaration of independence in 1991, Russification continued in a more subtle form. The Russian language was declared as the language of "social interaction" within the Soviet Union and as the language of "great Lenin." The practical result in Ukraine was that the Ukrainian language has been nearly eliminated from scholarship and higher education. In four Eastern regions of Ukraine (Khankiv, Zaporizhaha, Donetsk, and Luhansk), the percentage of students educated in the Ukrainian language of instruction at universities is on average less than 16%. In four other central regions (Kherson, Odessa, Dnipropetrovsk, and Mykoloiv), the percentage is only 37. Attempts to introduce Ukrainian as the language of instruction at universities is facing many difficult practical and psychological hurdles.

Years of geopolitical hegemony by Russia and absolute totalitarian control conditioned two generations of educators to accept supremacy of the Russian language as a vehicle for scholarly discourse. The general acceptance of the Ukrainian language will require considerable effort. It is not sufficient to declare in the Constitution Ukrainian as the national language. The general use of Ukrainian will occur only where the Ukrainian language will be utilized as the language of instruction at the institutions of higher learning. Only then will parents encourage their children, for pragmatic reasons, to study Ukrainian at secondary schools to improve their chance of admission to the institutions of higher learning.

ACKNOWLEDGMENT

We express our appreciation to professors John Fizer, David Muschinske, and N. K. Shimahara for helpful suggestions.

REFERENCES

Brukhovetsky, V. (1999, May 21). *Report of the President of UKMA*.

Cassirer, E. (1953). *The philosophy of symbolic forms*. New Haven, CT: Yale University Press.

Chas. (1995, April 28). Interview with minister Zhurovsky.

Chornovil, V. (1977). What Dohden Stenchuk defends and how he does it. In L. Jones & B. Yasen (Eds.), *Dissent in Ukraine: The Ukrainian-Herald* (Issue 6). Baltimore & Toronto: Smolosky Publishers.

Derkach, M. (1997). Ukrainian meandering and European ways of education. *Universum, 3*(4), 36-39.

Drobonokhot, M. (1995). On the way toward reconstruction. *Ridna Shkola, 4*, 2-5.

Dziuba, I. (1968). *Internationalism or Russification*. London: Weidenfeld and Nicholson.

Feldstein, D. I. (1977). Psychological characteristics of children's collective in the formation of collective qualities of personality of school age children. *Voprosy Psikhologii, 2*, 83-95.

Holowinsky, I. Z. (1988). Vygotsky and the history of psychology. *School Psychology International, 9*, 123-128.

Kobzar, B. (1999, June 9-16). How many entrances to thelabyrinth of a soul? Methodological foundations of the development of personality. *Osvita* (Education), 30-31, 451-452.

Kochenka, H. O. (1994). Some thinking about the development of Ukrainian scientific terminology. *Sucasnist, 7-8*, 173-182.

Kolaska, J. (1970). *Two years in Soviet Union*. Toronto, Canada: Peter Martin Associates Limited.

Kononenko, P. (1995). *State language official language*. Kyiv: Prosvita.

Kononenko, P., & Kononenko, T. (1999). *Issues of Ukrainian language in post-communist society*. Kyiv: Our Culture and Scholarship Publishing Center.

Krasovetsky, H. (1995). The problems of child collective in the context of school humanization. *Ridna Shkola, 2*(3), 8-15.

Lubar, O. O., & Fedorenko, D. T. (1994). Development of higher pedagogical education in Ukraine for the 21st century, a concept. *Ridna Shkola, 7*, 75-79.

Lutovinov, V. I. (1998). The inculcates of patriotism in the teaching programs of New Russia. *Russian Education and Society*, 6-14.

Martyniv, M. (1996). Shadows of state controlled schools. *Universum, 9*(10), 34-35.

Mynkiv, I. (1989). Do not idealize the past. *Catedra, 7,* 123-135.

Ovcharenko, M. (1987). The plight of the Ukrainian language Ukraine. In N. Chirovsky (Ed.), *Moscow's Russification of Ukraine* (pp. 17-37). New York: Ukrainian Congress Committee America.

Pambookian, H., & Holowinsky, I. Z. (1987). School psychology in the USSR. *The Journal of School Psychology, 25,* 220-221.

Paschenko, B. O. (1994). Painful lessons of the 1930's years. *Ridna Shkola, 7,* 2-4.

Pohribny, A. (1992). Education should serve development of the state. *Literaturna Ukrayina.*

Pohribny, A. (1994). Why did I leave the ministry of education? *Literary Ukraine.*

Rieben, R., & Carton, A. (Eds.). (1987). *The collected works of L. S. Vygotsky.* New York/London: Plenum.

Shevelov, G. Y. (1986). The language question in Ukraine in the twentieth century (1900 -1941). *Harvard Ukrainian Studies, 1-2,* 71-171.

Skyba, V. (1994). Political pathology of Ulanov-Lenin; sources and persistent agony. *Ridna Shkola, 7,* 60-74.

Solchanyk, R. (1980). Shkilnytstvo i movna polityka v URSR [Schooling and languag epolicy in Ukr. SSR]. *Sucasnist, 11,* 100.

Svoboda. (1996, July 31). Constitution of Ukraine, *145,* 3-6.

Svorak, S. D. (1997). Education in Ukraine after WWII. *Ukrainian Historical Journal, 2*(123), 28-42.

Talanchuk, P. (1992). Name ne treba kermuvatyskya trudnoshchamy [We should not be guided by hardships]. *Literaturna Ukrayina, 17,* 50.

The New York Times. (1998, August 15).

Tykhlovod, L. (1974). Literatura dla ditey propodvyh nerodu u Velykii Vitchyznianniy Viyini [Children's literature about victories in the Great Patriotic War]. *Doskhilne Vykhovannia, 10,* 43-49.

Yablonsky, V. (1995, June 21). Higher education in anticipation of new reformers. *The Voice of Ukraine.*

Yaroshevsky, M. G. (1974). Lenin and the problem of sociohistorical determination of the mind. *Voprosky Psikhologii, 1,* 3-23.

Notes: Ministry of Education of Ukraine, Personal Communication, 9-5-1995; 4-14-1998.

10

Local Identity and National Systems: The Case of Wales

Cardiff University School of Social Sciences

Over the past decade the British education system has become something of a "social laboratory" for scholars and policymakers keen to observe the operations of public services restructured on the basis of market principles. This is especially so in the case of education, where "choice" and "competition" have been the watchwords. Moreover, the British state has developed powerful instruments to hold schools accountable to the center and to parents. But what happens in subnations, regions, or territories within national systems where there are aspirations to create and maintain educational provision that is sensitive to the local needs, priorities, and values? And what arises where these issues are further complicated when local identities, as in the case of Wales, are in part created around language differences? In light of this, to what extent has Wales been able to forge an autonomous system of education? The purpose of this chapter is to provide some answers to these questions.

Wales can be defined territorially by its geographic boundaries; by a distinctive set of institutions that govern and organize its political, economic, and cultural relations; and by an ancient language-Welsh-that is the medium of instruction in about 30% of its schools. For more than a century, it has had its own education system, denoted by the existence of a federated University of Wales (founded in 1889), a department of state (the Welsh Office) created in 1964, which until recently was charged, among other things, with the planning and provision of education in Wales. It also has its own territorial schools' inspectorate, further and higher education funding councils, and a curriculum and assessment authority that oversees the development and implementation of the legislated National Curriculum in Wales.

Wales also has a national library and museum, and this year has its own elective legislative body, the National Assembly, to which power has been devolved from Westminster over activities formerly administered by the Welsh Office. There is also a Wales-focused political party, Plaid Cymru, which holds seats in the House of Commons and the Welsh Assembly, and one of whose key purposes is the defense of Welsh language and culture. National and local eisteddfoddau (music, drama, and verse competitions) provide other arenas for the transmission and preservation of linguistic and cultural traditions. There are also agencies such as the Cymdeithias yr Iaith Gymraeg (Welsh Language Society) and the Urdd Gobaith Gymru (the Welsh Youth Movement) whose focus is also the promotion of local linguistic and cultural traditions and who are also stout campaigners against the "Anglicization' of Wales.

At first glance, all the evidence suggests the existence of a robustly autonomous territory within the United Kingdom. The obvious comparisons here are the European regions of the Basque country and Catalunya in Spain, each with its own language and culture but that are also situated, like Wales, within a dominant national economy, political framework, language, and culture. In effect, these territories seek both the benefits of that relationship but also the space to determine their own present and future. Wales is an example of the tensions and challenges they all face. Wales can be identified by the Welsh language, its political institutions, and its cultural organizations. These both reflect and define distinctive local identities, values and communities. On this basis there is a strong claim for Wales to be regarded as a robust territorial entity within the United Kingdom. The situation is rather more complex and more fragile than first impressions may convey, and it is the sources and consequences of this order of things of that I want to focus on in this chapter.

The education system warrants particular attention here because, as sociologists of education have argued, education is a principal structure within which societies strive to create, maintain, and reproduce the dominant principles of social organization, relations, values, and practices (Althusser, 1971; Bernstein, 1975, 1990, 1996; Bowles & Gintis, 1976; Bourdieu & Passeron, 1977). Wales and the United Kingdom, in this regard, is an interesting arena insofar as it provides a start contrast to the United States. The central state in the U.K. since 1998 has progressively derogated powers of local education authorities and created an education market in which schools are expected to compete for students. The state has, in contrast, also assumed considerable powers to intervene directly in the operation of schools. These arrangements were justified by need to drive up standards in public schools (Firestone, Fitz, & Broadfoot, 1999; Fitz, Halpin, & Powers, 1993; Grubb, March, 1998; Whitty, Power, & Halpin, 1998). This process has, therefore, sharpened the tensions between local and national aspirations.

This chapter draws together several literatures and combines this with original research undertaken by the author and other colleagues at Cardiff University and elsewhere. It draws heavily on work by social scientists working in a number of disciplines in Wales, including economics, language, demography, political sociology, and geography. Finally, the paper draws on a body of work in the policy sociology that has been at the forefront of investigations of, and insights into, the rapidly changing ideological and political character of educational policy and policymaking over the past decade or so.

At this point I want to set out how I interpret the notion of "identity" and how that informs the structure and organization of this chapter. The interpretation derives from a number of sources, but the most important are Castells (1997) and Bernstein (1996). I also make reference later to other social theorists such as Beck and Giddens in further elaboration of the foundational statements I set out here.

One relevant strand of theorizing identity relates it to a family of concepts that includes, globalization, nation, nationalism, territories, colonialism, and post-colonialization. Castell's (1997) study is an example of this (see also Jenkins & Sofos, 1996; Lazarus, 1999; Tomlinson, 1999). For Castells, "identity" involved the social construction of meaning, by actors, around a social or cultural attribute that takes priority over other sources of meaning (Castells, 1997). I take this to include a sense of place and actors' relationships to it. In the post-structuralist mode, Castells further argued that all individual actors are bearers of multiple identities and that these are the outcomes of social processes of construction. He noted that identities have consequences for actors insofar as they become touchstones or reference points for the interpretations they make of the social world, making decisions and entering and/or understanding relationships. Most importantly, he noted that identities are constructed "in context marked by power relations" and therefore "who constructs collective identity and for what, largely determines the symbolic content of that identity and its meaning for those identifying with or placing themselves outside it" (Castells, 1997, p. 7). In short, some agencies have greater capacity to shape and reproduce identities than others and some identities have greater appear and therefore exert greater influence on meanings and action than others.

Bernstein's theorization of identity is embedded within his broader conceptualization of "pedagogic discourse" (Bernstein, 1996). Discourse and identity are the multiply mediated ends of meta and micro structures and processes within which dominant social forces (material and symbolic producers and reproducers) assemble discourses that are selectively appropriated and "recontextualized" by subordinate and less powerful agencies. A brief topical example might be history taught in U.S. schools. As a curriculum subject, it draws on scholarly research in the academy, but what then appears in school texts depends on the relative power of book publishers, curriculum designers, and local text book committees. What aspects of academic history thus make it into the classroom is the outcome of struggles between what Bernstein called "recontextualizing" agencies. The consequence is that those multiply mediated texts project to American students a sense of who they are-identity-and who belongs and who does not. A key point about Bernstein's theorization is that discourses project a limited range of identities and in consequence constrains the meanings around which actors constitute themselves.

When we synthesize these approaches, sociological work on identities takes as its point of departure the dominant discourses, the ensemble of meanings through which identities are projected, and the ensemble of institutions and agencies that maintain and reproduce them. In the case of Wales, this inevitably involves the study of its relationships with England and to the processes of, and resistance to, Anglicization, a word that condenses the considerable historical impact of England and English on social relationships, language, cultural forms, and religion in Wales. Wales is what it is to a considerable degree because of that dominating presence.

The rest of this chapter is organized into three parts. The first addresses the constitutional arrangements through which English influence in Wales was created and sustained. These are considered in the context of Welsh education and show how constitutional arrangements constrain the development of a distinctive system within Wales. The second part focuses on education and the reproduction of Welsh linguistic and cultural traditions. These issues are considered in a historical context of long-term demographic changes and transformation in the division of labor. The third part considers the tensions that exist in the education system in Wales, where schools are organized and operate on an agenda set out in England but where schools are also expected to promote the distinctiveness of Wales and Welsh culture.

WALES AND ENGLAND: THE TIES THAT BIND

Dotted through Wales one finds the massive presence of walled castles. The castles, such as those in Cardiff, Caerphilly, Pembroke, and Caernarfon, are material reminders of the longevity of an English presence in Wales. They represent early attempts to subjugate its princes, chiefs, and tribes to Norman and English domination. It is likely that the earliest phase of English rule in Wales was secured after the defeat of Gwynedd in 1292 (Adamson, 1991). What followed was the transformation of local rulers into feudal tenants of the English monarchy, and with it an imposition of all the obligations of fealty and rents, in cash and kind, that were part of feudal systems of landholding. It is the Acts of Union, legislated under the Tudors of 1535 and 1542 (Williams, 1990), however, that institutionalized the legal union of Wales and England, which is more widely interpreted as the "death of Wales" (Adamson, 1991). From this point in time, Westminster legislation applied in England and Wales and English institutions and language were the means and instruments of governance. This quick sketch does not do justice to the complex history of the English presence in Wales. It was resisted and its effects were chronologically and geographically uneven. The border areas were Anglicized earlier and more thoroughly than elsewhere for example. The narrative cannot be adequately dealt with here, but it is the framework that explains the scope and character of governance and administration in Wales.

We can identify two broad sets of institutions in Wales relevant to our discussion of education. The boundaries between the categories, however, are not always well defined. The first set is that primarily related to national policymaking. These are recontextualizing agencies (Bernstein, 1990, 1996) through which policies generated in the central state are interpreted and, in light of Welsh circumstances, adapted and/or implemented in Wales.

These include the Welsh Office; the Office of Her Majesty's Chief Inspector of Schools, the territorial schools inspectorate; the Qualifications and Curriculum Council for Wales; and other relatively small government agencies. The second group is territorial in origin and focus, and it is primarily concerned with the preservation and promotion of local economic, political, and cultural interests. Here I am thinking of agencies that include a national museum, the Welsh Language Board, the Welsh Development Agency, and the Land Authority for Wales. The two categories, the "recontextualizers" and "territorial promoters," are analytically useful, though they are by no means pure. They are all complex organizations and contain aspects of each other's primary function.

In an important sense they form a "field," using the Bernstein sense of an arena where agencies and actors are concerned with developing Wales economically, politically, and culturally, but within which there are struggles over what is Wales and over the sense of what being Welsh should be. My main argument, in the first part of this chapter, is that the agencies fundamentally involved in the governance of Wales and education in Wales-the recontextualizing agencies-have had very little latitude to assemble and promote policies that are fundamentally different from those formulated at the national level in Westminster. This arises, I suggest, by the combination of constitutional arrangements, where the key policy arena remains London focused, alongside far-reaching changes in the organization and operation of the public sector. Thus, in spite of the existence of publicly funded agencies promoting Wales and a sense of Welshness, their impact is constrained by a mode of governance where national modes of organization and values remain paramount. I now turn to develop this argument in more detail.

At the formal level, the transmission of national policy frameworks into the territorial context of Wales is relatively straightforward. Legislation is drafted jointly for England and Wales, often appearing in the same text. The contrast here is Scotland, where legislation is framed in separate bills and acts. Welsh exceptionalism is grounded in the powers given to the Secretaries of State to approve all legislation for Wales. Moreover, they are also able to adjust the implementation of such legislation in the light of local circumstances. Here, civil service officials have had a crucial role in advising ministers. The arguments for

Wales to be treated differently, however, have to be set alongside the convention of collective cabinet responsibility and the subsequent responsibility this places on ministers in the Welsh Office to implement parliamentary legislation. As Rees and others have argued, we have very little empirical research on the "assumptive world" of Welsh civil servants and on the character and quality of the advice given, via the usual channels, to ministers (Rees, 1997, October). There is, then, a qualified constitutional recognition for a distinctive application of national policy in Wales. That situation also applies to government agencies located in Wales. The latter, however, are constrained not only constitutionally but also in their resources to forge innovative approaches to local policy issues. These limitations are evidences when we consider the "big picture" of public-sector restructuring over the past two decades.

POLICY, GOVERNANCE, AND THE PUBLIC SECTOR

For insights into forms of governance in the public sector that have been incrementally established since the early 1980s, we can turn to writers in the fields of political science and public administration. Writers such as Gamble pointed to the seeming paradox of public-sector services being subjected to a "free market" and a "strong state" (Gamble, 1988). In the organization and provision of public sector services provision, in Rhodes' words, "fragmentation" and "centralization" coexist (Rhodes, 1997). What he and others (e.g., Ferlie, Asburner, Fitzgerald, & Pettigrew, 1996; Hood, 1991) in this genre suggest is that this is not a paradoxical or chaotic situation, but an extremely flexible and powerful form of governing.

To paraphrase a complex argument, the reasoning runs as follows: The creation of freestanding, autonomous institutions, where available resources are tied to "customer" use and satisfaction, has been accompanied by the embedding of an ensemble of ideologies and practices, loosely denoted as "new public management." This has three principal characteristics: managers are free to manage; managers have responsibility for institutional survival; and institutions are accountable, up (via meso-level regulation) and down (via customer/client, preferences). There are other versions of this, but the broad combination of "freedom," "audit," "accountability," and "quality provision" are also the key elements in these. More sensitive accounts also note the restructuring of professions and professional practices within public institutions and within private enterprise, from which the models for public management were derived.

What Rhodes and others went on to argue is that the combination of "autonomous," strong central regulation, and "new public management" give rise to a potent mix of self-surveillance and external regulation. Potent, because institutions and agents, at the "hub and the rim," "coproduce" the way public service provision is organized, sustained, and reproduced (see Offe, 1984). In this account, "governance" of a new kind weakens boundaries between state and civil society, the professional and the personal. In Foucault's terms, what we have here is a very distinctive form of "governmentality" (Foucault, 1977). The point to be made here is that while territorial agencies in their composition may have local appointees and personnel at the structural level, the mode of governance and values associated with it permeate national borders. It is in this context that claims for a Welsh dimension have to be considered, and moreover, it is at this level that reformers will have to aim in order to reconfigure the realm of policy and policymaking in Wales. What, then, have been the consequences for this restructuring for education in Wales?

NEW GOVERNANCE OF EDUCATION

The progressive attempts to restructure the U.K. national system of education commenced in legislation, with the introduction of the Assisted Places Scheme in the 1980 Education Act. That initiative was intended to increase parental choice via government financial support to enable financially needy families to use fee-paying schools (Edwards, Fitz, & Whitty, 1989). It was taken forward by the Education Reform Act, 1988, and subsequent Education Acts (Ball, 1990; Fitz, Halpin, & Power, 1993; Flude & Hammer, 1990; Maclure, 1988). The prolonged shift from locally planned and provided forms of schooling to an institutional arrangement compatible with a "marketized" system of provision is complex and contradictory. It has involved a reorientation not only of the post-war system of public service provision, but also the reorientation of "citizens" as "consumers," and a reshaping of what they can and ought to expect. The analytical framework for capturing the scope and character of the reform of education and the attendant reorientation is grounded in two linked concepts.

"Manufactured uncertainty," a term borrowed from Giddens (1994), is employed to describe the location of schools in education markets, the consequent shaping of school relations with each other and the impact of markets in the internal organization of schools. "Redefining pedagogical authority," owes much to state theory and to Bernstein (1996) and denotes two things. First, it involves the creation of a new layer of institutions within the central state and a subsequent redistribution of power and politics between these and conventional departments of government. Second, it refers to the increased central regulation of public meanings, discourses, and institutional practices at the expense of local and community-generated systems and practices. The introduction of a National Curriculum and associated testing procedures, and its regulation via an expanded program of school inspections, is a notable example. The process might all be understood as a set of standards-driven reforms, formal statements about "what every child should know" and what levels of attainment, as measured by national testing, each school should achieve. It is in this area that the Labour government has extended most policy direction established under previous Conservative administrations and set out in the Labour government's first white paper on education, Excellence in Schools (Department for Education and Employment/Welsh Office, 1997). I take it as axiomatic that each of these concepts denotes an associated discursive regime, embedded in policy texts that function to promulgate action; position institutions, agents, and privilege regimes of truth; identify and legitimate particular sources of authoritative knowledge; and prioritize certain voices. I will discuss each of these in more detail.

MANUFACTURED UNCERTAINTY

A sustained critique of Local Education Authorities (LEAs) and the so-called bureaucratic control of education commenced within one year of Thatcher's first government, although the ground had been prepared well in advance of that (Edwards, Fitz, & Witty, 1989). Policies that attempted to roll back the monolopy of LEA provision and the power of administrators and educational professionals include the Assisted Places Scheme (1981), reformed governing bodies (1986, 1988), City Technology Colleges (CTCs) (1986), grant-maintained schools (1988), Local Management of Schools (1988), and open enrollment (1988) (see Flude & Hammer, 1990; Maclure, 1988; Pierson, 1998).

In brief, the organization of state education in England and Wales features:

1.   A high degree of institutional autonomy. All schools manage their own budget and their internal affairs. Introduced by the Conservatives, these arrangements will continue under the Labour government's recent legislation within which schools designated "community," "foundation," or "aided." The legislation effectively removes the funding advantages previously enjoyed by grant-maintained schools.

2.   Schools are construed as individual cost centers that are market-driven by virtue of a per-capita funding regime. Failure to recruit the planned number of students is intended to translate directly into reduced staff and resources.

3.   Schools exist primarily in a competitive, not collaborative, relation with each other. In this situation institutional survival is paramount.

4.   Published performance indicators--examination results and inspection reports--have been created to establish a hierarchy of relatively "good" and "poor" schools.

The privileged figure on the landscape is "the parent," who is presented with a choice of schools in the state and the fee-paying sectors, which are intended to be diverse in terms of governance and the education they offer.

How, then, do these arrangements articulate to our organizing concept "manufactured uncertainty"? All the evidence suggests that schools are no faced with an insecure future and are required to manage risk without the safety net of LEA support in times of turbulence or crisis. Schools are expected to act like enterprises in the private sector, but they also face the same problems of survival. There is no guarantee for the great majority of schools that they will have sufficient students, year to year, to sustain previously existing levels of staffing. All the existing research on the impact of the 1988 Act suggests that schools are prepared to plot and scheme to preserve their "market share" (e.g., Fitz, Halpin, & Power, 1993; Gewitz, Ball, & Bowe, 1995; Woods, Bagley, & Glatter, 1998).

It can be argued that educational markets in Wales are somewhat different from their English counterparts. For example, the independent sector in Wales is less prominent than its English counterpart, where it educates about 8% of students compared with less than 2% in Wales. There are no CTCs in Wales, and grant-maintained (GM) schools accounted for about 1% of students in the maintained sector compared with about 4% in England. Only one GM school selected students on the basis of academic ability, compared with the 166 grammar schools in England that selected on academic ability. On the other hand, in Wales, the market includes a choice for parents between Welsh and English medium schools and, under measures promoted by Welsh Secretary John Redwood's "Popular Schools Initiative," funds were made available for "popular" or oversubscribed schools to expand their accommodation in order to admit more students.

On the basis of small-scale comparative research conducted in Cardiff and Bristol, there is evidence that "manufactured uncertainty" applies to state schools in urban South Wales as well as in England (see fitz, Firestone, & Fairman, 2000). State schools in Wales are equally concerned about the long-term future; they are concerned about their performance in public examinations and how parents will interpret these. they are also conscious of, and concerned about, attracting students who perform well academically. We have no evidence yet on the relative effects of market principles on schools and their operation in the more rural areas of Wales nor of the extent to which manufactured uncertainty impacts on the organization, curriculum, and admissions policies in rural schools.

REDEFINING PEDAGOGIC AUTHORITY

Perhaps the most striking and potentially far-reaching consequences of institutional reform run somewhat counter to the trends we have so far identified. First, there has been transformation of the state both in terms of institutional arrangements and an expansion of its capacity to regulate the various activities of schools. There has been the creation of meso-state-nonelected, ministerially appointed agencies, responsible for the provision of aspects of education, social, and welfare services. They are accountable upward to ministers, but have no clear lines of accountability downward to citizens and electors. In education in England, the funding of grant-maintained schools, and progressively, of LEA schools, was determined by the Funding Agency for Schools; teacher education is decided by the Teacher Training Agency, while the Qualifications and Assessment Authority monitors the National Curriculum and the national testing of students. Her Majesty's Inspectorate (HMI) in England and Wales has been succeeded by, respectively, the Office of Standards in Education (OFSTED) and the Office of Her Majesty's Chief Inspector of Schools (OHMCI) as the agencies responsible for the inspection of schools and teacher education.

There has been, then, a proliferation of what might be called, in Bernstein's terms, official pedagogic recontextualizing agencies (Bernstein, 1990, 1996), each concerned with a specific domain of education policy and practice. Inevitably, there has been an increase in the "noise" in the field as educational policymaking has been reconstituted, and as institutions have been repositioned. The prominence of the coordinating role of Prime Minister and his policy unit alongside the Education Secretary and the Department for Education and employment (DfEE) is one of the key features to emerge from these changes. Whatever the prevailing state of play, it is now clear that the central state has established a formidable institutional complex with which to regulate curriculum and pedagogic practices in schools. Central direction is conducted through:

1.   A National Curriculum (NC) that all maintained schools are required to teach, and associated testing procedures in which children undertake national tests at age 7, 11, and 14.
2.   Inspection, originally on a 4-, now 6-year cycle in England and a 5-year cycle in Wales, by OFSTED in England and OHMCI in Wales. Inspection reports are available to parents.
3.   Guidance on pedagogy, mainly a strong steer to adopt a more teacher-centered approach to classroom transmission,

via government-sponsored reports and by increasingly interventionist programs such as the national literacy and numeracy strategies in England (HMCI, 1995; Department for Education and Employment, 1998).

4. Target setting, where schools and LEAs set out publicly the percentages of students expected to achieve designated grades in public examinations, from ages 5 to 16 years.

The wider implications of the central regulation of education, however, are to be found in the range of educational identities that are projected in the combination of curriculum, pedagogic, and inspection policy.

In general terms the educational identities constructed in and through the NC, the inspection process, and pedagogic guidance correspond with what Bernstein called retrospective identities. "These . . . are shaped by national, religious or cultural grand narratives recontextualized to stabilise a past in the future. . . . With these identities the collective base is foregrounded much more than the exchange value of the identity" (Bernstein, 1996, p. 411).

Although aspects of schooling thus evoke a sense of a national or religious belonging (the retrospective identity), it can also be argued that identities that have an exchange value are those that schools under a market regime are required, and indeed choose, to promote. Bernstein clearly argued this possibility in his theory. I will develop this argument below.

There are important differences between England and Wales in terms of what constitutes the NC. The English version emphasizes a subject-based curriculum. Moreover, National Curriculum English makes Shakespeare and other writers in the "canon" compulsory reading for all school students. History is primarily a study state craft and the impact of British (read English) traditions overseas. Schools are also judged by school inspectors on their development of students' spiritual, social, moral, and cultural development and schools also have a statutory responsibility to conduct a daily act of worship, broadly Christian in character. The NC can be interpreted as revitalizing both nationalism and traditionalist subject knowledge. Alongside this, however, the government has attempted to foster modernization via the inclusion of technology as a National Curriculum subject, and has invited schools to adopt a technology focus through the Technology of Schools Initiative (Fitz, Halpin, & Power, 1997a, 1997b). The most recent of these initiatives was the creation of a National Grid for Learning. It aims to connect all schools to the Internet and provide "portals" to virtual teachers' centers and classrooms. All the policies apply in Wales.

Children in Wales, however, have been progressively given the opportunity to explore their own national identity via the study of Welsh, Welsh history, geography, literature, and music-the curriculum cymraeg. Welsh is a compulsory fourth core National Curriculum subject in state schools. The territorial schools inspectorate invigilate the extent to which schools reflect a Welsh ethos, via dual signing policies, cultural events, and wall displays. These are important departures from England's NC and may well prove vitally important in the claim for building distinctive programs of teaching, learning, and assessment in and for Wales. Nevertheless, the key principles of a subject-based curriculum with associated testing procedures, where children are subject to national tests at ages 7, 11, and 13 along with General Certificate of Education (GCSE) exams at 16, apply with equal vigor in Wales as they do in England.

There are territorial differences. For example, while the centrally defined and closely prescribed specifications of the national literacy and numeracy strategies are being implemented in england, schools in Wales are being offered more general guidance on ways of developing pupils' literacy and numeracy. The local view that these, in reality, are no more than English creations imposed on Wales was summed up by one delegate at a conference on education policy in Wales, who made a plea that such agencies should be rather more than subpost office branches of the one in London.

There is some evidence that these territorial agencies have developed policies, values, and operations somewhat different from the English counterparts. The schools' inspectorate in Wales is one notable example. All state schools in Wales are subject to full inspection, on a fixed cycle, conducted by contracted terms of inspectors, led by a Registered Inspector. This mode of inspection is very similar to that in operation in England. In most respects then, inspection processes, purposes, and effects are the same. Indeed, the Framework documents, on which inspection criteria and judgments are based, were written primarily by Her Majesty's Inspectorate in England. Nevertheless, local adjustments were made in response to OHMCI's assessment of what would work best in the Welsh context. To reduce pressures on small schools, it was decided that the original inspection cycle would be every 5, not 4, years. One other notable contrast is the care that successive Chief Inspectors have taken to report positive aspects of the performance of schools and avoid the headline-grabbing spin of their English counterparts' sharp criticism of teachers. The gentler touch may well reflect the longer involvement of the territorial inspectorate in offering direct advice to school aimed at increasing school effectiveness and improvement. It remains the case that inspection in Wales is very different from the system in Scotland and, in most key respects, resembles that in England.

School improvement and school effectiveness policies have been in operation in Wales rather longer than in England. Since the publication of the Loosemore Report in 1981, one policy thrust in Wales has been the determination that levels of attainment in school should at least match those achieved in England. That refrain is to be found in later policy programs such as "A Bright Future" (Welsh office, 1995, 1997a), "Building Excellent Schools Together" (Welsh office, 1997b), and Education and Training Action Group for

Wales Report (1998). The discourse of these documents is founded on claims that children in Wales perform less well than children in England and that its schools are less effective than similar schools in England. The "schooled to fail" myth has been finally laid to rest in some sustained and rigorous research by Gorard (1998). The "underachievement" claim, though, gave successive Welsh Secretaries a powerful lever to argue for school effectiveness and improvement policies designed to drive up school performance. It also enabled them to sidestep policies that might have involved some form of wealth and income distribution, or policies aimed at changing the social mix of schools. A similar strategy can be observed under the present Labour administration, exemplified in its first education act, the 1998 School Standards and Framework Act.

At the national level, the School Standards and Effectiveness Unit of the DfEE is emblematic of the government's main policy direction s(Department for Education and Employment, 1999). In England, in association with their LEAs, schools are now required to set targets for attainment in public examinations. The top-down approach is not so evident in the implementation of target settings in Wales, where schools were invited to establish their own targets, which were then modified, where necessary, by LEAs and then agreed to by the Welsh Office. Target setting in both contexts has to be set alongside the threat of "a zero tolerance" for schools deemed to be "complacent" or "underachieving." Responsibility for raising standards, then, lies with school and with teachers. Little attempt has bee made thus far to address the external factors--social class, poverty, family arrangements, school resources, and welfare programs--which, four decades of research suggests, has a determining effect on student performance (see Davies, 1999). Centrally determined standards, performance indicators, and sanctions have become powerful policy levers to make schools accountable upwards to the center and measures through which the scale and pace of pedagogic change can be regulated. There are acknowledged variations in how these operate territorial, and these variations are important, but it can be argued that the mode of governance embedded in these policies operates in Wales in much the same degree as in England.

In light of local capacities for agencies to adjust national policies, is there any evidence that this has produced school organizations, admissions policies, pupil grouping, school management, pedagogy, classroom practice, and assessment arrangements in Wales that differ from England? Although the research base is very thin, at this time, the answer would have to be no. In a small-scale investigation led by Firestone and Fitz into the local impact of national assessment policies in Bristol and Cardiff, the research team reported that there was no discernible difference in schools' interpretation of, and responses to, national assessment policy on either side of the border (Firestone, Fitz, & Broadfoot, 2000; Firestone, Winter, & Fitz, 2000; Firestone, Fitz, & Fairman, in press). The research focused on English-language schools only in Wales and did not include any school where Welsh was the main language of instruction. The research was conducted at schools and at the classroom level and involved interviews with key actors as well as classroom observation. In all the features of schools listed above, no significant differences were found in schoolwide or classroom-based policies and practices. The researchers were struck by the similarities and the absences of differences between the two sets of schools.

What Wales has witnessed over the past decade or so has been a new form of regulation by successive national governments. This, it can be argued, has two elements: regulation via markets and regulation through the state. Markets, whether these operate in the wealth-creating or the public-sector arena, act as constraints on the ensemble of relations actors and agencies may enter into and on the values that are esteemed. Competition, choice, and diversity in education then motivate schools and parents to act in ways that are not always necessarily self-seeking, but that nevertheless limit the kinds of relations these schools and communities have with each other. Moreover, in a situation of manufactured uncertainty, it is difficult to consider what counts as a good education and a good student outside the quantum of test results and a school's market reputation. Learner identities projected by this ensemble of policies in the end privilege performance in public examinations, and these are sustained and reproduced by schools whose funding and survival depend on doing well in the high-stakes assessment arena. The principles apply in Wales as much as they do in England.

REPRODUCING WALES: WELSH LANGUAGE AND EDUCATION

My analysis above suggests that in terms of governance, organization, and goals, there is very little difference between the state schooling in Wales and England. In this section I turn to a feature of education in Wales that is one of its defining characteristics. Here I refer to Welsh medium education, where Welsh is the language of instruction, and where Welsh is one of the four core national curriculum subjects and is required to be taught in English medium schools as a second language. Discussion of Welsh language and education is important because it was an entitlement hard won this century and because for some people in Wales, it is the most significant affirmation of their difference and identity. Welsh-language education, however, is also a "field," an arena constituted by field occupants and entrepreneurs who have invested heavily in the maintenance and reproduction of the Welsh language, via schools. It is also important to discuss education and language because, as I point out later, school shave become the major site for the reproduction of Welsh speaking and are major forces ensuring its survival.

Welsh is an ancient language and probably spoken throughout what was predominantly a rural and peasant society. It was the language of work and production, the family, and worship. From about the 13th century, it is likely that English increasingly became the language of the ruling class. From the Acts of Union onward, legislation was drafted in Norman English and English and applied in Wales, where the majority of speakers were probably monoglot Welsh speakers (see Williams, 1990). Up to the mid-19th century, "popular" education--in the factor or works schools, dame schools, instruction by wandering scholars, the monitorial schools, and the Sunday schools-was also conducted predominantly in the medium of Welsh. We have an official account of popular education in mid-19th century Wales, at the time when there was some state funding for popular education, but before mass state-supported education commenced in 1870 and before it was made compulsory in the 1880s.

The Reports of the Commissioners of Inquiry into the State of Education in Wales were published in 1847. The commission was established as a London response seeking causes for rural disturbances (The Rebecca Riots) and Chartist uprisings. In Wales the reports are known more simply as the "Blue Books," and for others, the publication is known as the "Treason of the Blue Books." For those familiar with 19th-century parliamentary commission reports, the Blue Books are very much of the genre. Working-class life and culture is usually represented as alien and dangerous. The commissioners record evidence, given by the gentry and local clergy, of working-class drunkenness, sexual license, blasphemy, fighting, and political radicalism. The reports, however, also faithfully record the poverty and exploitation that accompanied early industrial capitalism. Accounts of a similar tone can be found in the HMI reports of popular education in England at about the same time. It was the parliamentary commission reports, for example, that provided Marx and Engels with an empirical basis for their critique of the capitalist mode of production, and excerpts figure prominently in Das Capital.

The Blue Books attempted to portray a systematic account of schooling in Wales at the time of the commissioners' inquiry. What emerges is a form of provision not unlike that found elsewhere in Britain in that period. For a small fee, some kind of education was widely available, as and when families required it, usually when the family economy did not require the children's labor. Its inadequacies were systematically documented and in their conclusions the commissioners made, for the time, a powerful, forward-looking case for the proper funding of schools and for systematic and regulated teacher education (Jones, 1998). That is not what made the Blue Books what they are best remembered for, however.

In their reports the commissioners argued that Wales was sunk into ignorance because of its language, and immorality because of its Nonconformist religion. Welsh, they reported, was "manifold barrier to the moral progress and commercial prosperity of the people" (1846 Report, quoted in Welsh

Department, 1947, p. 12). In their view, this could be remedied by the introduction of English as the medium of instruction in schools and a sound religious (read Anglican) education. The Blue Books are now widely interpreted as the judgments of an English bourgeoisie on a language they could not speak, a literature they deemed unworthy of the name and forms of culture and worship they either could not comprehend or mistrusted. In the Blue Books we find this telling and very important vignette of a classroom:

> My attention was attracted to a piece of wood, suspended
> on a string around a boy's neck. This, I was told were the
> words "Welsh stick." This I was told was a stigma for
> speaking Welsh. But in fact his only alternative was to
> speak Welsh or say nothing. He did not understand English
> and there is no systematic exercise in interpretation.
> (1847 Reports, cited in Welsh Department, 1947, p. 17)

This, and variations of it, was the "Welsh not" in practice. The extent to which that policy was fostered in the monitorial and popular schools by teachers keen to suppress the use of Welsh and the degree to which schools were responding to parental aspirations that their children should learn English at school is not easy to determine. It is likely that some parents saw English as the means of securing economic advantage and social mobility. Either way, English was perceived as the language of power.

The Blue Books did not stamp out Welsh in schools. The spread of English as a medium of instruction was certainly expanded by the impact of the Revised Code of 1862. Under the Code, a portio of a teacher's salary depended on the number of children attaining age-related "standards" in the "3 Rs" (Welsh Department, 1947a, 1947b, 1947c). The tests were conducted in English and so there was no profit in, and indeed a considerable disincentive to, teach Welsh, or in the medium of Welsh. In effect, the Revised Code went a considerable way toward achieving some of the 1847 commissioners' gender ambitions for English to become the medium of instruction in all state schools. Indeed, the poet Matthew Arnold, one of Her Majesty's Inspectors at the time of the Revised Code, echoed the Blue Book sentiments that Wales would be a better place without Welsh.

At the present time, of the 1900 state schools in Wales, nearly 30% of primary school sand about 8% of secondary schools now teach solely in the medium Welsh, and a small number teach part of the curriculum in that language (Welsh Office, 1997a, 1997b, 1997c). The regional variations are considerable, however, with the greatest concentrations occurring west and north, while the fewest are found on the eastern boundaries with England, and on the southern, more densely populated coastal strip, which includes the urban centers of Cardiff, Newport, and Swansea. How these patterns emerged and how they shape opportunity and identity for school students is the issue I turn to next. My analysis adopts categories that have been employed by demographers and political geographers in their studies of Wales. I refer here to "language shift," to denote historical changes in numbers of Welsh speakers, Welsh and its relationship with the English, and the socioeconomic forces that determine its changing patterns of use and acceptance. "Language regeneration" refers to the resources that have sustained and reproduced Welsh-language use.

LANGUAGE SHIFT

The main narrative here is the decline of Welsh-language use in the 20th century. Whereas census data record about half the population in Wales using Welsh in 1901, that has declined to 18.5% in 1991 (Aitchison & Carter, 1998, pp. 167-169; Blackaby & Drinkwater, 1996, p. 159). Its most rapid decline occurred in the first 20 years of this century. Indeed, in mid- and southeast Wales, the areas transformed socioeconomically in the 19th century by the rise of extractive and heavy metal industries (coal and steel and allied industries) and its subsequent decline. Welsh fell into desuetude in the space of two generations. One commentator notes that in the heartland of the valley coal fields, union business-administrative and political-was conducted entirely in English by 1911, whereas 50 years before, Welsh miners organized themselves in Welsh (jones, quoted in Aitchison & Carter, 1998).

Census data, though, because of the way the forms are worded, tended to over report the extent of Welsh-language use. The questions ask about knowledge of Welsh rather than frequency of use, first language used at home or fluency, for example. Nevertheless, studies using other secondary data confirm the broad census trends, namely, considerable regional divergence in Welsh speaking. However, even in the heartland of Welsh-language use, in 1991, about 52% of the population are recorded as having no knowledge of Welsh. In areas with low densities of Welsh speakers (Gwent & South Glamorgan), about 94% of the population claim no knowledge of Welsh. How can we account for its decline then, from a pre-19th-century situation where monoglot Welsh regions thrived and where Welsh was the ubiquitous community language? Six socioeconomic factors seem to underpin the Welsh-English language shift.

The first factor is the introduction of English as the governing language of the ruling class. Second, the English settlement of Gwent, and the mid-18th century, and of other border regions increased the use of English as the language of the hearth, education, and worship. Third, and most crucially, was the industrialization of mid- and south Wales in the form of the iron works and mines. The subsequent in-migration from other parts of Wales and England brought about the Anglicization of the industrial valleys by the 1870s (Pryce,

1990) and consolidated English as the language of labor and community. The fourth factor is mass state education, introduced in 1870 and compulsory after 1880, that more or less ensured that all children were able to use English even if Welsh was the language at home. It remains the case today that all Welsh speakers are bilingual in English. The fifth factor is the creeping prevalence of popular culture through music, film, magazines, and later television, broadly English and American in origin and language. The last explanation is probably the most difficult to map. This refers to a popular sentiment, increasingly evident after the mid-19th century, that English was the language of progress, modernization, social liberation, and mobility. I'm not referring here to cultural critics such as Matthew Arnold, who argued that progress was a condition to be achieved only after the death of Welsh, but to popular perception that the acquisition of English was a precondition for improving one's lot. In consequence of these socioeconomic transformations, then, there were fewer and fewer compelling reasons to speak or write in Welsh.

Language use is also related to identity and to politics in rather complex ways. I can only outline the main themes here. If we take two recent electoral events, referenda, held to determine whether or not Wales would have its own legislative body, there is an interesting pattern in the votes for greater autonomy and in the distribution of the density of Welsh speakers. In each case, in 1971 and 1997, the strongest support for devolution came from areas with the greatest density of Welsh speakers, the least from the areas with the fewest. The 1971 referendum failed to yield a majority in favor of devolution. In 1998 the National Assembly was established, but by only the very narrowness of margins, decided in the end by votes from the last area to return in results, west (Welsh-speaking) Wales. Voters in the east and south, then still show a strong orientation toward Britain and to the national arena. On the other hand, it can be argued that mid-Wales has an English-speaking population, the so-called British Welsh (Balsom, 1985) that is fiercely Welsh in its loyalties and orientation. So-called Welsh Wales, the heartland of Welsh use, shows still the greatest opposition to cultural forms of Anglicization (Balsom, 1985) and greater loyalty to Plain Cymru than other parts of Wales.

LANGUAGE REGENERATION

The 1991 census data suggested that just fewer than one fifth of the population in Wales are now recorded as having a knowledge of Welsh. To repeat, this may be an overestimation of Welsh-language use for reasons I noted earlier. Language shift from Welsh to English, according to commentators, has not stabilized. Some also claim resurgence in Welsh-language use, especially in areas where previously there was a low density of Welsh speakers. A powerful framework of what might be called "language planning," (Baker, 1998, June), has been set in place to preserve and promote the Welsh language, and this may well explain some of the upsurge in Welsh-language use.

Measures to promote Welsh include:

1. Ysgolion Cymraeg (1947)-schools where Welsh is the sole or shared medium of instruction.
2. Welsh Office (1964)-the department of state, which has adopted and promoted the bilingual publication of official documents.
3. Mudia Ysgolion Meithrin (1971)-the Welsh-language nursery school movement.
4. Sianel Pedwar Cymru (1982) S4C-the Welsh language television channel. In addition, there are Welsh language radio stations, such as Radio Cymru and BBC Cymru.
5. Welsh Language Act (1993)-that established the rights of Welsh speakers to conduct business in the medium of Welsh.
6. Welsh Language Board (1993)-that promotes, monitors, and maintains the use of Welsh in public institutions.

The Welsh Book Council, Welsh churches and chapels, the National Eisteddfod, and local "eisteddfoddau" (local festivals) are other means by which Welsh is promoted. Organizations such as the Welsh Language Society have also acted as effective pressure groups in the political arena. The field effect of these organizations has been to maintain presence of Welsh-language issues at the forefront of policymaking in Wales. One consequence of this is that in Wales, all major institutions are bilingually signed, as are road signs, and official documents are available in Welsh and English.

And yet, the reproduction of Welsh-language use remains somewhat fragile. It is developing unevenly and, although it has a secure place in schools, in public life, and in the churches, that is not necessarily the case at home, in families. It is to these tensions I now turn.

Census data suggest a further slow decrease in the numbers of people able to speak Welsh. This was recorded as 20.9% in 1971, 18.9% in 1981, and 18.6% in 1991 (T. Rees, 1999). The census, however, also shows an increase in the number of 3- to 15-year-olds able to speak Welsh, from 18% in 1981 to 24.9% in 1991 (Rees, 1991). There is also some support for the argument that the teaching of Welsh in schools may well further arrest the decline in Welsh speaking. The proportion of students in classes where Welsh is the sole medium of instruction has risen from 14.9% in 1990 to 17.2% in 1995 (Rees, 1999). Equally, the percentage of students in classes where no Welsh is taught has dropped from 22.8% to 7.8% in the same period. The figures are especially important because previous data had suggested a Welsh-speaking population not only declining but also aging.

Yet these figures do not reveal other, perhaps disturbing, trends. I summarize these below:

> Although the number of school students learning in the medium of Welsh, and learning as a second language, increased, there is a significant fall in the number of students educated in Welsh as they move through school. At ages 7 and 11, about 19% of students are in classes where Welsh is the sole or part medium of instruction. In first year of high school, however, only 12% of students are taught Welsh as first language, a falloff of some 7% (Baker, 1998, June). By the end of secondary school (16 yrs), this has declined to 11.3%, and a further 23% are entered for GCSE exams in Welsh as a second language. Secondary education, therefore, is an arena where significant language shift still occurs, in spite of the recent growth in the number of ysgolion cymraeg.

> There are recorded decreases in the number of Welsh speakers in the areas directly adjacent to the core of Welsh-speaking Wales in the west and north and a complex pattern of decreases and increases in the core itself. In-migration by English speakers has had some effect here (Aitchison & Carter, 1998).

> There are increases in Welsh speaking in the Anglicized and urban areas of Wales, in the south and east, but from a very low base. In Gwent, for example, the proportion has risen from 1.9% in 1971 to 2.1% in 1991, while in the same period, there figures rose from 5% to 6.5% in South Glamorgan (Aitchison & Carter, 1998).

> However, 45.4% of male Welsh speakers in southeast Wales were in the professional and managerial classes, compared with 24.9% of male non-Welsh speakers (Blackaby & Drinkwater, 1996). A very similar pattern appears for female Welsh speakers, where the figures are 43.8% and 22.6% respectively. In the non-Welsh-speaking areas, and the above figures relate to an area where 95% of the population report no knowledge of Welsh, there appears to be an occupational advantage for Welsh speakers (Blackaby & Drinkwater, 1996).

> The family, as a site of language reproduction and regeneration, is waning in significance. Large-scale, long-term changes in family arrangements mean that the number of households without children and

households with one parent have an effect on the rate of intergenerational language transmission. Aitchison and Carter's study, based on 1991 census statistics, suggests that no Welsh is spoken either by adults of children in 75% of households in Wales. In all, about 6% of households have children who speak Welsh. This is regarded as a weak basis for language regeneration. On the other hand, there is evidence of the "school effect" in the households that have adults and children but where the adults do not speak Welsh. Of all the households in Wales, about 27% fall into this category; however, just under 10% of them contain children who speak Welsh. In other words, these children are learning the language outside the family.

What is apparent, however, is that Welsh is reproduced in middle-class families more frequently than in working-class families, and that even in families where neither parent is a Welsh speaker, slightly more children in middle-class families speak Welsh than in working-class families (Aitchison & Carter, 1998). These differences are small, but suggest the greater propensity of middle-class families to encourage Welsh speaking (Aitchison & Carter, 1998).

Ysgolion cymraeg, the Welsh medium schools in Wales generally, and in southeast Wales specifically, are claimed to be more successful as measured by public examination results than their English medium counterparts (Reynolds & Bellin, 1996). However, an analysis of examination performance related to the proportion of students in Welsh medium schools entitled to free school meals (a widely used indicator of low income and poverty, and to which exam results are inversely related) suggests that intakes of Welsh medium schools are different from their English medium counterparts, even when they are situated in the same catchment area. Welsh medium schools, overall, tend to have rather fewer students on free school meals than English medium schools (Gorard, 1998; Gorard & Fitz, 1998a). Moreover, when we take free school meals into account, one can demonstrate that Welsh medium is no more or less "effective" than English medium education. There are good and relative poor performers in each category.

Generally, then, it can be argued that Welsh medium schools have become the significant site for the reproduction of the Welsh language in circumstances where the family now has a diminished capacity to sustain it. However, the situation also seems to be that middle-class families are more likely to encourage Welsh-language use at home and are more likely to use ysgolion cymraeg in traditionally non-Welsh-speaking areas. We need a more detailed analysis of the socioeconomic composition of Welsh medium education before this can be argued conclusively, however.

One explanation of the above might lie in the occupational structure and the opportunities open to Welsh speakers in upper tiers of the public sector and in the broadcast media, where a command Welsh is an advantage. Social and cultural reproduction in middle-class families appears to include greater exposure to Welsh-language use, and that is logical where this opens the way to professional and managerial occupations.

CONCLUSION

Whatever its linguistic and cultural distinctiveness, in numerous ways, Wales remains bound in the Union with England. The larger picture of restructuring the public sector and the creation of a mode of governance that combines market regulation, disciplines, and values, alongside a powerful and increasingly interventionist state, is as much in evidence in Wales as it is in England. The emphasis on standards and accountability, the minute regulation of schools via target setting and output performance indicators, and the strategies devised to raise these operate territorially as well as nationally. The discourse of school improvement and school effectiveness and avoidance of any discussion about the impact of poverty on patterns of educational opportunity and achievement apply in Wales as well as England. Paradoxically, the embedding of school improvement/school effectiveness language in official discourse commenced somewhat earlier in Wales, at a time when Welsh schools, by comparison with their English counterparts, were reported to be underachieving. The dominating official discourse now produces a narrow view of what is the good school and the desirable student, and these are strongly performance-based.

At present, that framework overshadows any debate about what value schools should be transmitting and takes prominence over the promotion of, and investment in, the curriculum cymraeg. On this view, the learner identities, which are maintained and reproduced by schools in Wales, are very British and not distinctively Welsh. English and Welsh schools, moreover, are more similar than they are different in the process of social and cultural reproduction. Middle-class students, by any measure, fare better in the system; the relative attainment of boys and girls-where by most indicators, girls are doing better in national assessments-is much the same across the borders, and raising the attainment of minority ethnic students is a challenge to both systems. As I noted earlier, researchers have not observed any pedagogy in English medium schools, which could be identified as distinctively territorial.

The rise of the ysgolion cymraeg is a distinctive development, but has given rise to some tensions within the system. The development of Welsh medium schools is one of a number of state-supported responses aimed at arresting the language shift from Welsh to English. Crucially, it has ensured that there is a younger generation of Welsh speakers able to keep the language alive and to reproduce it. The language has been further secured by state measures to protect the right of Welsh-language users and through bilingual signing and documentation.

For the great majority of people in Wales, however, there is no compelling reason to read, write, speak, or understand Welsh. This is reflected in the data that suggest the diminished importance of the family as a source of language regeneration. It is quite simply not being used at home to any great degree. One can be economically active, politically and culturally engaged, socially mobile, and fiercely Welsh without knowledge of the Welsh language. For others, as some commentators note (Balsom, 1985; Day & Rees, 1989; Giggs & Pattie, 1992), "the Welsh language is a critical marker of Welsh ethnicity" (Day & Rees, 1989, p. 1), and that it is the key signifier of territorial and political and cultural identity. Who then, it must be added, has benefitted from the regeneration of Welsh on the considerable investment of state resources? One could suggest that Britain as a whole has been the beneficiary, insofar as one of the nation's ancient languages has been preserved and kept in daily use. On these grounds, where diversity and the right to be different is consonant with any form of democracy, the succession of language policies can be defended. There are some ambiguities in the promotion of Welsh as a language of public life and in the support for the ysgolion cymraeg.

There is evidence to suggest that Welsh speakers are relatively overrepresented in middle-class occupations and that middle-class families are more likely to reproduce Welsh-language use than their working-class counterparts. Moreover, there is a tier of positions available in public institutions to those who have knowledge of Welsh or who are willing or have the capacity to acquire it. There is also research that suggests that Welsh medium schools are less socially disadvantaged than English-language schools, insofar as they contain fewer children on free school meals. These features, taken together, hint that Welsh, as well as being the language of the community in the north and west of Wales, is also emerging as the language of a public elite. The major beneficiaries of language planning, it can be argued, have been the middle classes, especially those based in south east Wales. The further danger is that the more Welsh is promoted as the language of, or becomes a condition for, participation in public life, then the great majority will be excluded from it. Within this framework, Welsh medium education continues to receive a high priority, evident in the opening of three new Welsh medium schools in the greater Cardiff area, a locality where Urdu speakers and other non-English first-language speakers are as numerous as Welsh speakers.

The arena where these tensions will be addressed moves now to the newly established 60-member National Assembly, which has assumed responsibility for territorial educational provision. Primary legislation still remains the responsibility of the national government, and the Assembly Members can only interpret existing legislation. Local legislators, then, are constrained in the degree to which they can refocus existing policies. The Assembly itself is further affirmation of Wales as a distinct geographical and political entity. The education system will remain an arena for those seeking to build what is to count as Wales and Welshness within the constraints of a powerful discursive system outside its borders. The questions remain as to the extent to which the education system will reflect and sustain Wales as a diverse and plurally linguistic cultural and social entity.

REFERENCES

Adamson, D. (1991). *Class, ideology, and nation: A theory of Welsh nationalism.* Cardiff: University of Wales Press.

Ball, S. J. (1990). *Politics and policy making in education.* London: Routledge & Kegan Paul.

Balsom, D. (1985). The three Wales model. In J. Osmond (Ed.), *The national question again: Welsh political identity in the 1980s* (pp. 1-17). Llandysul, Wales: Gower Press.

Bernstein, B. (1975). *Towards a theory of educational transmission: Class, codes and control, Vol. 3.* London: Roudledge & Kegan Paul

Bernstein, B. (1990). *The structuring of pedagogic discourse: Class, codes and control, Vol. 4.* London: Routledge & Kegan Paul.

Bernstein, B. (1996). *Pedagogy, symbolic control and identity: Theory, research and critique.* London: Taylor and Francis.

Blackaby, D., & Drinkwater, S. (1996). Welsh speakers and the labour market. *Contemporary Wales, 9,* 159-170.

Bourdieu, P., & Passeron, J. C. (1977). *Reproduction in education, society, and culture.* London and Beverly Hills, CA: Sage.

Bowles, S., & Gintis, H. (1976). *Schooling in capitalist America.* London: Routledge & Kegan Paul.

Castells, M. (1997). *The power of identity, the information age: Economy, society and culture.* Malden and Oxford, England: Blackwells.

Davies, N. (1999, September 15). Schools in crisis. *The Guardian*, pp. 4-5. G. Day, & Rees, G. (1989). Editorial. *Contemporary Wales, 2,* 1.

Department of Education and Employment. (1997). *Excellence in schools.* London: Department for Education and Employment.

Department for Education and Employment. (1998). *The national literacy strategy.* London: DfEE.

Department for Education and Employment. (1999). *The standards site.* www.standards.dfee.gov.uk/library/publications/development.

Education and Training Action Groups for Wales. (1998). *An education and training action plan for Wales, a draft for consultation.* Cardiff, Wales: Manweb PLC.

Edwards, T., Fitz, J., & Whitty, G. (1989). *The state and private education: An evaluation of the assisted places scheme.* Basingstoke, England: Falmer.

Ferlie, E., Asburner, L., Fitzgerald, L., & Pettigrew, A. (1996). *The new public management in action.* Oxford: Oxford University Press.

Firestone, W. A., Fitz, J., & Broadfoot, P. (2000). Power, learning and legitimation: Assessment implementation across levels in the US and the UK. *American Educational Research Journal, 36*(4), 759-793.

Fitz, J., Firestone, W. A., & Fairman, J. (in press). Local leaders: Local education authorities, schools and policy implementation. In K. Riley & K.S. Louis (Eds.), *Leadership for a change.* London: Falmer Press.

Fitz, J., Halpin, D., & Power, S. (1993). *Grant-maintained schools: Education in the market place.* London: Kogan Page.

Fitz, J., Halpin, D., & Powers, S. (1997a). Between a rock and a hard place: Diversity, institutional autonomy and grant maintained schools. *Oxford Review of Education, 23*(1), 17-30.

Fitz, J., Halpin, D., & Powers, S. (1997b). The limits of educational reform in the UK: The case of grant-maintained schools. *International Studies in Educational Administration, 25*(1), 60-67.

Flude, M., & Hammer, M. (Eds.). (1990). *The education reform act: Its origins and implications.* London: Falmer Press.

Foucault, M. (1977). *Discipline and punish.* Harmondsworth: Penguin Books.

Gamble, A. (1988). *The free economy and the strong state: The politics of Thatcherism.* London: Macmillan.

Gerwitz, S., Ball, S., & Bowe, R. (1995). *Markets, choice and equity in education.* Buckingham, England: Open University Press.

Giddens, A. (1994). Living in a post-traditional society. In U. Beck, A. Giddens, & S. Lash (Eds.), *Reflexive modernisation* (pp. 1-55). Cambridge, England: Polity Press.

Giggs, J., & Pattie, C. (1992). Wales as a plural society. *Contemporary Wales, 5,* 25-63.

Gorard, S. (1998). "Schooled to fail?" Revisiting the Welsh school effect. *Journal of Education Policy, 13,* 115-124.

Grubb, N. (1998, March). *Making sense of education and training markets.* Paper presented at the Annual Meeting of the American Educational Research Association, San Diego, CA.

HCMI. (1996). *Annual report of Her Majesty's Chief Inspector of Schools: Standards and quality in education 1993/4.* London: HMSO.

Hood, C. (1991, Spring). A new public management for all seasons? *Public Administration, 69,* 3-19.

Jenkins, B., & Sofos, S. (Eds.). (1996). *Nation and identity in contemporary Europe.* London: Routledge & Kegan Paul.

Jones, G. E. (1988). What are Welsh schools for? Wales and the education reform act. *Contemporary Wales, 2,* 83-96.

Lazarus, N. (1999). *Nationalism and cultural practice in the postcolonial world.* Cambridge, England: Cambridge University Press.

Maclure, S. (1998). Through the revolution and out the other side. *Oxford Review of Education, 24*(1), 5-24.

Maclure, S. (1988). *Education re-formed.* London: Hodder & Stoughton.

Offe, C. (1984). *Contradictions of the welfare state.* London: Hutchinson.

Pierson, C. (1998). The new governance of education; the conservatives and education 1988-1997. *Oxford Review of Education, 24*(1), 131-142.

Pryce, W. T. R. (1990). Language shift in Gwent. c. 1770-1981. In N. Coupland (Ed.), *English in Wales: Diversity, conflict and change* (pp. 48-83). Clevedon, England & Philadelphia: Multilingual Matters.

Rees, G. (1997, October). *The educational policy process in Wales.* Paper presented at the Scottish Educational Forum semina, Educational Policy Processes of the U.K., Edinburgh, Scotland.

Rees, T. (1999). *Women and work: Twenty-five years of gender equality in Wales.* Cardiff: University of Wales Press.

Reynolds, D., & Bellin, W. (1996). *Welsh medium schools; why they are better, agenda.* Institute of Welsh Affairs.

Rhodes, R. A. W. (1997). *Understanding governance.* Buckingham, England: Open University Press.

Tomlinson, J. (1999). *Globalization and culture.* Cambridge, England: Open University Press.

Welsh Department, Ministry of Education. (1947). *Education in Wales, Addysg yng Nghymru.* London: HMSO.

Welsh Office. (1995). *A bright future: Getting the best for every pupil in Wales.* Cardiff, Wales: HMSO.

Welsh Office. (1997a). *A bright future; beating the previous best.* Cardiff, Wales: Welsh Office.

Welsh Office. (1997b). *Building excellent schools together.* Cardiff, Wales: HMSO.

Welsh Office. (1997c). *Statistics of education and training in Wales: Schools 1997.* Cardiff, Wales: Welsh Office.

Whitty, G., Power, S., & Halpin, D. (1998). *Devolution and choice in education: The school, the state and the market.* Buckingham: Open University Press.

William, G. H. (1990). The Anglicisation of Wales. In N. Coupland (Ed.), *English in Wales: Diversity, conflict and change.* Clevedon, England & Philadelphia: Multilingual Matters.

Woods, P., Bagley, G., & Glatter, R. (1998). *School choice: Markets in the public interest?* London: Routledge & Kegan Paul.

11

Bilingualism and Bilingual Education in China

Teng Xing
Weng Yanheng
Central University of Nationalities

Today the world is comprised of over 200 countries with more than 2,000 ethnic groups, which speak 6,000 different languages. With the development of science and technology and ever-increasing communication among diverse ethnic groups and nationalities, bilingualism or multilingualism is becoming a global mode of communication. Bilingual education has become a global challenge. All the ethnic groups across the globe, especially those that do not use the mainstream language, are in need of preparing the younger generation to learn at least one more language that plays an important role in world society. Mackey (1989), a well-known bilingual expert, suggested that bilingual education plays a critical role in promoting communication and understanding among ethnic groups and nationalities in multicultural societies. China, a vast country inhabited by one and a quarter billion people, is a multiethnic and multilingual land where Han Chinese represent nearly 92% of the population. The remaining 100 million people are made up of numerous minority ethnic groups, which are often identified in China as "nationalities," and they have developed a variety of complex languages. It is imperative for China to promote effective bilingualism to advance the modernization of the country and to provide efficient means of communication among ethnic groups.

The purpose of this chapter is to analyze the development of Chinese strategies to develop bilingualism, with particular attention to the evolution of bilingual policy and current efforts to promote bilingual education.

DEVELOPMENT OF BILINGUAL EDUCATION
IN CHINA

The development of bilingual education since 1949 can be seen in three contrasting periods: the first period from 1949 to 1957; the second from 1958 to 1976; and the third from 1977 to the present. Each period is characterized by different issues reflecting the development of political and economic policies in China. These three periods are briefly described below.

The First Period (1949--1957)

This period is most important in establishing formal bilingual education for the first time in the history of Chinese education. The Chinese government saw it as a critical educational commitment. Since 1949, when the People's Republic of China was founded, the new government sent a number of anthropologists, sociologists, and linguists to the minority group regions throughout China to survey different ethnic groups and languages and the general conditions of these ethnic groups. This national undertaking laid an important function for the government to develop minority group and language policy. To advance minority groups and achieve literacy among the minority regions, the Political Affairs Bureau of the government undertook the following measures:

> The central government formulated the necessary policies for the implementation of ethnic minority group autonomy in the People's Republic of China, including a measure for the elimination of offensive titles, names, and tablets on which discriminating expressions against ethnic minority groups had been inscribed. The government enforced regulations guaranteeing equal opportunities for ethnic minority groups living in different minority regions. The government also repudiated Mandarin as "the language of China," and rejected traditional discriminatory practice against the ethnic minority languages.

> In 1952, the First Constitution of China was promulgated, declaring that "each ethnic group has the right to develop its spoken and written language." This was written into the Common Program of the Political Consultative Council for the Chinese People.

> In 1953, the Minority Affairs Committee formulated a policy directing the government to provide assistance to all the autonomous ethnic groups to affirm and establish an ethnic minority language as the main language of communication within each region. According to this

policy, other minority languages could be used while communicating with other ethnic groups.

In 1951, the government Administrative Council produced a document titled "Several Determinations Concerning Minority Affairs," which mandated that a cultural and educational committee be established to study ethnic minority languages. The committee's major role was to coordinate the initiative by ethnic minority groups to develop their own written languages and to provide needed assistance.

Accordingly, the central government promoted a national policy on "ethnic minority self-determination" to achieve the minority groups' goal to develop their own written languages. In 1954, in its report on the development of written minority languages, the government put forward a proposal that "for those groups with no written languages the government will provide assistance to develop a kind of pin yin (phonetic symbols)." The government's campaign resulted in the creation of 14 written languages, including Jingpo, Bouyei, Yi, Naxi, Miao, Li, Hani, Lishu, Dong, Zhuang, Miao, Wa, Bai, and Zaiwa, in 12 ethnic minority regions. Meanwhile, the government's campaign led to improving the written languages of Uygur, Kazakh, Daizu, Lahu, and Kirgiz minority groups.

In 1951, the First Council for Minority National Education urged that ethnic groups with their own minority languages teach children in their own language, as long as the language is in common use, and that groups with only spoken languages should develop written languages. At the same time, ethnic groups were given an option to use Mandarin or the native language as the medium of instruction, depending on the circumstances of each school.

As a result of these policy initiatives, laws and regulations were created to promote minority languages, coordinate language development among China's minority groups, and provide flexibility in the choice of Mandarin and minority languages. All these developments not only improved the quality of teaching but also led to training large numbers of bilinguals, including bilingual teachers.

The Second Period (1958-1976)

This period represents a drastic shift in the government's policy, reversing its emphasis on local autonomy. The new policy undermined the important incipient initiatives to promote minority languages as well as the economy and culture of minority groups in China. In 1958 the central government replaced the accommodation policy of the previous period with an assimilation policy. It mandated that only Mandarin be used as the medium of instruction and as the common language regardless of the existing languages and cultures of minority groups. In 1958, the Second National Ethnic Minority Native Languages Council repudiated the previous policies on minority groups as a reflection of laissez-faire capitalism, which resulted in "the rubbish heap of history." Further, restrictions were placed on the use of newly created ethnic minority native languages, and many schools in the minority regions were closed down. During the Cultural Revolution that lasted from 1966 to 1976, government control of minority languages was intensified to an extreme extent. Using Mandarin as the only language for learning and teaching caused insurmountable obstacles for minority groups. Consequently, students' school achievement dropped significantly during the period, and basic education in the minority regions lagged behind immeasurably. By 1976, however, this reversal finally began to give way to new reform.

The Third Period (1977-present)

After the Cultural Revolution, the new Constitution of the People's Republic of China was promulgated. The constitutional pillar that "all ethnic minority groups have freedom to develop their languages" was reaffirmed. At the same time, the central government encouraged the development of a program for people in different ethnic regions to learn languages from each other. To promote the program, a special measure was created: the Law of Autonomy of Ethnic Minority Groups in the People's Republic of China, which was implemented in 1984. It requires that "the government teach and encourage cadres of all ethnic groups to learn spoken and written languages from each other." "Members of the Han Cadre," the law reads, "must learn minority languages; minority cadres should also learn commonly spoken Mandarin. Workers who can use more than two native languages in the autonomous regions should be rewarded." The law also underscores the importance of trust and respect for minority ethnic groups.

The Law of Autonomy of Ethnic Minority Groups reemphasized that "the autonomous units [regions] are guaranteed the freedom of using and developing ethnic minority spoken and written languages." The law also states that "the autonomous units can establish educational programs, set up schools, and make decisions on issues such as the educational system, school management, the content and languages of instruction, and student enrollment." The law requires that "in schools with a majority of ethnic minority students, teachers use teaching materials written in the minority native language and teach in their own language. Courses in Mandarin can be set up in the higher grades of primary schools and in middle schools."

Besides the above-mentioned laws, the government also developed a flexible policy to enable minority students to enroll in grades lower than those of Han students to meet their linguistic needs. In some regions mainly inhabited by minority groups, students are now permitted to take examinations in their own languages. As for teaching materials, in accordance with the law, local autonomy permits regional schools to make their own decisions regarding the selection of educational materials for a given unit of lessons, and the government offers financial support assisting them to establish publishing houses and committees to examine teaching material.

In sum, China's policy on minority languages has drastically vacillated since 1949, when legitimate status was granted to minority languages for the first time. The first reform of language education was audacious, taking steps toward recognizing the rights and needs of regional minority groups by promoting minority languages and bilingualism. The second period represented a major setback in the nation's minority education, disclaiming minority languages as the medium of instruction. This era led to the decline of minority students' school achievement and a crisis in language education as well as basic education in the minority regions. But the second language education reform, which began in the late 1970s, not only restored the initiatives begun in the first period but also promoted a new model of language education.

LANGUAGES, WRITING SYSTEMS, AND VARIETIES OF BILINGUAL EDUCATION IN CHINA

Fifty-six ethnic groups currently exist in China, of which Han is the dominant ethnic group. Constituting 8% of the whole population, the other 55 ethnic minority groups are distributed in the vast areas that comprise 64% of the country's land mass. According to ethnic linguists' research on language family taxonomy, there are 61 recognized languages in China. Moreover, there are still additional languages and some newly discovered languages that need to be studied, recognized, and classified. These 61 languages belong to 5 language families, according to the *Encyclopedia of China: Ethnic Groups* (Encyclopedia of China Press, 1986): Chinese-Tibetan, Altaic, Austronesian, Austro-Asiatic, and Indo-European. They are further classified into 10 language groups and 14 branches (Yan, 1990), as shown in Table 11.1.

Ethnic Patterns of Writing

Let us turn to ethnic patterns of writing. Except for Manchu and Hui, which use Chinese characters, other ethnic groups use 39 different minority writing character systems. These writing systems can be divided into two types, one of which was introduced prior to 1949, and the other of which is the Latin alphabetic writing system created after 1949. The Chinese writing systems are shown in Table 11.2.

TABLE 11.1

Language Families in China

Chinese-Tibetan family

	1.	Han language
	2.	Tibetan-Burmese group:
		a. Tibetan branch: Tibetan, Jiarong, and Moinba languages
		b. Jingpo branch: Jingpo language
		c. Yi branch: Yi, Hani, Naxi, Lisu, Lahu, and Jinuo languages
		d. Burmese branch: Zaiwa and Achang languages
		e. Branch uncertainty: Bai, Qiang, Pumi. Luoba, Drung, Tujia, and Nu languages
	3.	Miao-Yao group:
		a. Jiao branch: Miao and Bunu languages
		b. Yao branch: Yao and Mian languages
		c. Branch uncertainty: She language
	4.	Zhuang-Dong group:
		a. Zhuang, Buyi, and Dai languages
		b. Dong-Shui branch: Dong, Shui, Maonan, Mulao, and Lajia languages
		c. Branch uncertainty: Gelao language
Altaic family	5.	Mongolian group: Mongolian, Daur, East Yugur, Tu, Dongxiang, and Bonan languages
	6.	Turkic group:
		a. West Hun branch: Uygur, Kazakh, Salar, Uzbek, and Tatar languages
		b. East Hun branch: Kirgiz, West Yugur, and Tuwa languages

(Continued)

	7.	Manchu-Tongus group: a. Manchu branch: Manch, Sibo, and Hezhe languages b. Tongus branch: Ewenki and Oroqen languages
Austronesian family	8.	Western Malayo-Polynesia group: Amis, Bunen and Paiwan languages
Austro-Asiatic family	9.	Mon-Khmer group: a. Wa-Deng branch: Wa, Deang, and Brung languages
Indo-European family	10.	Slav group: Russian language Iranian group: Tamagy language
Not certain		Korean and Jing languages

Han people are spread throughout China, and because of their wide geographical distribution, they are extensively mixed with people of each minority group in minority regions. This pattern of settlement is often characterized in China as an overlap of "macro and micro structures of living." Moreover, there are few distinct boundaries among ethnic groups. This not only contributes to the complexity of language use but also creates various types of bilingual communities, resulting in the development of unique and entangled bilingualism in China.

Bilingual education in China is understood as the instruction of a minority language and the Han language or Mandarin.

Because of the varying historical developments of minority communities, the extent to which people use their own language and Mandarin in school and everyday life differs considerably. Some ethnic minority groups start with their home language at the beginning of school education and gradually introduce Mandarin, ultimately using Mandarin as the instructional medium. Minority groups with newly created writing systems in southern China follow this practice. Some other minority groups have their own educational systems from kindergarten to university and exclusively use their own language

TABLE 11.2

Minority Writing Systems

Ethnicity	Writing System	Ethnicity	Writing System
Han	Chinese character	Hui	Chinese character
Manchu	Chinese character	Mongolia	Mongolian, Tuotei, Mongolian
Uygur	Uygur	Kazak	Kazak
Kirgiz	Kirgiz	Korea	Korean
Miao	Newly created Quandong, Xiangxi, Qian-dian, Northeast Dian Latin alphabetic writings and phonetic square character	Jingpo	Newly created Jingo and Zaiwa alphabet
Buyi	Newly created Buyi alphabet	Hani	Newly created Hani alphabet
Dong	Newly created Dong alphabet	Tu	Newly created Tu alphabet
Dai	Daile phonetic character, Daina character, Jinping Dai character	Lahu	Lahu writing system

(Continued)

Xibo	Xibo writing system	Russian	Russian
Yi	Syllabic language	Yao	Newly created Latin alphabet, square Yao character
Lisu	Newly created Lisu Latin alphabet, Latin capital letters, Lisu bamboo slip	Bai	Newly created Latin alphabet square Bai character
Wa	Old writing system, newly created alphabet	Li	Newly created Latin alphabet
Maxo	Newly created Latin alphabet		

medium of instruction. However, they teach Mandarin as a separate course. Korean and Mongolian compact communities in the Yanbian Korean Autonomous Region and Inner-Mongolian Autonomous Region are the two successful examples of long-standing bilingual education in northern China.

Considering the deep-seated interest of ethnic minority groups in being an integral part of China, bilingual education has an important practical significance for them. First, bilingual education is indispensable for bilingual life in minority regions. The distribution of ethnic groups, including Han, shows characteristics of the overlapped macro-micro structures of living to which we earlier referred, where everyday communication among people in ethnic groups makes bilingualism in China extremely vital. Implementing a well-planned bilingual program in minority schools is essential to meet the everyday needs of all people. Second, bilingual education in minority schools is an effective way to develop ethnic education and to improve the quality of teaching. Third, effective bilingual education in schools in the minority regions is a foundation for multicultural education and for maintaining the traditions and cultures of the minority groups.

All in all, bilingual education in minority schools contributes to enhanced mutual understanding and respect as well as political and economic equality. Bilingual education is especially vital in minority regions where Han and other minorities live and interact in everyday life. Given the fact that there are 61 languages in China, bilingual education is complex and intimidating. Nevertheless, China has made impressive progress. Bilingual education varies from region to region, but there are two main categories of bilingual programs, which we will discuss below.

Transitional Bilingual Education

Transitional bilingual education is designed to provide a program in which students are guided to make transition from their native language to the standard Mandarin. A transitional bilingual education program begins with a single native language in the first grade and phases in a stage in which children are exposed to both the native and standard languages. This stage is gradually followed by a third stage in which Mandarin becomes the medium of instruction. Current bilingual education in southern China, for example, in Guizhou, Yunnan, and Hunan provinces, follows this model. We will briefly describe problems in transitional bilingual education and some counterstrategies to promote it, focusing on the Dai language.

Transitional bilingual education tends to be fragmented and often lacks continuity. It is not guided by a clear and carefully constructed plan that emphasizes the mastery of both languages. In this model students often fail to develop sufficient writing skills in their native language because not only is careful planning lacking, but also instructional time is insufficient. Moreover, few teachers have the competent training and skills requisite for transitional bilingual education. Further, because of the lack of isomorphism between the contents of the two languages, students have enormous difficulty in making transition from the native language to Mandarin. This results in poor skills in Mandarin.

To overcome these problems, "minority language assistant teaching," begun in the 1950s, is employed in transitional bilingual education. Teachers who are competent in two languages, for example, in Dai and Han in Yunnan Province, use Dai to assist students to learn linguistic skills, including the pronunciation, writing, and meaning of the characters of Mandarin.

Another strategy, teaching Mandarin with pin yin (phonetic symbols) and Dai characters, which indicate the meanings of words, has been endorsed by Yunnan Province. This teaching strategy began in the 1960s. To disseminate this strategy, the Yunnan National Affairs Committee compiled the *Han Language Reading Primer* as a textbook, which enables children to translate different native languages into the Han language. Later, a similar textbook, the *Handbook of Language Reading Primer*, with notations and explanations in pin yin and Dehong Dai, was published by the Yunnan Press for Nationalities. It became popular and widely used in the Dai region.

As related to the above strategy, the approach to teaching Mandarin with Dai notations of pronunciation and meaning was the textbook *Dai People Learn Han Language*, published by the Yunnan People's Education Committee and Yunnan Press for Nationalities. In this textbook, the Dai language and Han were alternately printed side by side. The aim of this book was to assist those who can read Dai to learn the pronunciation and meaning of Han characters. Although this text was not used during the Cultural Revolution, it was recompiled and published under a new title, *Dai-Han Conversation*, in the late 1970s and adopted as a popular textbook for elementary schools. It remains a useful tool for students who have learned the Dai language to study Mandarin, even without teachers.

Similarly, Dehong Province printed a *Bilingual Education in Reading Primer* in 1978 for those with knowledge of the Dai language to enhance their Mandarin skills. Using this primer, children who have learned Dai language or pin yin of Mandarin can develop skills to read Han characters and understand their meanings.

Teachers of transitional bilingual education needed texts also, and for them, the *Handbook of Simultaneous Translation of Dai and Han Languages* was published. In recent years, it was discovered that most of the teachers in Dehong Province had little Dai language skills: consequently, they could not use the *Bilingual Education in Reading Primer* to teach Dai and Mandarin. Hence, the experts in the province added pin yin under each Dai character, so that the teachers could read Dai following the pin yin notations. Subsequently, the Education Bureau of Dehong published a whole set of Mandarin textbooks for 9-year compulsory education in which this method was applied. *Handbook of Simultaneous Translation of Dai and Han* is based on this approach. This handbook is easy to follow. It takes teachers with knowledge of pin yin only a few days to comprehend. In one year the province was able to train 1,660 teachers to use this handbook. As a result, bilingual education in the province has been considerably improved.

This new approach to learning both languages with pin yin is noteworthy, as it promotes both oral and reading skills. It was designed to assist teachers to instruct Mandarin. It uses pin yin and the minority language as the tools to develop initial competence for learning Mandarin and to introduce reading and writing skills in Mandarin progressively. Because Dai children are not familiar with Mandarin, teachers must teach in the Dai language at the beginning of the first school year. Subsequently, teachers expose children to everyday Mandarin words or expressions. When children become familiar with them, teachers give lessons in Dai with some Mandarin expressions. As the use of Dai is gradually reduced, Mandarin progressively replaces Dai. This teaching approach has produced some positive results. For example, at an elementary school in Yunhu Village in Fapa District, Mandarin was used 60% of the time in instruction at the first-grade level by the end of the first school year. At the second-grade level, Mandarin was used 80% of the time in instruction, contributing to improving both language and math education.

While we have focused on provinces with large concentrations of Dai people, it needs to be pointed out that this approach has been applied in other provinces, using other minority languages, to improve bilingual education.

Language Maintenance Bilingual Education

Although the transitional approach we have just discussed aims to achieve a progressive replacement of the native language with Mandarin, a language maintenance approach is designed to promote acquisition of both languages throughout formal education. Located in mostly northern China, the ethnic minority groups that employ the maintenance approach have developed long-standing native languages and writing systems. This approach has been promoted by ethnic groups in several regions, including the Mongolians in the Inner-Mongolia Autonomous Region, the Uygurs in the Xinjiang Uygur Autonomous Region, the Koreans in the Autonomous Province, and the people of Jilin Province and the Tibetans in the Tibet Autonomous Region. Given the equal emphasis placed on the native and standard languages, these provinces allocate equal time to teaching each language at minority primary or middle schools. For example, 2,068 hours are allocated to the Mandarin program in Korean elementary and middle schools in Jilin Province each year, while 2,308 hours are spent to teach the Korean language. As a result, most Koreans in Jilin can communicate fluently in both Korean and Mandarin. Their fluency in both languages reflects the priority that Koreans place on bilingual education.

The Inner-Monogolia and Xinjiang Uygur autonomous regions and parts of Tibet have created a complete system of bilingual education, from primary school to university education. Under this system, in place for 20 years, natives have been schooled to gain fluency in both native languages and Mandarin. A remarkable development of bilingualism in these northern regions has contributed to enhancing communication and interaction between them and people in the political, commercial, cultural, educational, scientific, and technological fields. Well-developed bilingualism not only enables minority students to understand the Mandarin language and Han culture, but it also develops students' skills to reproduce their native languages and maintain their own cultures as well. Language maintenance bilingualism has proved to be very effective. People in all walks of life educated under this bilingual education system are well noted for their adaptability and respected throughout China. They are regarded as the talented minorities who contribute to modernizing minority regions.

Achievements of Bilingual Education in China

Over the past 50 years, governments in various levels in the ethnic minority regions have undertaken important initiatives both to promote minority languages and to develop bilingual education that have resulted in tangible achievements.

First we will point out significant accomplishments in promoting minority languages:

1. Ethnic groups have more freedom to develop their own spoken and written languages, and they have gained more respect for their own languages.
2. Minority languages in both spoken and written forms are more widely used.
3. Important progress has been made in documenting and standardizing minority languages.
4. The minority written languages systematized in the 1950s have been disseminated successfully.
5. Minority languages have been translated into Mandarin and popularized through films and the mass media. Literature in minority languages has been published.
6. School programs offered in minority languages have been improved, and consequently, bilingual education has advanced significantly in ethnic minority regions.
7. Human resources required for teaching minority languages have restored and strengthened. Professionally competent resources have significantly increased.
8. Collaboration across provinces has been fostered to promote native languages and bilingual programs.
9. Mutual learning programs have been created, providing both Han and minority people with opportunities to learn each other's languages. Such programs have enhanced interaction and social cohesion.

Now let us review some achievements in bilingual education. To illustrate them we will look at bilingual education in Liangshan, the Yi Autonomous Region of Sichuan Province. In this region bilingual education has been promoted through formal education as well as a social movement to eliminate illiteracy. Liangshan offers two types of bilingual education. In one,

Mandarin is used as the main instructional medium, and the Yi language is taught only as a stand alone subject in elementary and middle schools. In the other programs, the Yi language is used as the main instructional medium, and Mandarin is taught as a stand alone subject. The second program debuted in selected primary schools in 1984; by 1988 the number of elementary and middle school that offer the second program reached 521, with 30,107 enrolled students, constituting 28% of the whole Yi student population. This program was staffed by 638 Yi language teachers. On the other hand, as of 1997, 130 elementary and 10 middle schools offered the first program, enrolling 8,343 students who represented 12% of all students in the bilingual schools.

In 1996 the first cohort of students who participated in the first program graduated from high school; 38 students were admitted into colleges and 47 students were enrolled in polytechnic schools in Sichuan Province. As of 1999, 150 college students and more than 200 polytechnic secondary school students, the first to participate in the first bilingual program, graduated from their institutions. Some of them moved on to post-graduate work. This anecdotal story reveals important progress made in bilingual education in a minority region and represents advancement in the educational history of the Yi ethnic group.

Another important accomplishment in Liangshan is the creation of textbooks in the Yi language for all levels. Although the Yi minority group had developed a traditional writing system, there was no textbook available to Yi children in the early 1950s. Further, from 1958 to 1977, the period of regression in bilingual education discussed earlier, lessons were offered in all schools only in Mandarin, disregarding children's linguistic background and total lack of knowledge of Mandarin. This led to students' extremely poor school achievement; most students failed to graduate even from elementary school.

Against that educational history, the Sichuan government launched an ambitious undertaking to create a series of school textbooks in the Yi language in 1977, at a time when the central government's policy on bilingual education was shifting toward promoting minority languages. Since the Sichuan government initiative, Yi-language textbooks have been created for all levels, including the college and normal education level. Hence teacher education has been improved. Consequently, the Yi language has been "systematized and standardized" throughout the region. The Sichuan government just launched another 10-year initiative to publish a variety of teaching materials in language education, including bilingual textbooks, teachers' manuals, exercise books, supplementary readings, and reference books, as well as books for polytechnic and teacher training schools. All those initiatives reflect the region's commitment to improving language education, which has become a source of inspiration for other provinces throughout the country.

At the same time as bilingual education was advanced with strong support from the regional government, the movement to eliminate illiteracy became an important, large-scale campaign in Liangshan. In the early 1950s, more than 95% of farmers in the region could not read and write, and the mere 2% who could read knew only the traditional Yi written language. The latter learned Yi by osmosis, including imitation and personal examples as well as verbal instruction. In 1978 the State Council announced a policy to eliminate illiteracy. In 1982 the government of Liangshan created a literacy and professional education corps to set up 6,895 literacy classes enrolling 164,117 learners. Among them were 260 senior primary classes with 8,842 learners. Over 4,000 adult students graduated from such classes. Counties and towns also ran over 500 cultural and technical classes as well as various short-term classes, with an enrollment of 20,000 farmers.

The year 1990 was International Literacy Year. In that year, the Yi Autonomous Region offered 1,226 literacy classes, which enrolled 151,565 learners. The number of students at literacy schools reached 152,586, 60% of whom graduated. The region also built 126 new elementary schools enrolling 12,000 students. Since 1982 illiteracy has dropped 15% in the entire region. The region's 10 counties, 362 towns, and nearly 2,500 villages aggressively promoted the literacy movement, resulting in the fact that 95% of the inhabitants gained some form of literacy. The campaign not only created literate people but also helped farmers gain new knowledge and skills for more productive farming.

Issues in Bilingual Education in China

Tangible progress has been made in China's bilingual education over the past 50 years, especially since 1978. But there are a number of problems that remain to be addressed, problems common in other multiethnic countries as well. Two major issues, one from each type of bilingual program, will be discussed here.

As referred to earlier, there are two types of bilingual education in China: the transitional approach of southern China and the language maintenance approach of northern China. The ultimate goal of the transitional approach is to accomplish a complete assimilation of ethnic minorities into mainstream Mandarin culture. This approach considers minority languages as peripheral to study and work. Is the assimilation approach as beneficial to ethnic minorities? Let us look at the case of the Jinuo as representative of the other 30 ethnic groups in southern China. Their bilingual education is designed to assimilate children and adolescents into mainstream society so that the younger generation may encounter few cultural and social obstacles and participate in social and economic spheres of activity without constraints. However, their transitional bilingual education may lead to the loss of their traditional minority cultures.

The Jinuo is an ethnic group in Yunnan Province with a population of about 25,000. Like any other minority group, they have their own language, belief system, and cultural traditions. However, under the influence of China's economic reform policy and the pressure of accelerating social integration, leaders in this minority region began to place a priority on mastering Mandarin and mainstream culture as a critical path toward modernizing their region. These leaders exhorted their people to study Mandarin as the language of their future. Following that appeal, Jinuo people sent their children to Han schools to study Mandarin.

Jinuo's assimilation campaign is popular and represents educational trends in other southern minority regions. Maintaining a balance between preservation of traditional ethnic cultures and assimilation into majority society remains a big concern not only for anthropologists and educators, but also for government officials in the National Affairs Committee in China. The issue is how to improve and enrich ethnic minority groups that have lagged behind mainstream society without losing their cultures in the process. Anthropologists are concerned that these cultures will be lost in several decades if the current trend continues.

There are also major issues in language maintenance of bilingual education in northern China. Theoretically, this type of bilingual education is an ideal model in which equal attention is given to both native and Mandarin languages. It contributes to the acquisition of the two languages and preservation of the native and Han cultures. Accordingly, governments in northern regions have vigorously promoted the maintenance model. However, history reveals that there is an intense conflict in efforts to teach Mandarin and a native language at the same time. To understand the characteristics of this conflict, we need to pay attention to external factors: the process of social and economic integration under way in China that requires skills and knowledge necessary for advanced industries and transferable to any region. This process has been growing over the past 20 years in China, penetrating minority regions and influencing bilingual education.

For example, many schools for minority children in the Inner-Mongolia and Uygur Autonomous Regions have witnessed a significant decline in student enrollment. When we conducted fieldwork in northern minority regions, we asked parents why they did not send their children to schools for ethnic minority children. Their response was remarkably identical: graduates from native schools have greater difficulty in finding jobs than those from Han schools (Teng, 1998). Parents were deaf to officials' appeals to enroll their children in minority schools because they considered Han schools to be superior for studying the Han language. It is interesting to note, however, that those same officials enrolled their own children in Han schools while exerting pressure on other minority parents to enroll their children in native schools. This reflects a paradox in bilingual education policy in northern regions and a conflict between self-enhancement and enhancement of ethnic identity and culture.

We can explain this phenomenon by referring to Maslow's (1970) theoretical model of needs. Educational officials in these minority regions discussed above have met their basic physiological and safety needs. They have stable social positions superior to those of ordinary people, and need not be concerned with basic aspects of their families' welfare. Thus, they seek satisfaction of higher needs, such as ethnic esteem and belonging, characteristic of higher needs for self-actualization. They want to show that they are the representatives of their ethnic groups and their social esteem is embedded in specific ethnic groups. Without those groups they might lose their positions. So, on the one hand, their needs for ethnic belonging motivate them to maintain ethnic affiliation and their official position, which, in turn, enable them to improve their own economic and social benefits. On the other hand, because their children will face competition in getting good jobs, they choose to enroll their children in Han schools.

We suggest that when members of minority groups encounter a conflict between satisfying needs for ethnic belonging and individual survival, they choose individual survival needs first. When they meet these needs, they then seek higher needs, such as ethnic belonging. Student enrollment decline in native schools is mediated by the fact that many families of ethnic minority groups have financial difficulties. Their children are enrolled in Han schools to increase their chances of getting better jobs to meet their own survival needs. For the younger generation of ordinary people in minority regions, ethnic identity and esteem are not immediately obvious needs. In contrast, because the upper echelons of ethnic minority groups have already met their survival needs, they seek to satisfy higher needs for ethnic esteem and belonging. Therefore, they create more schools for minority groups and exhort minority children to go to those schools.

There are other problems related to language maintenance bilingual programs, which we will briefly mention here:

1. Learning two or three languages (native language, Mandarin, sometimes a foreign language) costs money and time. How to ensure that students can learn these languages well without sacrificing other subjects is an important issue.
2. Bilingual education requires greater resources than monolingual education. Ethnic minority regions are economically underdeveloped and often have financial difficulty in maintaining even monolingual education. Meeting the needs of bilingual education is highly challenging.
3. Teacher preparation for bilingual education is much more difficult than for monolingual education. It requires a great deal of resources and financial support.
4. China's economic development and changing labor market requires higher and transferable skills and knowledge to be acquired through schooling. This economically based trend challenges the goals of bilingual education.

Alternative Approaches to Bilingual Education

In our view cultural diversity is a symbol of progressive human life. Schools at different levels should be encouraged to make a twin commitment: maintaining cultural diversity while assimilating minorities into modern ways to improve their lives. Effective strategies for bilingual education are essential to facilitate this twin commitment regardless of ethnic region. We suggest the following alternative approaches, which fuse aspects of both transitional and maintenance bilingual education, for consideration. Local needs should determine which model is most suitable to a particular region.

> Elementary schools may use either the maintenance or the transitional model, depending on varying regional needs. Start with minority-Mandarin bilingual textbooks as instructional materials and then gradually introduce a Mandarin monolingual program, moving from the maintenance model to the transitional model of bilingual education.

> Elementary and middle schools may use either type of bilingual education to meet regional needs. Begin with minority-Mandarin bilingual textbooks as instructional materials and then introduce a Mandarin monolingual program at the senior high school level. This approach will provide a smooth transition to higher education.

> Offer a minority monolingual program in the first 3 years of elementary education, followed by bilingual education in the later 3 years, with minority-Mandarin bilingual textbooks as instructional materials. Mandarin will become the instructional medium at the senior high school level.

> In minority language or mainly minority language communities, minority-Mandarin bilingual textbooks may be used in the first 3 years at the elementary level. The instructional medium will be the minority language at this stage. Mandarin as an instructional medium will be gradually introduced at the higher elementary level. Textbooks for middle schools may be bilingual, but Mandarin will be used as the instructional medium. At the senior high school level, both textbooks and instruction may be in Mandarin, and a minority language will be taught as a stand alone subject. This approach will provide continuity in the acquisition of a minority language while increasing weight on teaching Mandarin.

SUMMARY

Over the past 50 years, the government has undertaken significant initiatives to develop bilingual education in China's minority regions, with two major goals: to maintain minority languages and develop their writing systems and to enhance minority people's acquisition of Mandarin. These two goals are imperative both the maintain cultural diversity and to provide minorities with social mobility and opportunities to participate in the national labor market. The national campaign to create bilingual education began in earnest in the early 1950s. Bold bilingual education efforts, however, were impeded for nearly 20 years from the late 1950s to the mid-1970s, during which time the central government mandated that only Mandarin be taught at school. After the Cultural Revolution, China's bilingual education gained new momentum with fresh initiatives.

Bilingual education is an exceedingly challenging undertaking in China, where there are so many ethnic minority languages. The Chinese have developed two major approaches to bilingual education: transitional and maintenance approaches. The transitional approach is meritorious in facilitating linguistic and cultural assimilation into the mainstream language and culture. But its drawback is that it may result in an eventual disappearance of cultural diversity. On the other hand, the maintenance approach is ideal in its intention to develop youngsters' skills in both the native and Mandarin languages. This approach, nevertheless, is adversely affected by labor-market and economic factors, which favor Mandarin as the universal language in the nation's advancing economy and industries. China's efforts to promote bilingual education are mediated by these external, complex factors as well as limited resources and support. But bilingual education must continue with vigor in China because it is an indispensable means to support cultural diversity and national integration.

Cultural diversity is a growing global phenomenon. It is a symbol of human progress. We must develop strategies to preserve it.

REFERENCES

Encyclopedia of China Press. (1986). *Encyclopedia of China: Ethnic groups*. Beijing: Encyclopedia of China Press.

Mackey, W. F. (1989). *Introduction to bilingual education*. Paris: UNESCO.

Maslow, A. (1970). *Motivation and personality* (2nd ed.). New York: Harper & Row.

Teng, X. (1998). Report on investigation of bilingual education in Hetian, Xinjian Uygur Autonomous region. *Journal of Ethnic Educational Study, 48,* 20-38.

Yan, X. (1990). On the responsibility of bilingualism. In Y. Xeuequn (Ed.), *Papers on bilingualism in minority nationalities in China* (pp. 6-20). Beijing, China: National Press.

CONTRIBUTORS

Fatima Abrahams is dean of the Faculty of Economic and Management Sciences at the University of Western Cape, South Africa. Prior to becoming the dean in 1999, he served as chair of the Department of Industrial Psychology from 1995 to 1998 and associate professor from 1994 to 1998. He received a Yale University doctoral fellowship in 1992--93 to conduct research. His publications include articles on cross-cultural and industrial psychology. His recent research focuses on race and psychology.

Uzi Ben-Shalom is a senior research officer in the Department of Behavioral Sciences, the Israeli Defense Forces. He is currently a doctoral student at the Hebrew University. His main research areas include ethnic identity, acculturation, and adaptation of immigrants.

Douglas E. Foley has been a professor of anthropology and education at the University of Texas in Austin since 1970. His specialties are American ethnic and race relations and American popular culture. He has published over 30 articles and the following ethnographies: *Philippine rural Education: An Anthropological Perspective; From Peones to Politicos: Class and Ethnicity in a South Texas Town, 1900--1989; Learning Capitalist Culture; and The Heartland Chronicles.* He is currently coeditor of the *International Journal of Qualitative Studies in Education.*

John Fitz is a reader in education at Cardiff University School of Social Sciences. His main research interest is policymaking in education at both national and local levels and school responses to external policy framework. He has undertaken funded research into the relations between state and private education, self-governing schools, and school inspection. His present research is an investigation of the educational markets and the stratification of schools. He is a regular visitor to the United States and keen observer of policy developments across the Atlantic.

Ivan Z. Holowinsky is a professor of educational psychology, Graduate School of Education and a member of the Graduate Faculty in Psychology at Rutgers University. He is a fellow of the American Psychological Association, American Psychological Society, American Association on Mental Retardation, and American Academy of School Psychology. Holowinsky was a Fulbright scholar to Ukraine in 1995. His research interests include mental retardation, developmental disabilities, East European psychology, and special education. He is author of *Psychology of Exceptional Children and Adolescents: U.S. and*

International Developments (1983) and coeditor of *Teacher Education in Industrialized Nations* (with N. Ken Shimahara, 1995).

Gabriel Horenczyk is a senior lecturer at the School of Education and the Melton Center for Jewish Education, the Hebrew University of Jerusalem, Israel. His teaching and research areas include the psychology study of cultural and ethnic identity; intergroup contact and cultural identity; and immigrants' acculturation and identity. He has recently coedited two books: *Language, Identity, and Immigration* (with E. Olshatain) and *National and Cultural Variations in Jewish Identity* (with S. Cohen).

Hiroshi Ikeda is a professor of sociology of education at the Faculty of Human Sciences, Osaka University, Japan. His primary research interest is education for Burakumin, a Japanese minority. He has conducted several prolonged research projects on minority education and Burakumin communities in the Osaka area. He has published a number of articles and monographs on this topic. Ikeda is a coeditor of *School Culture: Rethinking School Culture;* and *Construction of Community Education System* (all published in 1997).

Petro P. Kononenko is a professor of history and Ukrainian literature and director of the Institute of Ukrainian Studies at Taras Shevchenko National University at Kyiv, Ukraine. He is a member of the Executive Board of the International Academy of Slavic Studies and chief editor of the Journal of Ukrainian Studies. He is a recipient of the International Herder Prize, Doctor Honoris Causa granted by University of Tiblis, Georgia. Kononenko is author of numerous articles and monographs.

Vivian Ota Wang is an assistant professor in the Counseling/Counseling Psychology Programs and director of the Asian Cultural Studies Program at Arizona State University. Her scholarly interests focus on social justice issues related to multicultural health education program development and evaluation and racial-cultural identity in the United States and China. Her publications include "The House of God: The Fallacy of Neutral Universalism in Medicine" (2000); "A Paradigm for Racial-Cultural Training in the Development of Counselor Cultural Competencies" (with S. Tomlinson-Clarke, 1999); and "Curriculum Evaluation and Assessment of Multicultural Genetic Counselor Education" (1998) in the *Journal of Genetic Counseling*.

N. Ken Shimahara is a professor of education at the Rutgers University Graduate School of Education and a member of the graduate faculty of the Rutgers Anthropology Department. A recipient of a senior fellowship granted by the Japan Society for the Promotion of Science, he served as a visiting professor at the University of Tokyo in 1989, among other Japanese universities. His primary research interest is ethnographic research on schooling and teaching. His publications include numerous articles and 10 books, among them *Learning to Teach in Two Cultures: Japan and the United* (with Akira Sakai, 1995). He is the author of a forthcoming book, *Teaching and Social Change in Japan: A Cultural Perspective* (with Hidenori Fujita and Suk-Ying Wong).

Crain Soudien taught as a high school teacher for nearly 10 years and joined the School of Education at the University of Cape Town, South Africa in 1988, where he is now the Deputy Head. He is a political scientist by training but has migrated into sociology and is particularly interested in the relationship between school and social identity. He has written extensively on youth identity in the apartheid and post-apartheid school and is currently conducting a study of White youth in South Africa. He has a wide range of extramural activities, the most significant of which is his work in the museum field. He is a founder of a landmark museum in Cape Town, the District Six Museum. Soudien was educated at the University of Cape Town and The State University of New York at Buffalo in the United States.

James B. Stewart is a professor of labor studies and industrial relations and African and African American studies at Pennsylvania State University. He served formerly as vice provost for educational equity and director of Black studies. His publications include seven books and numerous articles in economics and Black studies journals. Stewart also served as editor of *The Review of Black Political Economy*. He has been a visiting faculty member at the Defense Equal Opportunity Management Institute and the University of the Western Cape.

Saundra Tomlinson-Clarke is an associate professor and director of training for the Program in Counseling Psychology in the Department of Educational Psychology at Rutgers University. She also serves as advisor to the Dean at the Graduate School of Education on diversity and recruitment. She is a licensed psychologist. Her research focuses on the influences of culture and diversity on student adjustment and development. She has also researched factors associated with multicultural competencies and counselor development.

Volker R. Wedekind is a lecturer in education at the University of Natal in South Africa. He is currently a Commonwealth Scholar in the Sociology Department of the University of Manchester doing biographical studies on teachers' lives. Research interests include social theory and issues related to race, nationality, and identity in schooling. Recent publications include chapters in B. Moon and P. Murphy (Eds.) (1999), *Curriculum in Context* and J. Mouton and J. Muller (Eds.) (1998), *Knowledge, Method, and the Public Good*. He recently completed a 5-year spell as coeditor of the *Journal of Education*.

Teng Xing is a professor and director of the Institute of Ethnic Education Studies at Central University of Nationalities. He was a Fulbright scholar in the Department of Anthropology, University of California--Berkeley. He is editor of *Ethnic Education*, a Chinese quarterly journal. His professional interests include minority education and multicultural and bilingual education in China and abroad. He is the author of many books, including *Ethnic Minority Education in China 1949--1999 (1999), Bilingual Society and Bilingual Education in Liangshan Yi Minority Group* (2000), and *Introduction to Ethnic Minority Pedagogy* (2000). Teng is currently working on a research project focused on higher education for ethnic minorities in China in the 21st century.

Weng Yanheng is a lecturer at the Institute of Ethnic Education Studies, Central University for Nationalities and a professor at the China Research Association of Bilingual Education for Nationalities. His current research focuses on theory and practice of bilingual education. Weng's publication includes *Encyclopedia of English Education in China* (published by Northwestern University in 1995).

AUTHOR INDEX

A

Aboud, F., 203, 204
Abrahams, F., 8
Adamson, D., 236, 256
Apple, M., 11, 12, 31
Arredondo, P., 206

B

Baldwin, J., 203
Banks, J., 11, 12, 58,
    194, 195, 202
Ben-Shalom, 4, 5, 11,
    57, 62
Bernal, M. A., 202
Bernstein, B., 18, 235,
    239, 242, 243, 256
Berry, 61, 62, 63, 64,
    65, 74
Blackaby, D., 252, 256
Branch, C., 203
Brown, M., 1
Brukhovetsky, V., 226,
    231

C

Campbell, D. E., 194
Carton, A., 215, 232
Cassirer, E., 215, 232
Castells, M., 235, 256
Cheatham, H. E., 206

Chinn, P. C., 195, 197, 204
Chisholm, L., 108, 132
Chornovil, V., 226, 231
Christiansen, I., 8, 188, 189
Christie, P., 106, 107
Clark, K., 203
Clark, M., 203
Coleman, J., 17, 32
Collins, C., 106, 107
Confucius, 38, 39
Cook, D. A., 195, 200, 206

D

Dante, A., 214, 216
Derkach, M., 228, 231
DeVos, G. A., 82
Diller, J. V., 202, 203, 204
Ding, W., 39, 52
Dostoyevsky, F., 215
Drinkwater, S., 252, 256
Duesterberg, L. M., 207
Dziuba, I., 218, 231

E

Edwards, T., 240, 256
Erickson, F., 22, 32

F

Fedorenko, D. T., 223, 228,
    231

SUBJECT INDEX

A

Acculturation, 61, 62
Adaptation, 62
Affirmative Action, 179
Affrikaans-speaking universities,
172
Afrikaner, 107
Afrocentric epistemology, 23
Anglicization of Wales, 234, 236
Aparatchiks, 220
Assimilation, 60, 61
in South Africa, 142-145
Assimilationist approach, 57-61
74
Atheistic Indoctrination, 223
Autonomous System of Education in
Wales, 233, 238

B

Barakumin in Japan, 6
Bell curve, 4
Biculturalism, 60
Bilingualism
in China, 10, 259
Ukraine, 225
in Wales, 246-254
Blue Books, 248
Bolshevik Revolution, 213
Broken Commandment, 83
Brown v. Board of Education,
194, 196

Buraku Liberation Movement, 84
Buraku youth, 81-100
Burakumin, 82-100

C

Central Committee of the
Communist Party, 223
Chinese Americans and ethnic
identity, 49, 50, 51
Chinese educational reforms, 40-45
Clark doll tests, 203
Collectivism, 221
Compulsory 9-year education, 42
Confucianism
and education, 37-38, 39,
40
and social relationships
38-39
Cultural difference, 205
Cultural identity, 59-78, 81-
Cultural identity, 59-78, 81-
100, 193-194

D

Decision of the CPC Central
Committee, 41
Deficit thinking, 22
Democratic diversity, 178
Depolitization, 223
Desegregation
in South Africa, 133, 136
140, 146, 150

287

Historically White Universities
(HWU's), 165, 166, 169, 172,
178, 184, 187
National enrollment patterns,
170-178, 184-186
Schools, 108-115
Soviet Republics, 220

T

Teacher training
in Ukraine, 228
in South Africa, 145-150
Territorial bilingual education, 268,
269
Tsarist Decrees, 217

U

Ukraine, 9
Sociopolitical history,
9
Ukraine's school system, 222
Ukrainian language at universities,
227
United States
Culture, 193-194
Demographics, 197-198
Educational equity, 196
Educational systems, 193,
200, 206
National identity, 196
Self identity, 203, 205

V

Vashchenko Educational Association,
230
Verkhovna Rada, 213

W

Welsh Development Agency, 237
Welsh Land Authority, 251
Welsh Language Act, 251
Welsh Language Board, 237, 251
World view, 205
Written langauges in China, 251

Y

Yi language, 272, 273
Ysgolion Cymreag, 251